Doing Business in India

In response to the increasing interest in the growth and developments in the Indian economy, and the dynamic nature of the rapidly changing Indian business environment, this textbook is designed as a comprehensive guide to doing business in the Indian context.

Written by academic experts in their respective fields, the book is divided into three parts: the Indian business context, conducting business in India, and India and the world. Key information is presented on a wide range of topics, including:

- The shortcomings and the opportunities associated with the Indian business environment.
- The economic development model in India.
- Critical skills for negotiation and incentives for foreign investors, including case studies of Italian companies that have entered the Indian market in different ways.
- Business culture in India, including particular customs and etiquette.

In addition to the pedagogical features, each chapter contains a set of key issues, and there is also a list of useful websites covering a wide range of business needs. This book introduces students to business in India, and will also be of use to investors, organisations and managers who are already doing business, or intend to, in India.

Pawan S. Budhwar is Professor of International HRM and Associate Dean for Research at Aston Business School, Birmingham, UK. He is Director of the Aston India Foundation for Applied Business Research. His previous publications include *The Changing Face of People Management in India* (Routledge, 2008) and *Human Resource Management in Developing Countries* (Routledge, 2004).

Arup Varma is Indo-US Professor of Management Studies at the Institute of Human Resources and Employment Relations, Loyola University, Chicago. His research interests include performance appraisal, and expatriate issues. His previous publications include *Performance Management Systems* (Routledge, 2008).

Doing Business in India

Building research-based practice

**Edited by
Pawan S. Budhwar
and Arup Varma**

Routledge
Taylor & Francis Group

LONDON AND NEW YORK

First published 2011
by Routledge
2 Park Square, Milton Park, Abingdon, Oxon. OX14 4RN

Simultaneously published in the USA and Canada
by Routledge
270 Madison Avenue, New York, NY 10016

Routledge is an imprint of the Taylor & Francis Group, an informa business

Typeset in Times New Roman by
Florence Production Ltd, Stoodleigh, Devon

Printed and bound in Great Britain by
CPI Antony Rowe, Chippenham, Wiltshire

British Library Cataloguing in Publication Data
A catalogue record for this book is available from the British Library

Library of Congress Cataloging in Publication Data
Doing business in India/[edited by] Pawan S. Budhwar and
Arup Varma.
    p. cm.
    Includes bibliographical references and index.
    1. Investments, Foreign–India. 2. International business
enterprises–India. 3. India–Economic conditions–1991–
I. Budhwar, Pawan S. II. Varma, Arup.
    HG5732.D65 2010
    330.954–dc22   2010015872

ISBN 978-0-415-77754-4 (hbk)
ISBN 978-0-415-77755-1 (pbk)
ISBN 978-0-203-84093-1 (ebk)

To those who have an interest in
doing business in India

In memory of my father, the
late Major Abhe Ram
P.S.B.

To my mother, Leelawati
A.V.

Contents

PART I
The business context   1

PART II
Conducting business in India   101

Figures

Tables

Boxes

Contributors

Olga Annushkina is Lecturer in Strategy, Bocconi University, Bocconi, Italy.

Jyotsna Bhatnagar is Associate Professor of HRM at the Management Development Institute, Gurgaon, India.

Pawan S. Budhwar is Professor of International HRM, Director of Aston India Foundation for Applied Business Research and Associate Dean (Research) of Aston Business School, Birmingham, UK.

Bhaskar Dasgupta is Global Head of the Programme Office, Global Finance, HSBC Holdings PLC, London, UK.

Debdeep De is Lecturer at Jaypee Business School, Jaypee Institute of Information Technology University, Noida, India.

Prasanta Dey is Reader in Operations Management at Aston Business School, Birmingham, UK.

Mamta Kapur is Senior Specialist at the Accenture Institute for High Performance, New Delhi, India.

Naresh Khatri is Associate Professor of HR in the Health Management and Informatics Department at the University of Missouri, Columbia MO, USA.

Devendra Kodwani is Lecturer at the Open University, Milton Keynes, UK.

Rajiv Kumar is Assistant Professor in the Behavioral Sciences Area at IIM Calcutta, India.

Vikas Kumar is Senior Lecturer in International Business, Faculty of Economics and Business, University of Sydney NSW, Australia.

Charmi Patel is Doctoral Researcher at Aston Business School, Birmingham, UK.

Rajesh Pillania is Assistant Professor of Strategy at the Management Development Institute, Gurgaon, India.

Debi S. Saini is Professor of HRM at the Management Development Institute, Gurgaon, India.

Sukanya Sengupta is Lecturer in HRM at Cardiff Business School, Cardiff, UK.

Ravi Shankar is Director of Jaypee Business School, Jaypee Institute of Information Technology University, Noida, India.

Ashok Som is Associate Professor and Co-chair in the Management Area at ESSEC Business School, Paris, France.

Mohan Thite is Senior Lecturer at Griffith Business School, Brisbane QLD, Australia.

Jacob D. Vakkayil is Assistant Professor in the Behavioral Sciences Area at IIM Calcutta, India.

Arup Varma is Professor of HRM at the Institute of Human Resources and Employment Relations, School of Business Administration, Loyola University Chicago, Chicago IL, USA.

Acknowledgements

For the past few years Routledge has wanted us to develop a volume like this. As we explored the possibility, we realised that there are a number of books on India that have emerged in the last couple of years. However, pursuant to our ideas, we are convinced that there still is a pressing need for a book of this nature. The present volume is unique in many ways – in terms of the content, depth, research-based evidence and clear takeaways.

Book projects such as this are an outcome of the efforts of a number of dedicated scholars. Given both the spread of topics covered in the volume and the scarcity of reliable information, it became imperative to invite leading scholars from the field in order to deliver a quality product. The majority of the contributions are original and have been specifically written at our request. We would like to thank all the contributors for being responsive to our demands, revising their chapters as per the referees' suggestions and for meeting rigid deadlines.

We would also like to thank all those who have helped us in various capacities, often behind the scenes, to bring this project to fruition. Our special thanks to Routledge for giving us the opportunity to develop this volume and also for being open to our proposal, and the numerous modifications. Finally, we would like to thank Dorothea Schaefter, Tom Bates, Bettina Gehrke, Urmila Chakraborty, Suzanne Chilestone, Madhavi Bhargava and Jillian Morrison at Routledge for their help and assistance at various stages of the production of this volume.

Pawan S. Budhwar
Aston India Foundation for Applied Business Research
Aston University, Birmingham, UK

Arup Varma
Loyola University, Chicago, USA

Foreword

Ravi Kant
Vice-chairman, Tata Motors

I am pleased to present a timely and topical book that should prove very useful to anyone interested in doing business in India. Pawan S. Budhwar and Arup Varma have brought together a group of renowned scholars, each an expert in their own right, and put together a comprehensive volume that covers all critical aspects of doing business in India.

The worldwide tribulations of 2009–10 have demonstrated the relative resilience of the Indian economy. Though the country is more closely linked to the global economy than ever before, the faster turnaround in India illustrates the efficacy of measured liberalisation of the past two decades, the manner in which Indian corporates have leveraged the scope and the ever increasing domestic market opportunities. Doing business in India – as also out of India – today is far easy and also far more rewarding. It will become even more so, given the inexorable progression of policy direction and citizen aspirations.

The one unstoppable change which will influence every other progression is what I describe as urbanisation of minds in a country with one of the youngest populations. Large swathes of the Indian population reside and will continue to live in rural habitations. But with the growing penetration of means of information dissemination – television, mobile phones, information technology – their aspirations are becoming as urbanised as in the cities. As one travels across the hinterlands, one will not fail to notice that the ubiquitous presence of telephone booths is increasingly getting supplemented with institutions of various scales, offering English education and IT education. They indicate two important trends – after taking care of basic needs, disposable incomes are on the rise, and people across the country are driven by the yearning to acquire capabilities to better capitalise opportunities. If there are areas where we witness unrest, it is because of the lack of these stimuli, and over a period of time will certainly get corrected.

Business success in the coming decades will require corporations to take cognisance of this transformation. It is not simply a question of creating products and services for consumption. Of course, that is a *sine qua non*. But those corporations will stand out which simultaneously integrate people and meet their aspirations to become productive members of the value chain. That will lead to the creation of a self-sustaining cycle.

I could offer an example from my company. In 2005 we launched the Tata Ace, a mini-truck for last-mile distribution. A substantial number of Ace customers are what we describe as first-time users – individuals who have bought an Ace to set up a small delivery business or a shop-on-wheels. In the future, as their incomes increase, many of them will buy our Tata Nano for their personal transport. We are trying to integrate them with the opportunities that the country has begun to offer by upgrading both the quality of their livelihood and the quality of their lives.

Last, but not the least, outstanding businesses will not only take advantage of change, but will also contribute to the change by steadfastly adhering to time-tested values. An informed society is an aware society. We already see its impact in the increasing influence of civil society in India's social, political and business ambience. Corporations, and their principles and practices, must contribute positively to the consolidation of right conduct.

I am happy that Budhwar and Varma have adopted a comprehensive approach in underscoring the needs and nuances of business in India with this insightful collection of work by eminent researchers. The choice of topics and the inclusion of specific information enhance the relevance of the book.

R.K.

Part I

The business context

1 Introduction

The business context

Pawan S. Budhwar and Arup Varma

Since the liberalization of its economy in 1991, India has emerged as a major player on the global economic front. Indeed, the World Bank and other bodies have projected that over the next decade India is likely to sustain its economic growth, and is likely to be among the top two or three leading economies of the world. Not surprisingly, such developments have led to a renewed interest in the Indian market, and foreign investors have been making a beeline to enter the lucrative Indian market. However, the pace of these developments has been rather rapid, and the relevant support systems to guide investors have not kept pace, and many are still evolving.

In a related development, the number of academic and other publications related to India has been on the increase over the last decade or so. These cover topics like the rapid economic developments in India (see Ghoshal *et al.*, 2001; Tharoor, 2007; Dossani, 2008; Nath, 2008; Kumar *et al.*, 2009); comparing India and China (Sheth, 2008; Gupta and Wang, 2009; Parayil and D'Costa, 2009), management in India (see Budhwar and Bhatnagar, 2009), areas of further development (see Murthy, 2009; Business Standard, 2010), and how to do business in India (see Budhwar, 2001; Cavusgil *et al.*, 2002; Kumar and Sethi, 2005; Millar, 2009).

Nevertheless, given the dynamic nature of the Indian business environment, which is changing rapidly on most fronts, there is a paucity of research-based evidence regarding available and emerging opportunities for foreign investors, and the key challenges/bottlenecks they might face in doing business in India. Indeed, potential investors would be well served by publications directed towards addressing the issues they might face, as well as suggestions on how to successfully navigate these. As the Indian economy grows at a rapid pace, businesses are facing numerous critical issues such as growing competition, increasing pressures to attract and retain talent, pressure for further reforms in different sectors, developments and deficiencies in infrastructure, divestments in public sector, corruption, and bureaucratic delays in the approval of proposals of foreign direct investments, etc. In addition, foreign investors would likely have to deal with issues such as corruption, bureaucratic red tape, limited infrastructure (power, transport), and union policies and practices that are sometimes counter to progressive business. Further, the nation has sometimes been slow to pursue the next generation of economic reforms, and suffers from poor implementation of dated legislation. In addition, while nationally millions graduate from high school and college each year, many of these graduates lack employable skills, and need further training.

Finally, India's geography offers both advantages and disadvantages. With thousands of miles of coast, and a diverse topography, India is indeed a land of opportunities for potential investors. However, it is also a nation bordered by unstable neighbouring countries, and suffers from poor border controls – resulting in regular insurgencies and a continuous in-flow of illegal immigrants (see Budhwar and Singh, 2007). Thus, potential investors would need to devise project plans and strategies that incorporate more than simple "business-oriented" steps. A more detailed presentation on the complex, uncertain and challenging aspects of the Indian business environment and ways of dealing with them is the focus of this volume.

Table 1.1 presents ranking of India by the International Finance Corporation (World Bank) on various parameters on the "ease of doing business" in comparison to 181 economies. The figures in the table are telling, and indeed, discouraging; however, given the opportunities India offers to foreign operators, the potential is immense, and those that make the effort are likely to be rewarded handsomely in terms of their bottom line. The key to success in India, however, lies not only in their own competencies, but also more importantly on how best they understand the Indian business context and efficiently function in it.

The importance of understanding a given "context," and developing appropriate management systems as a pre-requisite for success, is now well acknowledged in the literature (e.g., Locke and Thelen, 1995; Jackson and Schuler, 1995; Budhwar and Debrah, 2001; Schuler *et al.*, 2002). If foreign operators, while developing strategies for their Indian operations, do not

Table 1.1 India's ranking (against 181 economies) on doing business, 2009

Parameters of ease of doing business	Rank
Starting up	121
Dealing with construction permits	136
Employing workers	89
Registering property	105
Getting credit	28
Protecting investors	38
Paying taxes	169
Trading across borders	90
Enforcing contracts	180
Closing a business	140

Source: International Finance Corporation (2009).

carefully understand the Indian business context, the potential for missteps and eventual failure can be very high. This volume is specifically designed to provide information, which should prove extremely useful for MNCs and their decision-makers, as they formulate their India strategies.

We started by noting some of the shortcomings of the Indian business environment, and the potential pitfalls that foreign investors might face. We now address some of the tremendous strengths and related opportunities that are available in the Indian business environment. These include cheap resources, reasonably skilled talent, a massive national market (population 1.16 billion), a rapidly growing middle class (over 350 million) with increasingly stronger purchasing power, and one of the youngest populations in the world. In addition, India boasts one of the most diverse populations in the world, with a democratic political set-up, a free press, and a reasonably reliable judicial system, which though slow, is known to be robust. Further, Indians are known for their entrepreneurial abilities, and the willingness to learn, adapt and integrate into the global business systems. In addition, time and again India has shown the capacity to absorb global economic/financial crisis related ripples.

Due to its uniqueness in many ways, the economic development model pursued by India is considerably different to other emerging markets, which perhaps minimizes the impact of global events such as the late 1990s Asian economic crisis, the present global recessionary conditions, and was also less affected by the "Dubai debt crisis" of late 2009 on its economic growth. Broadly speaking, it characterizes the strengthening and enhanced contribution of the private sector organization, indigenous entrepreneurship, presence of massive local and national markets, increased support to encourage both foreign direct investments (FDI) – inward and outward and entry of multinational companies (MNC) to India, massive contributions from non-resident Indians to India's foreign reserves in the form of remittances sent from overseas, growth of the Indian multinational company, and increasing global leadership of specific sectors (such as the information technology, software, business process outsourcing, knowledge process outsourcing, pharmaceuticals, research and development, amongst many others).

Most aspects of the Indian economic model are strongly ingrained into the unique socio-cultural, political, legal and economic milieu of India; as a result, the challenges regarding developing a good understanding about the Indian business context and to successfully operate in it can be both complex and demanding for foreign investors. An attempt has been made in this volume to address such issues. It should contribute to better practice development. We believe this information should be useful for a variety of readers including top managers, researchers, consultants, students, and academics. This volume then provides latest research based evidence and consolidates it in a single source of information which helps to address questions pertaining to the "what", "why", "how" and "when" of doing business in India.

Overview of the volume

All but one of the authors contributing to this volume are Indian natives, and have been conducting research in their respective fields for a number of years. We believe this helps to minimize the "Western bias" for this project, and has enabled us to present a more realistic picture of the key issues facing foreign investors in India. The contributors were given a framework to develop their respective chapters – including key developments in the topic, a critical analysis of the existing literature, core opportunities, and key challenges for foreign investors. In addition, we asked them to develop a list of "key issues", which managers could use while operating in India, and provide a list of useful websites (which are placed before the index in this volume). This volume is divided into three parts – the Indian business context, conducting business in India, and India and the world.

In Chapter 2, Kapur and Pillania start off the volume by addressing the Indian economy and the emerging growth opportunities and challenges. They provide a succinct overview of India's economic growth and performance since independence in 1947, the important contributions of both domestic and international actors, and the role played by economic reforms in India's continuing development. They further discuss the underlying structural growth drivers of the Indian economy and discuss how the current growth momentum can be sustained. This chapter also discusses the impact of the global financial crisis on the Indian economy, and the key challenges that pose risks to India's economic growth.

In Chapter 3, Saini analyses Indian employment law in the context of the broad framework of social and economic justice as enshrined in the Constitution of India. In particular, he focuses his analysis on the working of the legal employment framework (i.e. relating to working conditions, the law of industrial relations, laws relating to wages and monetary benefits, and the law of social security) in light of the changing nature of the Indian economy. He also covers issues relating to the structure and functioning of various branches of Indian employment law, and assesses the hurdles that the Indian labour law framework poses in the smooth conduct of business. Saini summarizes his chapter by highlighting the salient aspects of the Indian employment law framework, weaknesses in its implementation, and how best to work within it.

In Chapter 4, Budhwar, Varma and Sengupta discuss the socio-cultural, political and institutional contexts of India. They analyse the historical developments in India, its political and legal structures, its societal values, along with corporate culture, and management behavior. For each aspect of the Indian business context, the authors highlight the unique features that are critical to understanding the issues involved in doing business in India. Based on their analyses, the authors present a list of key takeaways, which should prove very useful as a ready reference for foreign managers.

Khatri covers the sensitive and challenging topic of corruption and cronyism in India in Chapter 5. Given the common understanding that both corruption and cronyism are seriously ingrained in the Indian business environment, Khatri first examines the major factors that underlie cronyism and corruption in India. He then defines and distinguishes the concepts of corruption and cronyism from each other. The core discussion in the chapter is on the dynamics of corruption and cronyism in India. He ends the chapter with a list of key implications for managers and policy makers.

In Chapter 6, Kodwani discusses various aspects of infrastructure in India. He starts with a definition of infrastructure in the Indian policy framework, and accordingly groups the infrastructure services into three broad categories of energy, telecommunications, and transportation. Kodwani highlights the emerging business opportunities and the expected challenges investors might face in the each of these groups. He notes that a meaningful way to improve the infrastructure in India would be to involve the private sector and develop the public–private partnership (PPP) mode. He next discusses the salient features and uses of the PPP in India. Finally, he presents a list of useful tips for both the users and investors in the Indian infrastructure and provides references to useful resources.

In Chapter 7, Kumar and Annushkina discuss the dynamics associated with the entry mode options available to foreign investors. They discuss different entry modes suitable for India, with the help of two case studies – of Italian companies (Lavazza and Fiat) that have each entered India in different ways. They next highlight the inherent complexity in designing entry strategies, and the importance of accounting for industry and institutional factors in such an endeavor. Finally, they discuss the key challenges with each entry mode specific to the Indian context (in the form of key takeaways).

In Chapter 8, Shankar and De analyse the birth of the retail industry in India, and discuss changing consumer patterns. Next, they explore the strategies that might be adopted by foreign investors attempting to penetrate the Indian market. They also provide an introduction of the diverse Indian market, present a demographic profile of Indian consumers and discuss the changing consumption pattern of the Indian consumers, and what makes them unique. They further discuss the changing pattern of the Indian distribution system, which has been strategically evolving in response to the growth of the retail sector. Lastly, they highlight a number of policy issues core to the Indian retail sector and offer key messages for policy makers.

Dey presents information about project management for the Indian context in Chapter 9. He starts by alerting potential investors to the need for an effective project management mechanism in India, and discusses the potential pitfalls, which might include issues related to supply chain integration, relationship management, project planning, economic and political challenges, environmental regulation, and social needs. He next discusses an organization in the Indian oil industry, highlighting its project management experience, and also emphasizes the challenges of managing projects in India, and possible techniques and strategies for overcoming the challenges. Dey concludes the chapter with a list of dos and don'ts of managing projects in India.

In Chapter 10, Budhwar and Varma present core issues related to management of human resources (HR) in India. Initially, they explore the evolution of the HR function in the Indian context, followed by a discussion of the key factors determining human resource management (HRM) policies and practices in firms operating in India. They also discuss the nature of HRM systems prevalent in foreign firms operating in India, and provide a list of key suggestions for MNCs on developing HRM policies and practices appropriate for the Indian context.

In Chapter 11, Vakkayil and Kumar cover the important topics of conflict handling and negotiations in the Indian context. They present examples of conflict in the context of Indian businesses, both at the macro and micro levels, and discuss conflict management styles adopted by Indian managers. While doing so, they also explore the relationships between cultural values and conflict handling behaviours. Lastly, they provide guidelines for negotiation that should be of practical use to foreign managers operating in India.

Chapter 12 is devoted to outsourcing. Initially, Patel and Budhwar clarify the meaning of terms such as outsourcing, offshoring, ITO, BPO and KPO. They then provide information about the background and evolution of outsourcing/offshoring industry in India, highlighting why India is the favoured land for offshore outsourcing, and also discuss challenges this sector faces. The authors also explore the steps involved in starting an offshore outsourcing project in India, also addressing the common myths that vendors and clients might have about offshore outsourcing. Finally, they provide key takeaways for policy makers.

In Chapter 13, Bhatnagar and Som present two case studies of Indian organizations that have been successful because of the adoption of HR and OD interventions, resulting in efficient, effective and innovative HR systems. They further discuss how lessons from these companies can be utilized by others in the Indian context. Based on the analysis of the two case studies, the authors highlight the key implications for practicing managers, and discuss potential HR-related challenges for firms operating in the Indian business context.

In the next chapter (14), Varma, Dasgupta and Budhwar present information that should prove highly valuable for foreign managers in connection with adjusting, working and living in India. The authors cover topics such as religion, festivals, housing, shopping, medical care and insurance, as well as deal with etiquette and dos and don'ts of living in India. This chapter also presents, apart from key takeaways, an interview with an expatriate about his experiences of working and living in India.

In Chapter 15, Thite and Dasgupta focus on the nature and characteristics of multinational companies emerging from India. They track the global footprints of the Indian MNCs and identify the defining features that explain their internationalization strategies, the rationale behind these strategies and how they compare and contrast with different time periods. This chapter also pinpoints the crucial factors that underpin the success of Indian MNCs, as well those that threaten their future growth and viability.

References

Budhwar, P. (2001) Doing business in India. *Thunderbird International Business Review*, 43 (4): 549–68.

Budhwar, P. and Bhatnagar, J. (eds) (2009) *Change Face of People Management in India*. London: Routledge.

Budhwar, P. and Debrah, Y. (2001) Rethinking comparative and cross-national human resource management research. *International Journal of Human Resource Management*, 12 (3): 497–515.

Budhwar, P. and Singh, V. (2007) Introduction. People management in the Indian subcontinent. *Employee Relations*, 29 (6): 545–53.

Business Standard (2010) *India 2010*. New Delhi: BS Books.

Cavusgil, S. T., Ghauri, P. N. and Agarwal, M. R. (2002) *Doing Business in Emerging Markets: Entry and Negotiation Strategies*. London: Sage.

Dossani, R. (2008) *India Arriving*. New York: AMACON.

Ghoshal, S., Primal, G. and Budhiraja, S. (2001) *World Class in India*. New Delhi: Penguin.

Gupta, A. K. and Wang, H. (2009) *Getting China and India Right*. San Francisco: Jossy-Bass.

International Finance Corporation (2009) *Doing Business 2009 Data*. http://www.doingbusiness.org/ExploreEconomies/?economyid = 89 (accessed 27 November 2009).

Jackson, S. E. and Schuler, R. S. (1995) Understanding human resource management in the context of organizations and their environment. *Annual Review of Psychology*, 46: 237–64.

Kumar, N., Mohapatra, P. K. and Chandrasekhar, S. (2009) *India's Global Power-houses: How they are Taking on the World*. Boston MA: Harvard Business Press.

Kumar, R. K. and Sethi, A. K. (2005) *Doing Business in India*. Basingstoke: Palgrave Macmillan.

Locke, R. and Thelen, K. (1995) Apples and oranges revisited: contextualized comparisons and the study of comparative labor politics. *Politics and Society*, 23: 337–67.

Millar, R. (ed.) (2009) *Doing Business with India*. London: GMB Publishing.

Murthy, N. R. Narayana (2009) *A Better India, a Better World*. New Delhi: Penguin Books.

Nath, K. (2008) *India's Century*. New Delhi: Tata McGraw-Hill.

Parayil, G. and D'Costa, A. P. (eds) (2009) *The New Asian Innovation Dynamics: China and India in Perspective*. Basingstoke: Palgrave Macmillan.

Reddy, C. M. (2006) Globalization and human development in South Asia. In C.M. Reddy (ed.) *South Asia, 2006: Europa Regional Surveys of the World*. London and New York: Routledge, 3–13.

Schuler, R. S., Budhwar, P. and Florkowski, G. W. (2002) International Human Resource Management Review and Critique. *International Journal of Management Reviews* 4(1), 41–70.

Sheth, J. (2008) *Chindia Rising*. New Delhi: Tata McGraw-Hill.

Tharoor, S. (2007) *The Elephant, the Tiger and the Cellphone: Reflections on India in the Twenty-first Century*. New Delhi: Viking Penguin.

2 Economic environment and challenges

Mamta Kapur and Rajesh Pillania

The aim of this chapter is to provide a backdrop of the Indian economic environment that can help readers to assess the emerging growth opportunities and challenges. It is structured into five main sections. The next section outlines the basic contours of India's economic growth performance after independence, and briefly discusses the role of economic reforms. The second section reviews the macroeconomic trends that characterized India's growth performance in the post-independence period, with a special focus on the roles of domestic and international actors, including the part played by foreign investment, trade, and other dimensions of openness. It also outlines the underlying structural growth drivers that provide further reassurance about the sustainability of the current growth momentum. The third section discusses the magnitude of the impact of global financial crisis on Indian economy. The fourth section examines the key challenges that pose a risk to India's economic prospects but also provide opportunities for investors. The last section summarizes the chapter and lists the key lessons from it.

Economic reforms and performance

After attaining independence in 1947, India followed inward-looking and state-interventionist policies that constrained investment and undermined growth (Budhwar, 2001). As a result, in the first three decades after independence the economy grew at a disappointing growth rate of 3–4 per cent, which was popularly called the 'Hindu rate of growth' (Singh, 2008). During the 1980s a modest beginning was made towards some liberal changes helping the economy to grow at an average annual rate of around 5 per cent.

The major economic reforms beginning in 1991 gradually removed obstacles to economic freedom, and India started to steadily reintegrate into the global economy. The liberalization process that began with the onset of reforms in the early 1990s was characterized by gradual deregulation and delicensing of industry. India began to unshackle its closed economy by gradually lowering its very high trade barriers and boosting exports. Average tariffs fell to below 15 per cent from as high as 200 per cent as the country opened doors to global competition (Poddar and Yi, 2007). Contrary to negative perceptions that supported restrictions on foreign investment and technology transfer, the gradual opening up of the Indian economy introduced a competitive dynamic, which forced the private sector to restructure during the relative slowdown in growth and corporate profitability during 1997–2002. The increased competition from actual and perceived imports focused domestic firms on the need to improve efficiency as critical to survival. Increased openness also helped provide domestic firms with access to superior inputs, know-how and technology. Between 1992 and 2002 the economy grew at 6 per cent per annum as shown in Figure 2.1. There was some loss of the growth momentum in the latter half of the 1990s which coincided with the onset of the East Asian financial crisis and a sustained deterioration in the fiscal correction process, slowdown in agriculture growth and some slackening in the pace of structural reforms.

The year 2003 saw the economy ascend to a higher growth trajectory and grow at 8.5 per cent, the highest since 1999. During the following five years (up until 2008), the Indian economy leapfrogged at 8.8 per cent (Acharya, 2008). The drivers for the spurt in growth included sustained investment boom, increased productivity, an unusually buoyant global economy and a demand- and technology-driven growth of the services sector. The Planning Commission expected this economic boom to continue and envisaged growth of 9 per cent for the eleventh Five Year Plan (2007–12) rising to 10 per cent from 2012 (Planning Commission, 2006).

A detailed analysis of the growth trend suggests that per capita income also followed a similar pattern. The rate of growth of per capita income as measured by per capita GDP at market prices (constant 1999–2000 prices) grew by an annual average rate of 3.1 per cent during the twelve-year period (i.e., 1980–81 to 1991–92). It accelerated marginally to 3.7 per cent per annum during the

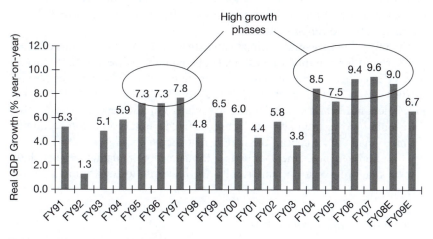

Figure 2.1 Trends in real GDP growth.

Source: CSO (2009); *Economic Survey* (2009)

next eleven years, 1992–93 to 2002–03. Since then, as the GDP growth started accelerating, the population growth rate moderated, giving a sharp impetus to the growth in per capita income – almost doubling to an average of 7.2 per cent per annum (2003–04 to 2007–08) (*Economic Survey*, 2007–08).

This fast-growing GDP and increasing per capita income coupled with a huge population makes India a big market for many goods and services and offers numerous investment opportunities.

India's growth performance: trends, growth drivers and opportunities

Consistent growth in savings and investment

A notable feature of the growth of the Indian economy has been the consistently rising trend in the gross domestic capital formation (GDCF) and the gross domestic savings rate. Gross capital formation (GCF), which was 25.2 per cent of the GDP in 2002–03, increased to 39.1 per cent in 2007–08 (*Economic Survey* 2008–09). Much of this increase is attributable to a rise in the rate of investment by the corporate sector. The rise in the rate of investment was primarily driven by the transformation in the investment climate, coupled with an optimistic outlook for the growth prospects for the Indian economy.

The growth in capital formation in recent years was amply supported by a rise in the savings rate. India's high savings rate has been a crucial driver of its economic boom, providing productive capital and helping to fuel a virtuous cycle of higher growth, higher income and higher savings. The gross domestic savings as a percentage of GDP at current market prices stood at 37.7 per cent in 2007–08 as compared to 29.8 per cent in 2003–04. The household sector remained the largest contributor to the savings pool, accounting for around 70 per cent of total domestic savings. The share of corporate savings in total savings increased from 14.1 per cent in 1991–92 to 24.9 per cent in 2005–06 (Kumar, Palit and Singh, 2007).

The improved investment climate and strong macro fundamentals also led to a surge in foreign direct investment. The combined effect of these factors was reflected in an increase in the investment rate from 25.2 per cent of GDP in 2001–02 to 35.9 per cent of GDP in 2007–08 (Mohan, 2008). The higher investment need absorbed the domestic savings and also generated an appetite for capital inflows from abroad. The gross fixed capital formation accounted for more than 90 per cent of the investment (*Economic Survey*, 2007–8).

The improved investment climate, strong macro fundamentals and high growth rate provide a big opportunity for investors to further invest in the country.

Growth led by the services sector

The continuing and consistent acceleration in growth of the services sector played an instrumental role in driving India's economic growth. The exceptionally rapid growth in India's services sector is reflected in the contribution of the sector to overall economic growth since 1991–92. The sector grew in this decade at an average of 7.9 per cent per annum, far ahead of agriculture (3 per cent) and manufacturing (5.2 per cent) (Banga, 2006). The growth in the services sector has been broad based. Among the subsectors, transport and communication have been the fastest growing segments within the services sector, with growth averaging 15.3 per cent per annum during the Tenth Five Year Plan period (2002–07) followed by construction (*Economic Survey* 2007–08). The impressive progress in the telecommunication sector and higher growth in rail, road and port traffic also played an important role in the growth of the services sector.

The services sector with its high growth rate and still untapped potential combined with increasing liberal FDI norms is a big opportunity for investors. Investors can think of joining hands with local players to explore opportunities for investment and growth.

Domestic consumption is a key source of growth

The Indian consumer market is on a growth trajectory that will make it one of the biggest by 2020, on the back of demographic and lifestyle changes brought by globalization and rising disposable incomes. Consumption comprises 65 per cent of GDP, of which the share of the private sector is 85 per cent (Global Insights, 2009). The number of affluent and consuming families in India has risen markedly since 1995. By 2016, 67–8 per cent of Indian households are likely to be middle-class or high-income households (Shukla, Dwivedi and Sharma, 2005).

Developments in the consumer markets are affecting other markets too. Customer service standards set in the consumer markets are becoming a benchmark in other industries, triggering off a process of 'retailization' across businesses as diverse as health care and banking. India's imminent urbanization process has implications for demand for housing, urban infrastructure, location of retail and demand for consumer durables. The boom in consumer goods is also having a trickle-down effect on other industries, fueling dynamic growth in entertainment, real estate and travel.

As India's investment-led economic boom slowed in the wake of the global financial crisis, relatively stable domestic consumption provided the cushion that helped the country to sustain its growth momentum. The foundations for continued consumption growth are in place: a billion-plus population, with the bulk of it entering the working age group, and a significant fiscal stimulus this year in the form of subsidies, a farm loan waiver and salary increases for government employees.

Rural India, home to about 720 million of the country's billion-plus people, is not just witnessing an increase in its income but also in consumption and production. Four consecutive years of positive growth in rural GDP has not just boosted sentiment but also spending power. Rural consumption (including government spending) is estimated to account for a little over 60 per cent of total consumption. The rural consumer spending in India has grown faster than that of urban consumers for the period 2002–07. The rural economy has got a further boost with the farmer loan waiver of US\$ 13.86 billion, the expansion of the National Rural Employment Guarantee Act (NREGA) to all states and the ambitious Bharat Nirman Programme with an outlay of US\$ 34.84 billion for improving rural infrastructure, road connectivity and digital access to villages for marketers.

India is then a big market for various goods and services, and not only a place for outsourcing. Rural markets are playing a important role in this growth. Investors can bring in their know how of operating in other emerging markets and join in exploring this big domestic market.

Growing fiscal imbalance

Despite fiscal consolidation constituting a major plank of the policy response to the macroeconomic crisis, the progress on fiscal correction was mixed during the 1990s, both at the central and state levels. By 2001–02 the fiscal deficit was nearly 10 per cent of GDP and the revenue deficit was at a record 7 per cent (Acharya, 2008). Despite considerable improvement in the fiscal scenario, both at the centre and in the states, India's combined fiscal deficit, as a percentage of GDP, still continues to be one of the highest in the world.

In view of increasing fiscal deficits and public debt over the period 1997–98 to 2002–03 and their adverse impact on public investment and growth, a renewed emphasis was laid on improving the health of public finances. In order to achieve this objective, the Fiscal Responsibility and Budget Management (FRBM) Act, 2003 at the centre and similar fiscal responsibility legislations at the state level guided fiscal consolidation. As a result, significant gains have been witnessed in the fiscal consolidation process since 2002–03. For instance, the tax–GDP ratio of the centre steadily rose from 8.8 per cent in 2002–03 to 11.8 per cent in 2007–08 (Mohan, 2008). The fiscal deficit of the centre as a proportion of GDP came down from 5.9 per cent in 2002–03 to 3.3 per cent in 2007–08. Similarly, the revenue deficit declined from 4.4 per cent in 2002–03 to 1.5 per cent in 2007–08 (*Economic Survey*, 2007–08).

This rising deficits and need for fiscal consolidation means government will have less money to spend on many programs but the country needs huge investment in many projects particularly infrastructure. This is going to bring in more disinvestment in public sector undertakings and more involvement of private sector. Public–private partnerships are going to increase which offers many investment opportunities.

Growing integration into the world economy

The Indian economy has undergone considerable structural transformation over the last decade. With growing importance of external trade and of external capital flows, India has steadily integrated into the world economy. The share of merchandise trade to GDP increased to over 35 per cent in 2007–08 from 21.2 per cent in 1997–98 (Subbarao, 2009). If the trade in services is included, the trade ratio is 47 per cent of GDP for 2007–08. During the period 2001–02 to 2007–08, India's export revenue almost quadrupled from US$ 43.8 billion to US$ 162.9 billion. India has developed a well diversified export profile over the past decade. The leading export categories include textiles and garments, gems and jewelry, and the export of engineering goods and chemicals and related products. The growth of service exports has also been remarkable throughout the period, particularly software exports. Software exports increased more than sixfold from US$ 5.7 billion in 2000–01 to US$ 37 billion in 2007–08, raising their ratio to GDP from 1.2 per cent to 3.2 per cent (Global Insights, 2009).

The rapid growth of the economy from 2003–04 to 2007–08 also made India an attractive destination for foreign capital inflows and net capital inflows increased from 1.9 per cent of GDP in 2000–01 to 9.2 per cent in 2007–08 (*Economic Survey*, 2008–09). Foreign portfolio investment added buoyancy to the Indian capital markets and Indian corporates began aggressive acquisition spree overseas, which was reflected in the high volume of outbound direct investment flows. Another important dimension has been the high degree of external dependence on imported energy sources, especially crude oil with the share of imported crude in domestic consumption exceeding 75 per cent.

FDI inflows continued to grow and were broad-based as it spread across a range of sectors including financial services, manufacturing, IT& ITeS and construction. It was accompanied by a surge in outward investment from a very low base, with net FDI continuing to grow at a good pace. In what can be seen as India's relative strength amid nations reeling under the onslaught of a global recession, foreign direct investment (FDI) worth US$ 11 billion flowed into the country between October 2008 and March 2009 even as foreign institutional investors (FIIs) pulled out US$ 8.3 billion through the portfolio route over the same period. For the full fiscal 2009, the FDI amounted to US$ 33.6 billion while FIIs pulled US$ 13.8 billion out of the country (*Economic Survey*, 2008–09).

The globalization of Indian enterprises and planting of the seeds for the creation of Indian multinationals has been another remarkable achievement of the past decade. Outward investment from India increased from US$ 1.4 billion in 2001 to US$ 15 billion in 2007. Indian companies have significantly increased their M&A activity over recent years, particularly in terms of cross-border acquisitions. The value of deals conducted by Indian companies grew at a compound annual growth rate of 28.3 per cent over 2000–07 to reach US$ 30.4 billion in 2007, of which US$ 22.6 billion represented cross-border transactions (Accenture, 2008).

Growing trade integration offers increasing trade opportunities whereas capital market integration offers opportunities for capital flows and investment. Investors can explore opportunities for investment in an increasing number of Indian multinationals that are going for more and more foreign money to meet their growing needs.

Impact of global economic crisis

Despite having no direct exposure to the sub-prime mortgage assets and a largely domestically driven economy (with merchandise exports accounting for less than 15 per cent of GDP), India could not escape unscathed from the global economic crisis due to its rapid and growing integration into the global economy. The recent contagion of the crisis has affected India in three ways – the tightening of liquidity, slowdown of trade, and the economic outlook. Firstly, as a consequence of the global liquidity squeeze, Indian corporates found their overseas financing drying up, forcing corporates to shift their credit demand to the domestic banking sector. The Index of Industrial Production (IIP) grew a mere 2.8 per cent in April 2008 to February 2009 compared with a robust 8.8 per cent growth in the corresponding period of the previous year. Secondly, the forex market came under pressure because of reversal of capital flows as part of the global deleveraging process. Simultaneously, corporates were converting the funds raised locally into foreign currency to meet their external obligations. Both these factors exerted downward pressure on the rupee. Thirdly, the Reserve Bank's intervention in the forex market to manage the volatility in the Rupee further added to liquidity tightening. The RBI took various steps to increase liquidity and also lower the cost of funds for companies and individual borrowers. It has reduced the repo rates (at which it acquires funds from bankers) from 9 per cent to 5.5 per cent, the reverse repo rate (at which it lends to banks) from 6 per cent to 4 per cent, and the cash reserve ratio (CRR) from 9 per cent to 5 per cent between the period October 2008 to March 2009 (Subbarao, 2009).

The trade suffered with the slump in demand for exports, with the United States, the European Union and the Middle East, which account for three-quarters of India's goods and services trade, in a synchronized downturn (Subbarao, 2009). Data on foreign trade available till February 2009 shows that exports posted negative growth for five months in a row since October 2008. Import growth, during this period, also weakened considerably and entered negative territory in January and February. During the first three quarters of 2008–09 (April–December 2008) the trade deficit increased considerably to US\$ 105.3 billion from US\$ 69.3 billion in the previous year. Meanwhile the current account deficit increased from US\$ 15.5 billion (1.8 per cent of GDP) during the corresponding period in 2007–08 to US\$ 36.5 billion (4.1 per cent of GDP) for the period April–December 2008. The capital account balance declined significantly to US\$ 16.09 billion (1.8 per cent of GDP) as compared to US\$ 82.68 billion (9.8 per cent of GDP) during the corresponding period in 2007–08 (*Economic Survey*, 2008–09).

Beyond the liquidity and trade issues, the crisis also spread through the economic outlook. The crisis of confidence in global financial and credit markets increased the risk aversion of the financial system in India and led to banks becoming highly risk averse while lending (Subbarao, 2009).

However, when compared to other emerging markets, India is in a relatively comfortable position to tackle the crisis, as is evident from Table 2.1. Though the growth rate has come down, it is still among the highest among the major global economies. The robust financial system coupled with the domestic demand has helped in reducing the impact. For investors, India is still one of the best options.

Key challenges

Building physical and social infrastructure

India's rapid economic growth over the past few years has put massive strain on the country's existing infrastructure, which has not been able to keep pace with development. The World Economic Forum's *Global Competitiveness Report 2008–09* identifies the country's inadequate infrastructure as the biggest problem for doing business in India (WEF, 2009). The Planning Commission estimates that, to cope with the growing demand, in the span of six

Table 2.1 Emerging markets' risk ranking, 2009

Country	Current account as % of GDP	Short-term debt as % of reserves	Banks' loan/deposit ratio	Overall risk ranking[a]
South Africa	−10.4	81	1.09	17
Hungary	−4.3	79	1.3	16
Poland	−8	38	1.03	14
South Korea	1.3	102	1.3	14
Mexico	−2.5	39	0.93	12
Pakistan	−7.8	27	0.99	12
Brazil	−1.5	22	1.36	10
Turkey	−2.3	70	0.83	10
Russia	1.5	28	1.51	9
Argentina	0.2	63	0.74	8
Venezuela	0.8	58	0.75	7
Indonesia	1.2	88	0.62	6
Thailand	0.3	17	0.88	5
India	−2.4	9	0.74	4
Taiwan	7.9	26	0.87	3
Malaysia	11.3	15	0.72	2
China	5.2	7	0.68	1

Note: [a] Higher score implies higher risk.

Source: *Economist* (2009).

years, India will have to step up investment in infrastructure from 5 per cent of GDP to 9 per cent of GDP. In absolute terms, it means an investment of US$ 500 billion (Chidambaram, 2008). Today, India's infrastructure investment program is struggling to find private investors needed to participate in expanding roads, ports, airports and power. The government has received bids for just twenty-two road projects out of sixty offered by the National Highways Authority of India (NHAI) in the last fiscal year. Many investors that had set their eyes on India have been battered by the global financial crisis and now find debt-heavy Indian infrastructure projects too risky. Indian companies, backed by still strong domestic banks, continue to invest, but they aren't able to invest enough to meet the country's vast expansion plans (Anand, 2009).

India ranks 128 out of 177 countries in the UN's Human Development Index (UNDP, 2008). The reason for poor performance is a result not only of the lack of resources but also poor governance. Moreover, levels of malnutrition and immunization have stagnated during the last decade. Around 25 per cent of India's population is malnourished and lives below the poverty line. More than 230 million people in India are nutrition-deficient or food-insecure (MSSRF, 2009). Further with rapid urbanization, the incidence of lifestyle diseases is expected to further rise. According to industry estimates, over the next six years about US$ 78 billion worth of investment would be required in the Indian healthcare sector. However, the government spending in the healthcare sector still lags behind other developing nations. As a result, private sector participation in this sector is crucial to meet the shortage of quality healthcare facilities – it is expected that of the US$ 78 billion investment, up to US$ 70 billion may come from the private sector (Ernst & Young, 2008). Though India offers demographic dividends, and can be a source of qualified labor for the world, the literacy rates are amongst the lowest of the major economies of the world (World Bank, 2008).

India then needs huge investment in infrastructure, both physical and social. Coupled with the government limitations on spending, this offers a big opportunity for investors. Though earlier there were difficulties, now the new government has given it a priority and efforts are underway to speed up projects and make it more investor friendly.

Enhance competitiveness of the manufacturing sector

Having carved a niche for itself as a global outsourcing hub for services, India needs to enhance the competitiveness of the manufacturing sector to sustain the high level of economic growth in the future. Manufacturing in India contributes to only 16 per cent of GDP, vis-à-vis over 25 per cent in other Asian countries (CII, 2009). There is huge scope for scaling up activities in this sector but key issue remains competitiveness. With competitive pressures increasing from around the world, there is an urgent need for India to build its domestic innovation capabilities and to develop a healthy innovation ecosystem for future growth. The Indian businesses need to continuously enhance their design and engineering skills and develop new capabilities for product and technology innovation to carve a niche in the global market.

Indian firms are trying to catch up with global best practices. This offers opportunities for investors to invest in training and consulting services to help Indian firms become more competitive and be prepared to meet the challenges of global markets and compete successfully against global players.

Making agriculture more productive

Despite the services sector being the growth engine for the Indian economy, the importance of agriculture sector cannot be undermined as it accounts for the livelihood of more than 52 per cent of India's work force. However, the performance of the agriculture sector over the past decade has been far from satisfactory. Agriculture in India continues to be constrained by stagnation of yields, inadequate irrigation infrastructure, declining size of land holdings, inefficient distribution network, lack of technology-led agricultural extension support, inter-state barriers to trade in agricultural products and inadequate linking of farms with the markets. These impediments have led to a deceleration in agriculture growth from 3 per cent in the 1980s to 2 per cent in the last decade. In 2007–08, when the Indian economy grew at 9 per cent, agriculture grew at a meager 3.7 per cent. Agriculture in India still continues to be dominated by small land holdings, and per capita productivity rose by only 7 per cent between 1995 and 2004, compared with 25 per cent in China over the same period (WEF, 2009).

Currently, agriculture is heavily dependent on monsoons. India also has one of the highest wastages in the world, touching nearly 90 per cent in some cases. This offers investors opportunities to invest in bringing best practices into agriculture, particularly in agriculture supply chain and food processing industries.

Fiscal consolidation

The recurring fiscal deficit remains one of the primary constraints on growth, as deficits divert resources from critical development spending. The revenue and fiscal deficits in the revised budget estimates for 2008–09 are significantly higher than the budgeted level as well as those of the preceding year (Budget, 2009). The bloated deficit figures are also because of the three fiscal stimulus packages announced in December 2008, January 2009, and February 2009, apart from the implementation of the Sixth Pay Commission, agricultural debt waiver, and oil and fertilizer subsidies. The fiscal deficit for 2009 stood at 6 per cent and the current year's deficit (centre and states combined) is likely to be over 10 per cent – among the highest in the world – with severe consequences for industry as the government borrows more to cover its expenses. Going forward, the challenge for fiscal policy will be to maintain a balance between short-term goals of boosting demand to revive the economy with the long-term need to restore fiscal consolidation process.

Conclusion and key issues

The aim of this chapter was to provide a backdrop of the Indian economic environment that can help readers to assess the emerging growth opportunities and challenges. This chapter was structured into six sections. The section on economic reforms and performance outlined the basic contours of India's economic growth performance after independence, and briefly discussed the role of economic reforms. The Indian economy was suffering from inward-looking and state-interventionist policies till the major reforms of 1991.The economic reforms has resulted in better economic performance. The third section reviewed the macroeconomic trends that characterized India's growth performance in the post-independence period, with a special focus on the relative roles of domestic and international actors, including the part played by foreign investment, trade, and other dimensions of openness. Strong growth in savings rate coupled with investment, fast growth in services; strong domestic consumption; and global integration have driven the country to this stage. The following section discussed the magnitude of impact of the global financial crisis on Indian economy. Though the effect is there, India is still among the best performing major global economies. The fifth section examined the key challenges of infrastructure, competitiveness of the manufacturing sector, productivity of agriculture and fiscal consolidation that pose risks to India's economic prospects. These challenges also offer big business and investment opportunities. This last section summarizes the chapter and lists the key lessons from the chapter.

Key issues

- India is a big opportunity for investors in terms of a supplier of goods and services, as well as talent but also a big market for goods and services.
- Over the last two decades, economic reforms have played a key role in boosting the economy, and, going forward, this remains the key for sustainable economic progress of the country.
- India's medium and long-term growth prospects remain promising, as the country continues to enjoy impressive growth in consumer spending, bolstered by long-term fundamentals including demographic dividend, rising per capita income and rising urbanization.
- The fact that India is yet to fully utilize its growth potential offers growth opportunities. Despite being one of the fastest-growing economies in the world, India's per capita GDP at market exchange rates remains fairly low. The low per capita income masks considerable pockets of wealth that exist in India, often alongside the vast masses of the poor. The low income level along with a huge population offers opportunities for investment for productivity and low cost innovations.
- Infrastructure, both physical and social, needs immediate attention as lack of quality infrastructure exerts pressure on the competitiveness of Indian manufacturing as well as exports in terms of increased costs. This requires

huge investment, which is not possible through government alone and thus offers a big investment opportunity for investors.

- The manufacturing sector needs to enhance competitiveness whereas the agriculture sector needs to improve productivity and reduce wastage. Both these sectors offer investment opportunities particularly for training and consultancy for bringing the global best practices and investments in supply chain and food processing industry.
- Understanding the Indian market is critical. It is not only urban India, but also rural India, which offers increasing opportunities for investment.
- Collaboration is the key to manage the complexities of diversity of India and government regulations. Dual challenges of understanding the expectations of a highly diverse population and the ability to predict, prepare and act on the growth opportunities would require businesses to be in the right places at the right time. In some cases, a collaborative network of strong regional players may be helpful to reach, connect with and do business in the local conditions.

References

Accenture (2008) *High Performance through Mergers and Acquisitions: India's New Dynamics*. Retrieved May 2, 2009, from Accenture India. Website: http://www. accenture.com/NR/rdonlyres/69D1B1F5–8EAE-48D7-A865 F96FCCCD60CE/ 0/9065_IndiaMADynamics_final22.pdf.

Acharya, S. (2008) *India's Macroeconomic Performance and Policies since 2000*. ICRIER Working Paper 225. Retrieved May 2, 2009, from ICRIER website: http://www.icrier.org/publication/WorkingPaper225.pdf.

Anand, G. (2009, April 28) *India's Infrastructure Funds Fall*. Retrieved June 17, 2009, from *Wall Street Journal* website: http://online.wsj.com/article/SB1240860599714 60379.html.

Banga, R. (2006) *Critical Issues in India's Services-led Growth*. ADB INRM Policy Brief No. 2. Retrieved May 5, 2009, from ADB website: www.adb.org/Documents/ Papers/INRM-PolicyBriefs/inrm2.pdf.

Budhwar, P. (2001) Doing Business in India. *Thunderbird International Business Review*, 43 (4): 549–68.

Chidambaram, P. (2008) *Sustaining Growth amidst Global Uncertainty*. Retrieved May 9, 2009, from Finance Ministry website: http://financeminister.gov.in/26.03.2008_ fm_statement.html.

Confederation of Indian Industry (CII) (2009) Communiqué. Retrieved May 2, 2009, from CII website: http://www.cii.in/documents/Communique/communique_May 09.pdf.

CSO (2009) *Important Statements on NAS 2009*. Retrieved May 12, 2009, from MOSPI website: http://mospi.nic.in/nas_2009_10feb09.pdf.

Economic Survey (2007–08), chapter 1, State of the economy. Retrieved May 11, 2009, from Government of India website: http://indiabudget.nic.in/es2007–8/esmain.htm.

Economic Survey (2008–09), chapter 1, State of the economy. Retrieved June 11, 2009, from Government of India website: http://indiabudget.nic.in/es2008–9/chapt2009/ chap12.pdf.

Economic Survey (2008–09), chapter 1, State of the economy. Retrieved June 11, 2009, from Government of India website: http://indiabudget.nic.in/.

Economist (2009, February 26) *Domino Theory: Where could Emerging-market Contagion Spread Next?* Retrieved June 17, 2009, from the *Economist* website: http://www.economist.com/businessfinance/displayStory.cfm?story_id = 13184631.

Ernst & Young (2008) *Investment and Financing in Healthcare Sector*. eHealth, 3 (4), http://www.ehealthonline.org/pdf/april08.pdf.

Goldman Sachs (2003) *Dreaming with BRICs: The Path to 2050*. Retrieved June 11, 2009, from Goldman Sachs website: http://www2.goldmansachs.com/ideas/brics/brics-dream.html.

IHS Global Insights (2009) *Economic Growth: Recent Developments: India Country Intelligence Report*. Retrieved June 5, 2009, from Global Insights website: http://www.globalinsight.com/Highlight/HighlightDetail2350.htm.

Kumar, R., Palit, A. and Singh, K. (2007) *Sustainability of Economic Growth in India*. Centre for International Governance Innovation (CIGI) Working Paper No. 25. Retrieved June 11, 2009, from CIGI website: http://www.cigionline.org/publications/workingpaper.

Mohan, R. (2008) *The Growth Record of the Indian Economy, 1950–2008: A Story of Sustained Savings and Investment*. Retrieved June 11, 2009, from RBI website: http://rbidocs.rbi.org.in/rdocs/Speeches/PDFs/83118.pdf.

M. S. Swaminathan Research Foundation (MSSRF) (2009) *Report on the State of Food Insecurity in Rural India*. Retrieved June 11, 2009, from MSSRF website: http://www.mssrf.org/fs/atlas4.htm.

Planning Commission (2006) *Eleventh Five Year Plan*. Retrieved June 1, 2009, from Planning Commission website: http://planningcommission.nic.in/plans/planrel/fiveyr/11th/11_v3/11th_vol3.pdf.

Poddar, T. and Yi, E. (2007) *India's Rising Growth Potential*. Retrieved June 11, 2009, from Goldman Sachs website: http://www2.goldmansachs.com/ideas/brics/book/BRIC-Chapter1.pdf.

Shukla, R. K., Dwivedi, S. K. and Sharma, A. (2005) *The Great Indian Market*. New Delhi: NCEAR.

Singh, N. (2008) *India's Development Strategy: Accidents, Design and Replicability*. WIDER Research Paper 2009/31. Retrieved June 3, 2009, from WIDER website: http://www.wider.unu.edu/publications/working-papers/research-papers/2009/en_GB/rp2009–31/.

Subbarao, D. (2009) *India: Managing the Impact of the Global Financial Crisis*. Retrieved from Lecture Notes Online website: http://rbidocs.rbi.org.in/rdocs/Bulletin/PDFs/SPCH1704–2.pdf.

UNDP (2008) *Human Development Report 2008*. New York: UNDP.

World Bank (2008) *World Development Indicators*. Washington DC: World Bank.

World Economic Forum (WEF) (2009) *Global Competitiveness Report 2008–2009*. Geneva: World Economic Forum.

3 Employment law framework

Structure and potential hurdles

Debi S. Saini

India has a comprehensive framework of employment legislation, which is aimed to provide social justice to the working class. We will be using employment law and labour law interchangeably in this chapter. This branch of law enjoys a special place in the Indian legal system. As per this thinking, most labour matters have been kept out of the jurisdiction of civil courts. Special adjudicatory bodies have been created under different pieces of labour legislation for expeditiously adjudicating labour claims. The Indian judiciary has played a significant role in interpreting these laws for the benefit of the employers as well as the working class.

This chapter seeks to analyse the structure of Indian employment law in the context of the broad framework of social and economic justice as enshrined in the Constitution of India. An attempt has also been made towards analysing the working of the employment law framework for employers in view of the changing needs of the global economy. The issues discussed relate to the structure and functioning of various branches of Indian employment law, i.e. the law relating to working conditions; the law of industrial relations, the law relating to wages and monetary benefits, and the law of social security. It also assesses, in the form of an overview, the hurdles that the Indian labour law framework poses in the smooth conduct of business. The concluding part of the chapter summarizes the salient aspects of the Indian employment law framework.

Context of employment legislation

The contents of most labour laws in the country are rooted in the constitutional obligation of the Indian state to dispense social, economic and political justice. The Constitution also guarantees to citizens certain fundamental rights which are enforceable against the state. These rights, among others, relate to equality before law and rights as to certain freedoms such as: speech; association; movement throughout the territory of India; residence anywhere in India; engaging in profession, trade and business; protection of life and personal liberty; and adopting any religion. The Constitution of India also confers a fundamental right on children below the age of fourteen years whereby it envisages a prohibition on all employers from employing them in factories and hazardous employments.

Chapter IV of the Constitution contains the Directive Principles of State Policy – most labour laws have their source in these directives. These directives consist of a number of articles in the Constitution such as right to just and humane conditions of work, maternity relief, work, living wage, social protection for the sick, and so on. In a way they lay down a welfare agenda to be practiced by the state instrumentalities. Interestingly, this part of the Constitution is not enforceable in any court of law but is mainly a directive by the Constitution that the state shall pursue policies in consonance with these prescriptions so as to render social justice to the citizens. Despite this, the Supreme Court of India has held that the Directive Principles of State policy is of fundamental importance in the governance of the country. The judiciary has frequently reminded the state of its obligation to enact laws in the spirit of these Principles. Many times, the Supreme Court has declared certain pieces of legislation as violating certain parts of the Constitution including the Directive Principles of State Policy.

For the sake of convenience, various pieces of labour legislation in India can be divided into four categories: law relating to conditions of work; law of industrial relations; the law of wages and monetary benefits; and the social security law. The basic scheme of the Constitution is to confer lawmaking power both on the federal (central) as well as the state legislatures. Most labour matters find place in the Concurrent List of the Constitution, which entitles both sets of legislatures to enact laws on such subjects. States have been conferred this power so as to make laws to suit the indigenous situation and local power realities. Consequently, India has about sixty pieces of central labour legislation and nearly 200 pieces of state labour legislation. Some of these laws were already in existence at the time of independence; more were added to give way to the philosophy of welfare state as enshrined in the Constitution. Economists and labour academics have often argued that Indian labour is over protected. They have also felt a dire need for carrying out labour law reforms in order to meet the needs of the changing global economy. Some of the most salient pieces of Indian labour legislation can be listed as follows (Saini, 2009; Saini and Budhwar, 2007):

- Apprentices Act, 1961
- Beedi and Cigar Workers (Conditions of Employment) Act, 1966
- Bonded Labour System (Abolition) Act, 1976
- Building and other Construction Workers (Regulation of Employment Service) Act, 1996
- Child Labour (Prohibition and Regulation) Act, 1986
- Cine Workers and Cinema Theatre Workers (Regulation of Employment) Act, 1981
- Contract Labour (Regulation and Abolition) Act, 1970
- Dangerous Machines (Regulation) Act, 1983

- Dock Workers (Regulation of Employment) Act, 1948
- Dock Workers (Safety, Health and Welfare) Act, 1986
- Emigration Act, 1983
- Employees Provident Fund and Miscellaneous Provisions Act, 1952
- Employees' State Insurance Act, 1948
- Employment exchanges (Compulsory Notification of vacancies) Act, 1959
- Employers' Liability Act, 1938
- Equal Remuneration Act, 1976
- Factories Act, 1948
- Industrial Disputes Act, 1947
- Industrial Employment (Standing Orders) Act, 1946
- Inter-state Migrant Workmen (Regulation of Employment and Conditions of Service) Act, 1979
- Labour Laws (Exemption from Furnishing Returns and Maintaining Registers by Certain Establishments) Act, 1988
- Maternity Benefit Act, 1961
- Mines Act, 1952
- Minimum Wages Act, 1948
- Motor Transport Workers Act, 1961
- National Commission for Safai Karamcharis Act, 1993
- Payment of Bonus Act, 1965
- Payment of Gratuity Act, 1972
- Payment of Wages Act, 1936
- Plantations Labour Act, 1951
- Public Liability Insurance Act, 1991
- Sales Promotion Employees (Conditions of Service) Act, 1976
- Trade Union Act, 1926
- Weekly Holidays Act, 1948
- Workmen's Compensation Act, 1923

The most important source of labour law in the country is legislation. However, the federal as well as the state governments have been conferred rule-making powers so as to supplement the basic law laid down in different pieces of legislation. These rules and regulations are also referred to as subordinate legislation or delegated legislation as they are enacted by the executive branch of the state. Thus almost each piece of legislation enacted by a legislature has commensurate rules that are to be read along with the legislation to get a comprehensive picture. Another very important source of labour law in India are the decisions of the higher judiciary. India follows the common law system and not the civil law system. The common law system puts great importance on the decided cases as an important source of law. The higher judiciary – consisting of the Supreme Court and the High Courts of different states – has delivered hundreds of thousands of decisions in post-independence India to clarify the intentions of the legislature in different branches of law.

A large number of these decisions are in the domain of the labour legislation. Specifically, labour in the organized sector also gets benefits under collective bargaining agreements, which helps in improving the terms and conditions as implied in their contract of employment.

The law relating to working conditions

Working people in India are employed in different sectors, including factories, shops and establishments, plantations, railways, motor transport undertakings, mines, etc. In fact, presently nearly 60 per cent of the Indian work force is employed in the agriculture sector. However, there is almost no labour legislation which applies to this sector. Among others, one of the key reasons for this is that most holdings are very small, and most employees and employers in this sector are poor or very poor. This sector has thus been largely left out of the ambit of labour legislation. Some of the main pieces of legislation regulating working conditions for different sets of employers are discussed as follows.

The Factories Act, 1948

The Factories Act, 1948, was one of the first pieces of labour legislation enacted after independence. Factories fall under the organized sector in India. The principal definition under the Act is of the term 'factory'. It means premises or precincts whereby a manufacturing process is carried on with the use of power by ten or more persons or by twenty or more persons without the use of power. The term 'manufacturing process' also carries a very wide connotation. It includes even pumping of water, oil, repair work shops, etc., besides conversion of raw material into finished product for use, sale or otherwise disposal. Similarly, the term 'worker' under this Act has a wide definition. It means a person employed in the manufacturing process and includes even those persons who are employed by or through a contractor in the principal employer's factory.

The main provisions of the Factories Act are those related to: health, welfare, and safety of workers; conditions under which women work; working hours for adults and children; leave with wages for workers; protection against hazardous operations; payment of over time; inspection of the work in factories by inspectors; and the role of other authorities under this law. The Act obliges every employer to register his factory and obtain a license from the State government before the employer seeks to set up a factory. In this regard the occupier of the factory has also to obtain the approval for the site to be used for the construction of factory premises. The Act also provides for certain obligations of every occupier before the factory starts working.

Provision has been made for certain number of annual leaves with wages for workers, depending on the number of days worked. A factory worker can be asked to work for a maximum of nine hours per day, and forty-eight hours per week. And, a rest interval of half an hour after every five hours of work has to be provided. The total spread over of work in a day can not exceed ten and a half hours. Employers wanting their workers to work overtime must pay double the normal rate. Every employer must provide a week off to all workers. Children who have not attained the age of fourteen years are not permitted to be employed in a factory.

The provisions relating to health of factory workers include certain requirements as to: rest, waste disposal, handling of dust and fumes, ventilation, artificial humidification, provision of drinking water, provision of latrines and urinals, and avoidance of overcrowding. The Act also provides for certain welfare facilities such as washing and drying of clothes, providing the facility of sitting to workers in certain cases, shelters, canteens, lunch rooms, first aid appliances, and crèches for women workers' children below six years of age.

Under the safety provisions, this Act provides for detailed specifications about the space to be provided to every person working in a factory; installation of machines, their fencing and working; installation and maintenance of hoists, lifts, chains, ropes, lifting machines, etc.; opening in floors, pits and sumps; precautions in case of fire; and maximum weight that a worker can be asked to carry. This Act was substantially amended in 1987. This amendment was consequent to the Bhopal gas disaster that involved a factory of Union Carbide in the city of Bhopal in which nearly 8,000 people died and many thousands got disabled. This disaster also led to introspection by the Indian government about the adequacy of the provisions of the Factories Act. The amendment was carried out in 1987, and chapter IV-A was inducted in this Act. This amendment tightened the provisions related to hazardous processes. Sections 41-A to 41-H were added. Two new schedules were added, which are known as the First Schedule and the Second Schedule. The first schedule is applicable to hazardous processes and applies to twenty-nine industries. The second schedule contains the permissible level of certain specified chemical substances in the work environment. Among other things, there are provisions relating to the site appraisal committees, compulsory disclosure of certain types of information by the occupier so as to ensure safety of workers, permissible limits of exposure of chemicals and toxic substances, rights of workers to participate in management related to safety matters, and workers' rights to be warned by the occupier in case of imminent danger to their life. Section 111-A of the Act gives a right to the worker to get information related to his or her health and safety at work. They also were given the right to be trained by the employer in matters related to health and safety.

The Amendment Act of 1987 substantially enhanced the penalties that can be inflicted on persons responsible for the violation of this Act. After the amendment imprisonment has also been enhanced up to two years and a fine of Rs 100,000 can be inflicted for certain violations of the Act.

The legislation relating to shops and establishments

The shops and establishments legislation in India is not a central legislation. Rather, each state legislature had the power to enact a law in this regard. Different states have also framed their own rules applicable to the shops and establishments. Most states have somewhat similar legislation related to shops and establishments with minor differences here and there. Most workers who are employed in shops and establishments are believed to be in the informal sector; however, there are certain larger establishments as well such as motor transport companies, insurance companies, etc. So it covers larger as well as smaller shops and establishments. Interestingly, the establishments which do not fall under the definition of the factory as per the Factories Act, 1948, as they employ lesser number of workers, get covered under the shops and establishments law. Most such pieces of legislation have made provisions related to compulsory registration of shops and establishments. They have also made provisions related to the hours per day, as well as per week, that a worker can be asked to work. Comprehensive provisions have been laid down related to the spread over of work, rest interval, opening and closing hours, days on which the shops/establishments must be closed, provision of national and religious holidays, provision of overtime, etc.

The Mines Act, 1952

The Mines Act, 1952 provides for health, safety and welfare of workers employed in mines. The term "mine" refers to carrying on of any operation for excavation that goes on for the purpose of searching for or obtaining minerals. It also includes, among other things, all borings, boreholes, oil wells and accessory crude conditioning plants within the oilfields, etc. Further, it includes any premises that are connected with mining operations and near or in the mining area.

This Act provides for various health and welfare provisions for those working in mines. They include, among others, supply of drinking water, medical appliances and conservancy. There is also a provision for giving notice to the appropriate authorities if any accident takes place or a worker catches any disease. The overtime rate is also provided at a rate twice the daily wages that a worker receives. This is for both – workers working above the ground and workers working below the ground. There is a prohibition for women to work below ground. A person who has not attained the age of eighteen years is not allowed to work in a mine. However, there is a provision that apprentices and trainees who are not below the age of sixteen years can be allowed to work provided they work under proper supervision of the manager. The mines workers are entitled to annual leave with wages. These leaves have to be calculated at the rate of one day leave for every fifteen days of work.

The Plantation Labour Act, 1951

The conditions of work of workers employed in plantations are regulated by the Plantation Labour Act, 1951 (PLA). The Act applies to plantations of coffee, rubber and cinchona. All plantations are required to be registered with a registration officer appointed under the Act. The provisions of PLA mainly deal with health and welfare measures. The term plantation has been defined as 'any plantation to which this Act, whether wholly or in part, applies and includes offices, hospitals, dispensaries, schools, and any other premises used for any purpose connected with such plantation . . .'.

The health and welfare measures provided under PLA include: drinking water, medical facilities, crèches, recreational facilities, educational facilities, and housing for workers and their families. The welfare measures also include supply of umbrellas, blankets and raincoats. The Act envisages that employers shall provide and maintain necessary housing accommodation for every worker including his or her family residing in the plantation; and for everyone residing outside the plantation in case he or she has put in six months of continuous service in the plantation and desires to reside in the plantation. Among others, the Act had made provisions for working hours, weekly holiday and leave with wages. A child who is less than twelve years of age is not allowed to be employed in a plantation. The employer has to provide free educational facilities for workers' children who are between the age of six and twelve years. Provisions have also been made for regulating working hours, weekly holidays and leave with wages. The Act also provides for inspecting, medical and other staff that facilitates the process of securing compliance with various provisions of the Act.

The Contract Labour (Regulation and Abolition) Act, 1970

Especially after the onset of the globalization process, the number of workers employed by employers through contractors is on the rise. Most of these workers work under difficult conditions and get low wages. The Contract Labour (Regulation and Abolition) Act, 1970 (CLA), seeks to regulate the employment conditions of such workers, though this Act came into existence in the heydays of the welfare state era. As per CLA, all employers employing contract labour are required to register themselves with the registrar appointed by the appropriate government concerned. And the contractor working for the principal employers must obtain a license from the appropriate licensing authorities. One of the principal provisions of the Act relates to the payment of wages to the contract workers in the presence of the principal employer's representative. Such representative has to certify that wages were paid to the workers concerned in his/her presence. It is also important that the employer should employ contract labour in a legal way that is permissible under the law. There have been cases of sham contracts brought to the attention of the courts, whereby the courts declared that such contract workers would be deemed to be workers of the principal employer. Therefore, employers need to be extremely careful in employing contract labour by following the details of the law as laid down by the judiciary through decided cases.

The Act provides for certain health and welfare measures for contract labour as provided in chapter V of the CLA. Among others, a canteen is to be provided by the contractor in case 100 or more contract workers are employed. In case the contract labour is supposed to halt at night for the purpose of work the contractor is to provide rest rooms for them. It is also provided that first aid facilities should be readily made available for contract workers. Among others, the welfare facilities to be provided by the contractor include: wholesome drinking water, latrines and urinals, and washing facilities. The Act provides that if any of these facilities is not provided by the contractor it is the duty of the principal employer to provide them. Of course, he is entitled to recover the money so spent from the contractor concerned while paying the bills of the contractor.

The Inter-state Migrant Workmen (Regulation of Employment and Conditions of Service) Act, 1979

Indian industries employ a good number of inter-state migrant workers. The conditions of work of these workers are regulated by the Inter-state Migrant Workmen (Regulation of Employment and Conditions of Service) Act, 1979 (ISMWA). This Act was enacted with a view to protecting the migrant workers from exploitation. The Act seeks to provide them certain minimum conditions of employment. It applies to every establishment and contractor who employ five or more interstate migrant workmen. Among others, the Act provides for compulsory registration of the principal employer and licensing of the contractor concerned. It is also envisaged that all the liabilities of migrant workers shall stand erased after the completion of the contract of employment.

The Act provides for issuing a passbook to every inter-state migrant worker, which shall contain full details about his or her employment, payment of displacement allowance, payment of journey allowance and payment of wages during the period of the journey, suitable residential accommodation and medical facilities, protective clothing, and equal pay for equal work irrespective of sex, etc. The responsibility for payment of wages to the contract workers is of the contractor, which he is supposed to do in the presence of a representative of the principal employer.

Child Labour (Abolition and Regulation) Act, 1985

It is believed that the largest number of child workers in the world is to be found in India. The Child Labour (Abolition and Regulation) Act, 1985 (CLARA), was enacted to safeguard their interests. This law prohibits the employment of children below the age of fourteen years in factories and hazardous employments. Such employments, among others, include glass and glassware, fireworks and match making, and carpet weaving. In those cases where children are allowed to work, the Act regulates their employment. The working hours for children have also been fixed. It is provided that the total spread over a day, in the case of child workers, is not to exceed six hours. Provision has been made for a weeks holiday. Health and safety measures are to be provided for all children as per the provisions of the Act. Stringent punishment is provided for violation of the Act.

The law regulating employee relations

The Indian labour law system provides for three principal industrial relations laws, which seek to regulate employer–employee relations. They are: the Trade Unions Act, 1926 (TUA); the Industrial Employment (Standing Orders) Act, 1946; and the Industrial Disputes Act, 1947 (IDA). All these three laws have been in existence for a long time; in fact, they are all pre-independence pieces of legislation. The salient features of these three laws are discussed below:

The Trade Unions Act, 1926

The Trade Unions Act, 1926 (TUA), seeks to provide for registration of trade unions, and thus to create a countervailing power in favour of the working class in the game of industrial relations. Interestingly, this Act provides that all employees employed in industry including managers can become members of trade unions. It even makes it possible to have a trade union in which workers, managers and employers are members. In actuality it is mostly the workers who become members of a trade union. It is provided that any seven or more members can register a trade union. But this is subject to a minimum of 10 per cent of the workers who are employed in industry or 100, whichever is less. When a trade union is registered it acquires a corporate status or what may be called a legal personification through the act of incorporation under the TUA. Among others, the law lays down the rights and liabilities of a registered trade union. Perhaps, the most important right of a registered trade union is the immunities it enjoys from certain civil and criminal wrongs that amount to conspiracy under the Indian Penal Code, and are committed in furtherance of a trade dispute. The Act also provides that a certain number of outsiders can become members of a trade union. They are called special members. These special members can be only those who are members of the executive of a trade union.

The TUA confers immunity upon a registered trade union and its members against certain civil and criminal acts – which amount to becoming a conspiracy – done in furtherance of a trade dispute provided the act concerned is not an agreement to commit an offence. The rationale of providing for such immunity is to allow a registered trade union and its members their right to withdraw labour if they perceive exploitation, and use that situation of work stoppage as a tactic in the bargaining process. The Industrial Disputes Act, 1947 (IDA), is the principal legislation that deals with processing of industrial disputes in India. Though IDA is silent about the manner in which an industrial dispute can be espoused, the Supreme Court of India has held that an industrial dispute can be espoused by about 20 per cent or more of the workforce that can be called as substantial number of persons. Thus, espousal of an industrial dispute or collective bargaining is possible without forming a trade union. However, in reality this rarely happens.

Recognition of a trade union is purely a discretionary matter for the employer; it/he can refuse to recognize a union or unions without any legal consequences. The TUA does not contain any provisions for recognition. Recognition is something that workers can gain through show of their strength. In the post-globalization scenario, most employers including multinational companies are pursuing 'no union' strategies by creating and implementing appropriate human resource management (HRM) strategies. This has led to a lower incidence of union formation and recognition, especially in the private sector.

The Industrial Employment (Standing Orders) Act, 1946

The objective of the Industrial Employment (Standing Orders) Act, 1946 (IESOA), is to define with sufficient precision the conditions of work for different categories of workers and to make them known to them so that they develop some amount of consciousness about their employment rights. This Act applies to industrial employments that employ 100 or more workers. But many state governments have extended its applicability to establishments employing lesser number of workers. The term 'workman' has the same meaning as in the Industrial Disputes Act, 1947 (IDA). This legislation envisages a certifying officer appointed by the appropriate government whose job is to receive draft standing orders from the employers, making them known to the union concerned or to workers if there is no union, hear both the sides, and eventually certifying the standing orders that s/he considers just and fair for both sides. The matters about which the standing orders can be certified have been provided in the Schedule to the IESOA. Various matters that find place in this schedule, among others, are: classification of workmen, rules of discipline, working of shifts, workers' attendance and lateness, conditions for applying for leaves, disciplinary action and termination of employment, and means of grievance redressal. In case a worker is suspended for committing misconduct s/he has to be paid suspension allowance as per the provisions of the Act. The Act also provides for suspension allowance to be paid to a worker while s/he remains suspended for disciplinary action. After certification, each of the standing orders is deemed to be written in the contract of employment of the worker concerned.

The Industrial Disputes Act, 1947

Perhaps the most important of all labour laws in India is believed to be the Industrial Dispute Act, 1947 (IDA). Until about twenty years ago the IDA was believed to be the ultimate source for all personnel managers. That was so in the era of license and control by the government. All conflict resolution was reactive in nature and conflicts were resolved by using the various provisions of the IDA. However, after globalization came into vogue, a shift is discernible in the management style of especially the enlightened employers: they are becoming less and less legalistic in their approach to conflict management and have begun investing more into people development and using alternative means of managing industrial conflict including containing the countervailing power of workers.

The hallmark of the IDA is statutory machinery for dispute processing and resolution. This machinery envisages conciliation, adjudication and arbitration as the key methods of resolving industrial disputes in case mutual negotiation fails to deliver. The machinery contemplated in the IDA applies to individual as well as collective and interest as well rights issues. The IDA provides for seven forums for dealing with disputes or matters related to them. Works committees are to be appointed by every employer who employs 100 or more workers in an industry. The provision of conciliation relates to appointment by the appropriate government of a conciliation officer (CO) and constitution boards of conciliation (BOC). COs are normally appointed for different regions to handle industrial disputes in their region. They are government officers, who are expected to facilitate dispute resolution between the disputant parties. A BOC is not a standing body like a CO; it has to be appointed as per the demands of a particular dispute. A BOC consists of three or five members with equal representation from the employer and workmen concerned and one independent person. However, the system of BOC seems to be dead in the country, as no such BOCs have been appointed in the last three decades or so.

In cases where a dispute is not resolved through the mediation of the conciliation machinery it can go for adjudication. Three adjudicatory bodies have been envisaged in the IDA; they are: labour courts, industrial tribunals, and national tribunals. Their jurisdictions are different, which are provided in the Second Schedule and the Third Schedule of the Act. The former contains rights matters that fall in the jurisdiction of labour courts and the latter enumerates interest matters that can be processed only by an industrial tribunal. However, industrial tribunals can even decide rights matters contained in the Second Schedule. Unlike civil courts, adjudicatory bodies under the IDA cannot be activated by the parties themselves. An industrial dispute can be processed and decided by an adjudicatory body only if it has been referred to it by the appropriate government in its discretion. The IDA defines the term 'appropriate government,' which is aimed to clearly provide as to which government will have the jurisdiction in conciliation and adjudication of a particular dispute. The adjudicatory bodies are not strictly judicial in nature, but are only quasi-judicial. They deliver awards that bind the disputant parties.

The IDA also makes provision for arbitration of industrial disputes by a mutually agreed arbitrator. The arbitrator under the IDA is selected by the disputant parties. But they have to approach the appropriate government for notifying the arbitration agreement in the government's gazette. The arbitrator is expected to process the dispute with much less legal formalities and can also be quicker in delivering his decision. However, in actuality the method of labour arbitration in India is almost dead. This is mainly explained by the fact that parties fear that the arbitrator may be influenced by the other side. Such fears are more noticeable among workers. But to some extent the system of labour arbitration still survives in Mumbai–Thane–Pune industrial belt of India.

Wages and monetary benefits law

The following four pieces of legislation are worth mentioning in the category of the law relating to wages and monetary benefits. These are: the Minimum Wages Act, 1948; the Payment of Wages Act, 1936 (POWA); the Payment of Bonus Act, 1965 (POBA); and the Equal Remuneration Act, 1976 (ERA). Some of the salient features of these pieces of legislation are discussed below:

The Minimum Wages Act, 1948

The Minimum Wages Act, 1948 (MWA), aims to fix minimum wages for workers employed in the employments listed in the two schedules attached to this Act; these schedules consist of two parts – Part I and Part II. Part I contains, among others, the following industries: woollen carpet making, rice mill, flour mill, municipality, public motor transport, construction and maintenance of roads, docks and ports, and most mines. State governments have amended the schedule to this Act so as to add to it additional industries. Part II includes employments that are mostly related to agricultural operations. The appropriate government fixes the minimum wage, which can be central as well as a state government in their respective jurisdictions.

The Supreme Court of India has held that that 'no industry has a right to exist unless it is able to pay its workmen at least a base minimum wage' (*Crown Aluminum Works* v. *Their Workmen*, [AIR 1958, S.C. 30]). At least on paper, the minimum wage payment is an important aspect of industrial working in the country.

The MWA envisages two methods of wage fixing: the committee method, and the gazette notification method. Any of these two methods can be adopted for fixing and revising the minimum wage. The minimum wages under the Act can be fixed in the form of a time rate or a piece rate (with a guaranteed time rate) and an overtime rate. As has been held by the Indian Supreme Court, it is mandatory on the part of the employers to pay minimum wages; and anyone who is not able to pay minimum wage has no right to carry on his industry. Wage rates under the Act can be fixed per hour or per day or per month or even for any longer period. So as to ensure that minimum wages fixed under the Act are actually paid by the employer, a quasi-judicial body is provided for in the form of the authority to hear and decide claims related to delay in payment of minimum wage or payment of less than the minimum wage or unauthorized deductions.

The Payment of Wages Act, 1936

The Payment of Wages Act, 1936 (POWA), is one of the earliest labour laws that was enacted in colonial India. Its objective was to ensure that the employer actually pays wages to the worker on time, pays them in current coin, and does not make impermissible deductions from them. The Act applies to factories, railways and other establishments. Every employer is obliged to fix a wage period which can not exceed one month. In case an employer employs less than 1,000 workers, it/he must normally pay wages before the expiry of the seventh day from the last day in the wage period. In other cases, they must be paid before the expiry of the tenth day from the last day in the wage period.

The Act contains detailed provisions listing permissible deductions that the employer can make from the worker's wages. Some of these include: fines; absence from duty; damage or loss of goods entrusted to employed person; accommodation and service; recovery of advance; recovery of loans; income tax, etc. Employers are obliged to maintain registers and records, which help in facilitating inspection of these books and registers. The Act envisages a quasi-judicial body to hear and decide claims of workers related to non-payment or delayed payment of wages or undue deductions.

The Payment of Bonus Act, 1965

The Payment of Bonus Act, 1965 (POBA), envisages a scheme of sharing the gains of industry between the employer and the employee in a specified way. The Act applies to all factories defined under the Factories Act, 1948, and all establishments wherein twenty or more persons are employed on any day during the accounting year. It provides qualification of the employee for making him entitled to get bonus under this Act. As per this, he must have worked for at least thirty days in a year. If an employee was dismissed for any fraud or riotous behaviour while on premises; or for theft, misappropriation or sabotage of any property of the establishment; s/he may be disqualified to receive bonus.

POBA talks of payment by every covered employer of minimum annual bonus even in situations of losses. It is for this reason that minimum bonus in India is treated as a deferred wage. But in the initial five years of the existence of the establishment, bonus will be payable only in case the employer has allocable surplus that is calculated as per the scheme of this Act.

The Equal Remuneration Act, 1976

The Equal Remuneration Act, 1976 (ERA), applies to all establishments whether belonging to the public or the private sector. It envisages a duty on the part of all employers to pay equal remuneration to men and women for doing the same work or work of similar nature. Broadly speaking, for determining whether the work done is the same or of similar nature, it is important to see skill, efforts and responsibilities of the employees concerned. The Act prohibits discrimination between men and women even in matters related to recruitment for doing the same work or work of similar nature.

The social security law

In Western countries social security is known to be a separate branch of law; but this is not so in India. Here it is treated as part of labour law. There are two known aspects of social protection mechanism: social insurance and social assistance. As far as the organized sector workers in India are concerned, social security can be divided into three categories: states' creation of statutory unilateral liability of the employer in case of certain specific contingencies; social insurance schemes; and the provident fund. So far as the employer's unilateral liability is concerned four main laws can be said to fall in this category. They are: the Workmen's Compensation Act, 1923 (WCA); the Maternity Benefit Act, 1961 (MBA); the Payment of Gratuity Act, 1972 (PGA); and some parts of the Industrial Disputes Act, 1947 (IDA). In the second category falls the main social insurance law of India, i.e. the Employees' State Insurance Act, 1948 (ESIA). Some countries in South Asia provide social security to organized sector workers through some special funds called provident funds. In India, this fund is envisaged under the Employees Provident Funds (and Miscellaneous Provisions) Act, 1952 (EPFA).

The Workmen's Compensation Act, 1923

The Workmen's Compensation Act, 1923 (WCA), is one of the earliest labour laws in India. It fixes a unilateral liability on an employer for any injury or death resulting from an accident that takes place in the course of employment and arises out of an individual's employment related duties. While in case of injury compensation is payable to the injured worker himself or herself, in case of death it is payable to his or her dependents. Apart from injuries resulting from accidents, protection has also been given in case of occupational disease occurring in certain circumstances. The employments that are covered in this Act include, among others, factories, mines, plantations, railways, construction, electricity generation, cinemas and circus. Many other categories of employment that are considered as hazardous have also been included for coverage (see Schedule II of the WCA). Normally, persons employed in clerical capacity are excluded, though not in all situations. Also, if a person is covered under the Employees' State Insurance Act, 1948 (ESIA), s/he cannot get any benefit under the WCA.

It is important to note that the employer's liability under the WCA towards his workers is not related to his negligence. It depends on the interpretation of a much wider term, i.e. 'arising out of and in the course of employment'. This implies that it is enough if there is a nexus between the accident and the employment. Compensation is determined with reference to workers' wages and a relevant factor appropriate to the worker concerned (which depends on the age of the worker). Younger workers have a higher relevant factor. So other things being the same if two workers die in an accident getting the same wages, the younger one will get higher amount of compensation as her/his relevant factor is higher. Compensation is payable in four types of situations: death; permanent total disablement (100 per cent); permanent partial disablement; temporary disablement. Mostly, the only accidents that are covered are those that take place within the premises of the workplace; but in some situations the principle of 'notional extension of employer's premises' is applied to cover accidents taking place outside the employer's premises. All workers are covered under the Act despite their wages, but a notional ceiling of Rs 4,000 per month is put by the Act for the purpose of calculation of compensation.

Employers can escape liability under this act by contracting out their liability by compelling the worker to sign a 'no claim' bond. To prevent that from happening, such contracting out has been prohibited.

The Employees' State Insurance Act, 1948

The Employees' State Insurance Act, 1948 (ESIA), is the principal social insurance law in India. The hallmark of this law is an employee state insurance scheme (ESIS) that is administered by the Employees State Insurance Corporation (ESIC). This is perhaps the only social security law in India which has an insurance element in it. In order to obtain the benefits envisaged, the employees must have paid contributions as per the scheme of the Act. The contributions are payable by the employer as well as the worker. Presently the rates of contribution made by the employer for each employee are 4.75 per cent of the employee's monthly wages. The employee has to contribute 1.75 per cent of her/his monthly wages. The employer is responsible to make the payment for his own as well as his contractor's workers. Of course, he can recover it from the contractor while paying the contractor's bills or otherwise.

The ESIA initially covered factories employing twenty or more persons. Later on its application was extended to other power-using factories which employ between ten to nineteen persons, shops, hotels and restaurants, and cinemas. It covers employees getting a salary of up to Rs 7,500 per month. Unlike most other labour laws, the ESIA covers all employees irrespective of their designation provided their salary is below the specified wage limit. Unlike the other unilateral liability laws, the ESIS envisages making available a number of benefits to the employees covered. The amount of benefit that an employee beneficiary gets under this Act is proportionate to the average daily wage that the employee concerned receives.

The employer has to deposit the ESI contribution in the ESI Fund. This fund is administered by the ESI Corporation (ESIC). The benefits provided under the ESIS are sickness and extended sickness benefit, maternity benefit, disablement benefit, dependants' benefit, reimbursement of funeral expenses, and medical benefit. Sickness benefit is payable when an employee produces a certificate to that effect. It is payable at the standard benefit rate (SBR). Roughly, this rate is about 50 per cent of the employee's wages. For knowing one's SBR, one has to look into the Standard Benefit Rate table. The ESIC runs and manages its own hospitals and dispensaries throughout India which make available medical treatment to the beneficiary employees.

The Employee Insurance Court decides any dispute arising under the ESI Scheme. Civil courts do not have any jurisdiction in matters related with the ESIS. Penalties for violation of the Act have been specified in the Act.

The Employees' Provident Fund (and Miscellaneous Provisions) Act, 1952

Two of the key pieces of legislation that deal with provision of social security are ESIA and the Employees' Provident Fund and Miscellaneous Provisions Act, 1952 (EPF Act). The EPF Act applies to factories related with any of the industries that are specified in Schedule I to this Act provided twenty or more persons are employed in it; and to other establishments employing twenty or more persons that may be specified by the central government through a notification. The Act covers employees whose salaries do not exceed Rs 6,500 per month. However, voluntary coverage is permitted; and employers wanting to cover their employees are free to do so.

Three important schemes are envisaged under this EPF Act. These are: the Provident Fund Scheme; the Deposit-linked Insurance Scheme; and the Employee Pension Scheme.

The main scheme of this Act is the Employees' Provident Fund Scheme (EPFS). It is a savings scheme in which both the employees and employer make regular contribution to a fund. Both these contributions are credited to the account of the employee concerned. Normally, the employer deducts the employee's contribution from his monthly salary and the employer makes a matching contribution. The rate of contribution is 12 per cent of wages for employees employed in the notified industries where the number of persons employed is fifty or more. Notified industries are those industries which have been notified by the central government for enhanced contribution under the EPF Act. Their paying capacity is known to be better than the others. So far, the central government has notified 172 categories of establishments in relation to which employers are to make enhanced contribution. Other establishments have to contribute 10 per cent of the employee's salary as the employer's contribution with matching contribution from the employee.

The EPF Act envisages the Employees Provident Fund Organization (EPFO) for the purpose of administering this Act. The EPFO works under the direction of the Central Board of Trustees and various committees constituted for this purpose. The Board of Trustees (BOT) is an autonomous body with a separate legal personification.

The Maternity Benefit Act, 1961

The Maternity Benefit Act, 1961 (MBA), aims to protect the earnings of women employees in relation to pregnancy and childbirth related issues. This Act regulates women workers' employment in certain establishments for a certain specified period before and after child birth. The benefit under this Act is payable under three situations: childbirth, miscarriage or sickness arising out of pregnancy. Like some of the other social security laws, the MBA also imposes a unilateral responsibility on the employer to pay maternity benefit to women employees covered. The Act applies to those factories, mines, circuses, plantations, and shops and establishments which employ ten or more persons. But in case a woman employee is covered under the ESIA, she will not be entitled to benefit under the MBA.

The MBA provides the maximum period for which the maternity benefit is allowed under this Act. It is twelve weeks in the case of childbirth, of which not less than six weeks shall precede the date of the expected delivery. Leave with wages at the rate of maternity benefit for a period of six weeks immediately following the day of her miscarriage is payable to the woman concerned in case of miscarriage. For illness arising out of pregnancy, delivery, premature birth of a child or miscarriage, the rate of maternity benefit is admissible maximum for a period of one month. This Act provides a fast-track method of maternity benefit payment in case of any dispute. The woman concerned can make a complaint to the inspector concerned who has been conferred quasi-judicial powers for ordering the release of maternity benefit by the employer.

The Payment of Gratuity Act, 1972

Gratuity is a benefit that is payable by the employer to his employee on termination of the employee's service. It is regulated by the Payment of Gratuity Act, 1972 (PGA). It is a unique kind of protection prevalent in the Indian organized sector. It involves payment of money in lump sum to a person covered who has delivered more than five years of continuous service to the employer. The Act applies to factories, mines, oilfields, plantations, ports, railway companies, shops and other establishments which employ ten or more persons.

Though mostly it is paid at the time of termination of service of the employee due to superannuation, or retirement, it is also payable in situations of resignation, death or disablement caused by any accident or disease. The rate of gratuity is fifteen days' wages for every completed year of service or part thereof, in excess of seven months. Interestingly, under the PGA, there is no wage ceiling for coverage. The maximum amount of gratuity payable under the Act is Rs 350,000 with effect from 24 September 1997. The maximum limit is due for revision any time.

The PGA also makes provision for forfeiture of gratuity wholly or in part. This can be done in case the service of an employee is terminated by the employer for any act or wilful omission or negligence that has caused any damage or loss to the employer's property. The employer can also forfeit gratuity if an employee indulges in any riotous or disorderly conduct or other act of violence or for moral turpitude in the course of employment and the employer has terminated his services on account of that. Similar to other labour statutes, the PGA also creates a quasi-judicial body in the form of 'controlling authority' to decide any disputes related to non-payment of gratuity as per the Act.

Chapters V-A and V-B of Industrial Disputes Act, 1947

Unlike in the developed world there is no system of unemployment insurance or assistance in India. However, limited protection is available to certain categories of already employed workers. This protection is envisaged by the IDA. Chapters V-A and V-B of this law deal with the issue of payment of compensation in case of lay-off, retrenchment and closure of an industry. The retrenchment/closure compensation is payable to a worker affected at the rate of fifteen days' wage for every completed year of service.

Key hurdles and caveats

In some situations, the provisions of Indian labour law are proving to be an impediment for businesses. These are discussed below.

Among others, problems are faced when an employer wants to close his operations or lay off or retrench workers so as to carry out a re-engineering programme. The requisite permission from the government is sometimes difficult to obtain. The relevant part of the IDA in this regard is Chapter V-B. This chapter envisages that an employer shall have to obtain permission from the government in case of layoff, retrenchment, and closure of any factory, mine and plantation that employs 100 or more workers. It has been found that this legal process has led to unnecessary harassment of many genuine employers. It is a reality that a lot of arbitrariness is often exercised in handling the permission issues. Sometimes decisions are taken by government officials on extraneous considerations. Many organizations that are perennially sick are denied the permission. In this connection, there has been some discussion that the limit of 100 or more workers should be increased to 300 or more workers; though at one time the government was contemplating making it for 1,000 or more workers.

Jet Airways – one of the best private airlines in India – was compelled to retrench about 1,000 air hostesses and other staff members due to the crippling effect of the downturn on this airline. The provisions of the IDA about obtaining permission from the government did not apply in this case as it was not a case of a factory, plantation or a mine. Still the central government put pressure on the airline to take the employees back, as national elections were about to be announced and the ruling party did not want industrial unrest in the country at that point in time. The new economic policy of India, announced in 1991, promised reform to make exit for organizations easier, but these promises have not been carried out, even after the pursuit of the liberalization and globalization agenda for twenty years. In fact, the concept of coalition governments that has surfaced as a living reality in India partly explains the lack of determination on the part of the government. It is interesting to note, however, that changes in the government's labour policy have been more at the executive and implementation level and not through passage of laws carrying out certain amendments in them. Globalization philosophy is difficult to sustain if firms do not have the requisite flexibility in the formal labour market. The presence of chaotic competition caused by the new realities is bound to compel employers to search avenues of flexibility so as to try to excel. Therefore a review of the existing structure of retrenchment and closure law is long overdue.

Also, critics believe that the Indian organized sector provides too much job security to workers without relating it to performance, accountability and productivity. Especially in the public sector, the impact of this state of affairs is far worse. These realities result in indiscipline, inertia and inefficiency. Consequently, these laws have a debilitating effect on labour mobility, which is an essential prerequisite of efficient working of firms in a competitive environment. On the contrary, countries like China are able to restructure their labour market much more rationally as per the needs of globalization.

Another area that requires government attention is section 9-A of the IDA. This section envisages twenty-one days' notice that an employer must give to union and workmen in case he wants to make any change in workers' service conditions. When this is so done workers raise an industrial dispute about the change, and many times employers miss some critical opportunities to make their competitive position better. This tends to become a big stumbling block in managing change.

The multiplicity of labour laws in India is a big hurdle for employers. This has made the system very complex for ordinary managers as well as workers. Many of the problems in this regard relate to applicability of these laws; definitions of various terms like worker/employee, appropriate government, wages; different administrative structures for enforcement of these laws; and creation of special dispute resolution bodies, etc. This leads to excessive role for lawyers, which should be avoided so as to promote a greater degree of voluntarism in IR. For example, the term 'wages' has been differently defined under different Acts. Also, some laws cover employees receiving monthly wages as low as Rs 6,500 per month (e.g. the Payment of Wages Act, 1936), others cover even clerical and administrative employees (e.g. the Employee State Insurance Act, 1948; the Employees' Provident Fund Act, 1952; the Payment of Gratuity Act, 1972; and the Maternity Benefit Act, 1960). For some there is no wage limit for coverage (e.g. highly paid pilots are workmen under the IDA).

In order to help make sense of the complexities, the judiciary has delivered a plethora of case law. Many of these decisions are not quite easy to comprehend, which adds to the existing confusion of the employers. This has made the grasping of labour laws a very complex affair. In fact, labour law complexity tends to convert union leaders into full-time pleaders who have set up labour law practice as a vocation, even though they should be busy resolving workers' grievances or organizing them for collective bargaining.

However, there are some silver linings for the employers so far as their competitive position vis-à-vis workers is concerned. Recent signals from the judiciary in the labour field are encouraging from the employers' point of view. Some of these recent labour judgements reflect the belief that the judiciary is more sympathetic with the employers' predicament in the era of globalization and realizes their susceptibilities in the new environment. The number of strikes resorted to by workers is declining and employers have successfully used lockouts to counter the union power. Increasingly, the judiciary is upholding employee dismissals, perhaps to help recalibrate the balance of power between unions and employers.

Key issues

- All employees working for MNCs in Indian locales are covered by Indian labour laws, irrespective of their country of origin, or citizenship.
- Labour law is treated as a distinct branch of law in India. For most labour matters civil courts' jurisdiction is barred; rather quasi-judicial bodies have been created under different pieces of labour legislation to settle different types of labour disputes.

- Prior approval of the state government for the particular site and construction plans of a factory premises is required before starting any manufacturing operations in India.
- Especially since 1987, the Factories Act, 1948 makes it mandatory for factory owners to ensure much higher standards of safety of their workers than before; and stringent penalties have been provided for violation of the law.
- It is not obligatory on the part of an employer to recognize a trade union except in states like Maharashtra and Madhya Pradesh where a recognition issue can be taken for adjudication by a labour court.
- Labour courts and industrial tribunals in India have the power to reinstate a worker if they feel that s/he was wrongfully dismissed by the employer.
- An employer wanting to make any change in any service conditions of its workers must give at least twenty-one days' notice as per the requirements of the IDA before effecting such a change.
- While taking disciplinary action against a worker for committing misconduct, an employer is expected to impose such punishment that is proportionate and not excessive to the gravity of the offence.
- It is lawful for employers to lay off and retrench workers, or to close the business's operations, as per the provisions of the IDA; however, in certain situations as envisaged in Chapters V-A and V-B of the IDA, they require permission of the government do so.
- In case an employer runs a factory, plantation or a mine and employs 100 or more workers in it, and wants to lay off or retrench some workers or wants to close his establishment, he/it has to obtain permission from the appropriate government to do so. But there is no requirement for obtaining such permission if the employer employs such number of workers in say an airline or a travel agency or a software company, etc., i.e. establishments that do not fall under the category of a factory, plantation or mine.
- Workers employed by an employer through a contractor are not workmen under the IDA; so they cannot raise any industrial dispute against the principal employer. Thus, they need to bring their concerns and problems to the attention of the contractor. But they are considered as workers under the Factories Act. This simply implies that these workers must be allowed to work in the factory subject to the same health, welfare and safety conditions as are available to the workers directly employed by the principal employer.
- An employer can enter into a settlement with workers or union privately without involving the conciliation officer, but it is more desirable to settle before a conciliation officer as conciliated settlements under the IDA have wider applicability on all present and future workers.
- The employers covered are supposed to pay minimum wages to their workers. They are also required to pay minimum bonus to their workers

even in situations when they are suffering losses unless they are in the infancy period of initial five years. Thus, minimum bonus under Indian law is a deferred wage. The logic of this deferred wage is the presence of low level of wages in India in general. However, for those companies that are able to earn an allocable surplus under the Payment of Bonus Act, 1965 (PBA), and have to pay bonus as per the provisions of the PBA, bonus is profit sharing.

- The PBA applies mainly to establishments in the private sector. It is applicable to establishments in the public sector only if it produces goods or renders service in competition with the private sector and the sale of goods or services that are sold in competition with the private sector is not less than 20 per cent of its total sale.
- The Indian system of social security in the organized sector can be divided into three broad types, namely: creation of employer's unilateral liability through legislation like the WCA, PGA, MBA, etc.; social insurance legislation like the ESI scheme; and creation of provident fund under the EPF Act. India has yet to have a fully developed social security system on the pattern of the developed world. There is a need to develop an integrated system of social security so as to avoid complications from which the present system suffers (Saini, 2001).
- For the purpose of coverage, the definition of the term 'wage' is not uniform under all these laws. Also, coverage of workers under these laws is different. POWA has a wage limit of Rs 6,500 per month for its application. POBA covers employees getting up to Rs 10,000 per month. For coverage under MBA and PGA there is no wage limit. The WCA also does not envisage any wage limit for coverage; but there is a notional ceiling of Rs 4,000 per month on wages only for the purpose of calculation of compensation under this Act.
- Different pieces of employment legislation in India have different applicability. While some Acts apply to all workers/employees (e.g. MBA or PGA or TUA), others apply to only non-managerial employees (e.g. IDA, IESOA).
- Despite a comprehensive system of employment legislation in India, most employers including MNCs are able to maintain peaceful industrial relations and are able to pursue 'no union' strategies. It is suggested that employers must intertwine these policies with thoughtful HRM strategies and by carefully aligning them with business goals. Otherwise, employers are likely to face serious repercussions, and pay a high price for these failures, as in the case of Honda Motor Cycle & Scooters India (HMSI) in Gurgaon in July 2005.
- The judicial branch of the Indian state has appreciated the vulnerable position of employers in the game of industrial relations in view of the rising competition, and more judicial decisions are being delivered that emphasize the need to focus on productivity and social justice rather than social justice alone.

References

Saini, D. S. (2001) *Social Security – India: International Encyclopaedia of Laws*, ed. R. Blanpain, The Hague: Kluwer.

Saini, D. S. (2009) Labour law in India: structure and working. In P. Budhwar and J. Bhatnagar (eds) *Changing Face of HRM in India*, London: Routledge, 60–94.

Saini, D. S. and Budhwar, P. (2007) HRM in India. In R. S. Schuler and S. E. Jackson (eds) *Strategic Human Resource Management*, 2nd edn, Oxford: Blackwell, 287–312.

4 Socio-cultural and institutional context

Pawan S. Budhwar, Arup Varma and
Sukanya Sengupta

Given that socio-cultural and institutional factors strongly determine the relevance of management systems for a specific context (see, e.g., Budhwar and Sparrow, 1998; 2002a), this chapter aims to present and discuss the scenario related to the socio-cultural, political and institutional context of India. In this chapter, we discuss and analyse historical developments in India, its political and legal structures, its societal values, along with corporate culture and management behaviour. Finally, based on our analyses, we present key issues, which we believe will prove very useful for decision makers.

Historical background and setting

Recognised as one of the most ancient civilizations, India has a continuous and documented history from about 2000 BC (see Husain, 1992). The name India is derived from Sindhu (Indus), the great river of the north-west. India borders Bangladesh, Bhutan and Myanmar in the east, China in the north and north-east, Pakistan in the west and north-west as has the island of Sri Lanka to the south. It occupies a strategic location in South Asia for international trade. The Indian peninsula is surrounded by the Bay of Bengal in the south-east, the Indian Ocean in the south and the Arabian Sea in the south-west and by the great Himalayas in the north and north-east. India, with an area of 3.3 million km², is the second largest country in Asia and the seventh largest in the world. The country extends up to 3,200 km from north to south and over 3,000 km from east to west.

Since ancient times India has been invaded by foreigners, starting from 1500–1200 BC by the Aryans from central Asia, and later on by Alexander in 325 BC, Genghiz Khan in AD 1221, the Moguls in the fifteenth century, and the British in the eighteenth century. India is the birthplace of three of the world's major religions, Hinduism (about 7,000 years BC), Buddhism (487 BC) and Sikhism (AD 1699). These three religions have significantly impacted the social, political and economic landscape of the country. Despite such a long history, the first Westerner to arrive by sea was the Portuguese explorer Vasco Da Gama, who arrived in 1498 (Thomas and Philips, 1994; Budhwar, 2003).

The British entered India in 1603 with the establishment of the East India Company. The Company established its rule in the states of Bengal and Bihar in 1757 after the battle of Plassey. After putting down the famous revolt of 1857 by Indian nationalists, the East India Company was replaced by the British Crown (see Budhwar, 2001). Finally, India achieved independence from the British in 1947. As part of the independence agreement, Pakistan was carved out of India, and Jawaharlal Nehru was elected the first Prime Minister of India. On 26 January 1950 India revealed its new constitution and became a republic. In 1961 Goa was liberated from Portuguese rule and became an integral part of India. Sikkim became an Indian state in 1975.

In many administrative and constitutional affairs India still follows British traditions (see Basu, 1998; Jones, 1989). The constitution of India established the nation as a sovereign socialist secular and democratic republic (Basu, 1998). It comprises twenty-eight states and seven union territories. Its total population is about 1.14 billion (as at 2008), making it the second most populous country in the world, and the world's largest democracy. The percentage share of the six main religious groups is about: Hindus (83 per cent), Muslims (12 per cent), Sikhs (2 per cent), Christians (2 per cent), Jains, Buddhists, and others less than 1 per cent. Indians speak over 179 different languages (out of which seventeen are denoted as major languages) and 844 different dialects. The constitution recognises Hindi and English as the two official languages – not surprisingly, India has one of the largest English-speaking populations in the Asia-Pacific region. The literacy rate for over fifteen years of age is around 53 per cent, but literacy is unevenly distributed. According to the 2001 census, southern states like Kerala have rates higher than 90 per cent; while some states like Bihar and Rajasthan have an overall literacy rate of around 39 per cent (with a female literacy rate around 22 per cent).

Politics

India follows the Westminster model, with Parliament being the supreme body consisting of two houses – Rajya Sabha (the Upper House) and Lok Sabha (the Lower House), the government being formed by any political party or coalition of parties securing a majority in the Lok Sabha in national elections. The President is the constitutional head, while the Prime Minister is the executive head of the government. Both are elected for a period of five years. Apart from the execution of power, the President has the power to grant pardons or remissions of punishment or to suspend the sentence of any person convicted of any offence. The President also appoints the Prime Minister, other central government Ministers, the Attorney General, judges of the Supreme Court, the Comptroller and Auditor General, governors of all states and the three chiefs of the army, navy and air force. A multi-party system prevails both at the centre and state level. Presently there are nine national parties, with Congress and the Bharatiya Janata Party (BJP) being the dominant ones. Other minor national parties include the Bahujan Samaj Party, the Communist Party of India,

Nationalist Congress Party, Rashtriya Janata Dal, Samajwadi Party and Janata Dal. Over the last couple of decades none of the parties has secured a clear majority. Not surprisingly, the present government (as of mid-2009) is an alliance led by Congress and other political parties.

Among the major political issues affecting the business climate is the non-existence of a stable government with a clear majority in the centre. Rapid changes in economic policies with the change of each government and poor co-operation between central and state governments also affects business. Further, disputes with Pakistan over Kashmir, with China over border jurisdiction and with Bangladesh and Myanmar regarding illegal migrants and sharing of river waters disturb the economic and political stability of the country. Since partition with Pakistan in 1947, India has fought three wars with Pakistan (1947, 1965 and 1971) and the Kargil conflict in 1999 and one with China in 1962 – however, India did not initiate any of these wars. In 1971, India played a major role in the independence of Bangladesh from Pakistan, and in 1988 its forces were sent to Sri Lanka to fight the Liberation Army of Tamil Tigers (LTTE). India successfully conducted nuclear tests in 1974 and 1998 and is now recognised as a nuclear power, and also boasts a highly developed space research programme. India, however, has sought peaceful solutions with all its neighbours. In this spirit, India and Pakistan signed the Simla Agreement in 1972, and in February 1999 the Lahore Declaration, to settle their differences peacefully. However, this declaration ran into trouble when in June 1999 pro-Kashmir independence militants (apparently backed by the Pakistan army) entered Kargil (north of Kashmir). This insurgency nearly resulted in the fourth war between the two nations. To improve relations and lessen the risk of clashes along the disputed borders, India and China signed a Peace and Tranquillity Agreement in 1993 and another pact in 1996. India is also an active member of South Asian Association for Regional Co-operation (SAARC) and the Non-aligned Movement.

Legal system

The legal system is based on the 1950 constitution and, reflecting India's colonial inheritance of the English common law. Further, India has a three-tier legal system. The Supreme Court is the apex body, followed by the state High Courts and Subordinate (or District) Courts. For special events different commissions and tribunals are set up. The constitution of India officially grants its citizens the fundamental right to equality, freedom against exploitation, freedom of religion and freedom of speech, along with the right to property and cultural and educational rights (Basu, 1998). The judicial and legal systems are very strong and are capable of bringing even top officials to justice. However, due to the misuse of power by ruling political parties it is difficult for common citizens (who do not have close links with politicians or civil servants) to get their work done. There are also serious problems related to child labour, human rights, working conditions and minimum wages. Details on Indian labour legislation are covered in Chapter 3 of this volume.

Societal culture

Husain (1992) presents one of the most comprehensive reviews of Indian society and Indian national culture. According to Husain, the analysis of the national culture of India started about 5,000–6,000 years ago. It was during this period that holy books of *Vedas* were written and Indian culture was referred to as 'Vedic culture'. This was followed by the advent of Buddhism, and the national culture inherited a strong influence of the doctrine of Buddhism. The impact of Buddhism stayed for a short period and was replaced by 'Hindu culture'. In contrast with the 'Vedic culture', this doctrine has been termed the 'Puranic culture'. This cultural life was disturbed before the establishment of the Delhi Sultanate (around the tenth century AD) after which the Hindu–Muslim culture was erected, known as 'Hindustani culture'. This culture was not based on any particular religion, but on some sort of nationalistic feelings in the political sense. The British left a strong impact of the British culture (primarily in the form of red tape-ridden bureaucratic system and large amounts of legislation), which is still very prominent in India. Hence, over a period of time, the national culture of India has continuously transformed from one type to another (for details see Husain, 1992; Thomas and Philips, 1994; Budhwar, 2001; 2003).

Given the above-mentioned incursions and cultural changes, it is not surprising that Indian society is a mixture of various ethnic, religious, linguistic, caste and regional collectivities, with numerous inter-group differences as a result of historical and socio-cultural specificity. It is a panorama, which has absorbed diverse languages, cultures, religions and people of different social origins at different points of time. These diversities are reflected in the patterns of life, styles of living, land tenure systems, occupational pursuits, inheritance and succession rules (Sharma, 1984). Indeed, a number of commentators have explored various dimensions in trying to conceptualize Indian culture. For example, Myrdal referred to India as a soft state where people are so dependent on the state as to cease tackling their own problems with local initiatives. Kennedy emphasized the 'tender-mindedness' of Indians, which stands against taking bold decisions. Research by Sinha (1990) also confirms the 'soft work culture' characteristics of Indian organizations, as evidenced by the dependence of one set of people or group on another for regular guidance (e.g., subordinates' almost complete dependence on superiors).

On the basis of Hofstede's (1991) four initial dimensions of national culture, Kanungo and Mendonca (1994) have shown significant cultural differences between India and Western countries. India stands relatively high on uncertainty avoidance and power distance and relatively low on individualism and masculinity dimensions. Relatively high uncertainty avoidance implies an unwillingness to take risks and accept organizational change. The relatively low individualism implies that family and group attainments take precedence over work outcomes (Sharma, 1984). The relatively high power distance implies that managers and subordinates accept their relative positions in the organizational hierarchy and operate from these fixed positions. Thus, obedience is due to the holder of the position, not on a rational basis, but simply by virtue of the authority inherent in that status (Budhwar and Sparrow, 2002b). Finally, the relatively low masculinity score implies that employees' orientation is towards personal relations rather than towards performance (Kanungo and Mendonca, 1994: 450).

On the same lines, other researchers (see, for example, Sharma, 1984; Sinha and Kanungo, 1997; Tayeb, 1987) report that on average Indians resist change, hesitate to delegate, or even accept authority, are fearful of taking independent decisions, are protective of those with lower status, and frequently surrender to their superiors. A possible explanation for such behaviour can be traced to the long imperialist history of India. From the tenth century till 1947 foreigners (Thomas and Philips, 1994) ruled India. Similarly, the traditional hierarchical social structure of India has always emphasized respect for superiors – be they elders, teachers or superiors at work. No doubt this behaviour is influenced by the nature of Hinduism, as evidenced by the caste and social system (Budhwar *et al.*, 2000; Sahay and Walsham, 1997).

To summarize, Indians are known for their obedience to seniors, dependence on others, a strong belief in fate, a low ability to cope with uncertainty and reluctance to accept responsibility. In addition, they are often less disciplined, more modest and reserved than most nationalities (see Tayeb, 1987). There is also a great deal of collectivism, caste consciousness, friendliness, and clan orientation. Females are highly respected in Indian society, but respect does not always translate into equality in the workplace, in earnings or in society in general (see Devi, 1991; Budhwar *et al.*, 2005). Women are still expected to be more submissive and obedient, though these attitudes are changing, if primarily in urban areas. At the negotiating table, Indians are slow starters, unlike Westerners – indeed, like other Asians, Indians grow up bargaining for everything, thus learning patience, and the ability to hold out for better terms. In general, Indians are very hospitable and are highly tolerant of individuals of other nationalities, (see Budhwar, 2001), and social relations are very important in the business world.

From the above discussion it can be deduced that the Indian societal culture has a lasting impact on most management functions such as staffing, communication, leadership, motivation and control. Staffing for top managerial positions among Indian organizations (especially in the private and public sectors) is generally restricted by familial, communal and political considerations. Authority in Indian organizations is likely to remain one-sided, with subordinates leaning heavily on their superiors for advice and directions. In the next section, we discuss Indian corporate culture and the basis and evolution of management behaviour.

Corporate culture, managerial values and behaviour

As stated above, power based hierarchy exits in most Indian organizations. As a result, Indians are disposed to hierarchical relationships, and for this reason they usually work well individually rather than in groups (Sinha and Sinha, 1990), which is ironic, given that Indians are also considered collectivist. Furthermore, management in India is often autocratic, based on formal authority and charisma (Budhwar and Khatri, 2001). Family norms emphasizing loyalty to the family authority figure or superior in an organization underlie the limited decision-making experience, and unfamiliarity with responsibility found with most employees (Kakar, 1971). Consequently, decision making is very centralized, with much emphasis on rules and a low propensity for risk (Hofstede, 1991; Tayeb, 1987). In addition, complicated family ties coupled with strong authority figures are responsible for a paternalistic managerial style in India (see Saini and Budhwar, 2008).

It has been argued that since the original source of power in India is family and friends, nepotism is common both at the lowest and highest levels. Furthermore, it is often asserted that, within Indian organizations, expert power is frequently relegated in favour of position power (see Bass and Burger, 1979). Consequently, it is difficult for non-family members to advance into upper management positions particularly in private businesses. Furthermore, managerial thinking in India is also subject to a conflict of cultures, arising because the managers have often been trained in the West or in Indian colleges that have adopted Western education models (Garg and Parikh, 1986; Neelankavil *et al.*, 2000). Thus, Indian managers frequently internalize two sets of values: those drawn from the traditional moorings of the family and community, and those drawn from modern education, professional training and the imperatives of modern technology (Budhwar and Sparrow, 2002b). These two sets of values coexist and are drawn upon as frames of reference depending on the nature of problems that people face.

In the context of culture and organizational functioning, many suggestions have been put forward to help managers move toward more effective leadership. Tripathi (1990) suggests, 'indigenous values, such as familism, need to be synthesized with the values of industrial democracy' (also see Saini and Budhwar, 2008). Similarly, as mentioned above, Sinha (1990) proposes that, while a leader in India has to be a 'nurturant type', taking a personal interest in the well-being of each subordinate, he or she can use that nurturance to encourage increasing levels of participation. Sinha and Kanungo (1997) observe that the manager may achieve this by directing subordinates to work hard and uphold an excessive level of productivity, reinforcing each stage with increased nurturance.

As indicated above, Indian society is a mixture of various ethnic, religious, linguistic, caste and regional collectivities, which further differ due to historical and social-cultural specificities. It is thus often described as a panorama, which absorbs diverse languages, cultures, religions and people of different social origins at different points of time. These diversities are reflected in patterns of life, styles of living, land tenure systems, occupational pursuits, inheritance and succession rules. The idea of unity is inherent today in India's constitution, which pronounces values of secularism, socialism and democracy as its main ideals. British rule in India accentuated some of these socio-cultural and economic differences (Sharma, 1984).

Hierarchy and inequality are deeply rooted in India's tradition and are also found in practice in the form of unequally placed caste and class groups. These have created and endured a unique equilibrium because of the organic linkages and interdependence of different socio-economic groups (Jain and Venkata Ratnam, 1994). However, as discussed above, Indian society has undergone major changes due to foreign invasion, migration, natural calamities, struggle for power, and the policies of the Mughal and the British Empires. Changes in the post-independence era have occurred mainly due to the economic planning (spearheaded by the Five Year Plans) and development schemes in the fields of industry and agriculture (Datt and Sundharam, 2007). The post-independence era has witnessed the emergence of new forms of social and economic disparities. Most of the developmental programmes have helped the traditionally better off more, than those who were downtrodden and who genuinely needed social and economic betterment. However, those covered by the category of 'reserved class' (i.e. scheduled castes, scheduled tribes and weaker sections of society) benefited in the fields of education and employment. Overall, however, the most needy and deserving have not benefited as much as they were entitled to (Jain and Venkata Ratnam, 1994).

Over the years, both academics and practitioners have shown interest in exploring the impact of Indian national culture on management policies and practices (see, for example, Daftur, 1993; Mankidy, 1993; Sharma, 1984; Sparrow and Budhwar, 1997; Budhwar and Sparrow, 1998; 2002b). These writers have found the impact of Anglo-American and Japanese models of management on Indian HRM practices and policies. They have argued that despite the heterogeneity of languages, dialects and customs in India, there exist common attitudinal and behavioural patterns that knit most of the people together to give a sense of uniformity.

In comparing the Indian and American managerial styles, Sharma (1984) found a number of differences that have a strong theoretical and historical base and have an empirical support. For example, the average American is achievement-oriented and is consequently geared to work at a level of maximum efficiency. In comparison, an average Indian is essentially 'fatalist', and believes in the theory of 'predeterminism'. As a result, an average Indian has an infinite capacity to suffer, a tough resilience in the face of all the hazards, which a scarce economy and an indifferent society expose him to continuously, almost on a daily basis. It is not surprising then, as inheritors of such a legacy, Indian managers often vacillate and probably dither when crucial decisions are to be made (Sharma, 1984: 73). Nevertheless, in the present competitive context, such findings can be seriously challenged. However, there is a scarcity of research in this regard.

As compared with Americans, the gap between the ownership and management is less in India. Apart from merit, relations matter a lot, change is not accepted so easily, as a result of which the optimum level is achieved very rarely. The proprietor-manager of today has still to grow out of his trading and speculative attitudes. Along these lines, Silveria (1988) has also argued that the East India Company left a lasting impact on both, Indian managers and the Indian government. For example, the typical public servant demonstrates similar 'mistrust' of the general public as was shown by the Company towards the Indian natives. The Company also left India with a legacy of red tape-ridden bureaucratic system that they themselves inherited from the Mughuls. Silveria further blames the British rule for leaving Indian culture without an industrial culture, as a result of which, even after gaining independence, Indian businessmen continued to think and behave like traders and commission agents rather than entrepreneurs and industrialists (Silveria, 1988: 8–9).

In this connection, Kanungo and Mendonca (1994) have also argued that societal norms (through the socialization process) have a significant impact on work behaviour and job performance of individuals, and groups in organizations. Individuals enter an organization with certain beliefs, expectations, attitudes and values regarding work, based on their socio-economic background, which influence their work behaviour in either a positive or negative direction.

Since Indians are socialized in an environment that values strong family ties and extended family relationships, they are more likely to develop stronger affiliative tendencies or greater dependence on others. Thus, in the work context, interpersonal relations will likely be more salient to them and as a result, their job-related decisions might be influenced more by interpersonal considerations than by task demands (Kanungo and Mendonca, 1994: 448).

It is thus clear that cultural influences shape employees' needs and expectations, their hopes and aspirations, and their perceptions of what constitutes desirable forms of conduct. Further, managers' beliefs, values and assumptions about jobs and employees are also a product of cultural influence (Hofstede, 1991). Naturally, the HRM policies and practices are an outcome of such managerial beliefs, values and assumptions. In India, in general, employees are seen as a relatively fixed resource, with limited potential, and organizations are encouraged to take a passive/reactive stance to task performance. Thus, success is judged on moralism derived from tradition and religion, people orientation is paternalistic and consideration of the context overrides principles and rules (Kanungo and Jaeger, 1990; Saini and Budhwar, 2008).

We honestly believe that there could not be a more plausible explanation (than the one given above) for the average Indian's resistance to change, his willingness to delegate, or even accept authority, his fear of taking an independent decision, his protectiveness towards his subordinates, and his almost abject surrender to his superiors. In addition, the Indian ethos leads to strict observance of rituals by the average Indian, though he may disregard these in practice, preach high morals against his personal immorality, and make near-desperate efforts at maintaining the status quo while talking of change (Daftur, 1993; Sharma, 1984).

In addition, the Indian management culture is characterized by the principle of 'particularism' and 'stability' as compared with the West, where 'individualism' and 'mobility' characterize the philosophy and practice in organizations (Sharma, 1984). Researchers (see Mankidy, 1993; Krishna and Monappa, 1994) have also shown the influence of the Japanese models of management in Indian organizations. The main Japanese concepts, which are adopted in Indian organizations, are the 'quality circles', 'lifelong employment', Kaizen, 'just in time', total quality management and seniority-based wage systems. Though these concepts have been adopted in Indian organizations, these have not been as successful as they are in Japan. The main reason behind this failure is the cultural difference between the two countries. Indian organizations lack commitment towards individual goals and their integration with the organizational objectives. Understandably, the success or failure of Japanese management systems elsewhere would depend to a large extent not only on the inherent characteristics of those practices themselves but also on the extent to which Japanese techniques can be adapted to the peculiar conditions of alien environments (Hofstede, 1991).

Jain (1991) made an attempt to check if there is a coherent human resource management (HRM) system in India. He concluded that in India there is no coherent or unified management system, which can be called 'Indian management'. This has been mainly due to the existence of inconsistencies and contradictions which abound within the Indian management system. The main reason for such inconsistencies is the unsuccessful attempt to implement Western management theories and concepts in the Indian socio-economic and cultural environment (Sparrow and Budhwar, 1997). India has two management systems operating side by side: the philosophy is paternalistic but the organizational structure is bureaucratic and hierarchical in nature (Saini and Budhwar, 2008). Indian decision making, thus, is a process of consultative activity but the final decision is always made at the top.

The above analysis presents an overview regarding the socio-cultural and managerial behaviour in India. Nevertheless, it is important to remember that the work processes and work dynamics are changing very rapidly in India, especially in all the professionally run organizations, which primarily consist of foreign firms. However, the number of Indian firms attempting to professionalize is rapidly increasing due to increased competition and a desire and need to improve to survive and flourish. In such organizations, many aspects of the above-presented scenario are changing fast where constructs of empowerment, delegation/decentralization, team working, both ways of communication (downwards and upwards), active employee involvement, 360° feedback, participative management style, performance-based systems, etc., are strongly emerging. It seems that management systems in India are at a crossroads of traditional and modern/Western principles. This also confirms that India is able to accommodate and adapt to West-based management principles, perhaps with minor amendments. This is clearly evident from recent research findings from the BPO and IT sectors and multinational companies (see Budhwar *et al.*, 2006; Bjorkman and Budhwar, 2007; Budhwar and Bhatnagar, 2009).

Business customs and etiquette

Business hours in India vary between the central government and state government offices. Central government offices are open Monday to Friday from 9.30 a.m. to 17.00 p.m. all the year round and from 9.30 a.m. to 13.00 p.m. on Saturdays. The state governments follow the same pattern during the winter season, whereas during the summer they work from 7.30 a.m. to 13.30 p.m., with minor local variations. For cash transactions, all the banks function from 10.00 a.m. to 14.00 p.m. Monday to Friday and 10.00 a.m. to 12.30 p.m. on Saturdays. Indeed, such norms are being changed with the developments in the BPO sector, where people are working round the clock to cater to the needs of global clients. Even the rigid Factories Act, 1948, has been modified to allow females to work evening shifts to meet such market demands (see Saini and Budhwar, 2007). Next we present some more specifics about India that would be very useful for the global businessperson. First, India is four and a half hours ahead of GMT during the summer time and five and a half hours during the winter, and the country's international telephone code is +91. The standard electricity supply is 220 V a.c., 50 Hz.

In order to do business in the country, businesspersons need visas and letters of invitation from local sponsors, which are very easily obtainable. The country formally forbids the import of pornographic material (although it is locally available on the 'black market'), drugs and firearms. Depending on the season, Indian males wear shirts, ties, suits, Nehru jackets and trousers, while female wear varies from the traditional salwar-kameez or saree to suits, shirts and trousers. Some women in metropolitan areas wear skirts, t-shirts and blouses.

There are over fifteen national holidays (including religious holidays). The official system of measurement is metric, although numbers are frequently written in lakhs (100,000) and crores (10 million). Females are highly respected in Indian society, as evidenced by the number of female deities in the Hindu pantheon, though respect does not always translate into equality in the workplace, in earnings or in society in general. Women are still expected to be more submissive and obedient, though these attitudes are changing, the more so in urban areas. At the negotiating table Indians are slow starters (like other Asians making extreme offers, Indians grow up bargaining for everything; this brings patience and the ability to hold out for better terms) in comparison with Westerners. Social relations are very important in business management. In general, Indians are very hospitable and are highly tolerant of the foreign population (Budhwar, 2001; 2003).

For the expatriate employee a work permit is required, and a residence permit is required beyond a period of three months. Government approval is required for the appointment of expatriates to high managerial positions. Permission is also required from the Reserve Bank of India, where repatriation of salaries in foreign exchange is envisaged.

In India, personal greetings are both warm and friendly. Hindus generally fold both hands and say, 'Namaste', to greet others. Generally young people touch the feet of elders to get their blessings. Exchange of gifts is a common practice when visiting friends or relatives. Men shake hands and, in cases where they are well acquainted with others, they may also exchange hugs. Women follow the same practice. Indians use hand gestures frequently during conversation, but pointing at someone is considered impolite. Members of the opposite sex generally do not touch in public, even when married (though this norm is changing with the new generation and in metropolitans). Traditionally, married females, especially in villages, cover their heads, which is usually an extension of the saree or the scarf that accompanies the salwar suit, but this is not practised at the workplace or in urban settings. In public places, females and children are given priority (for example getting seats on buses or trains, buying tickets, etc.).

India is a secular country without a state religion, and a very open society, and there is no requirement to practise any religion. However, Indians have deeply spiritual traditions and religion plays an important role in everyday life. Due to its diversity of religion and the importance of spiritualism/beliefs in Indian society, many religious holidays and celebrations are observed year-round in one part of the country or other. Religious holidays are based on lunar calendars; therefore their occurrence varies from year to year. In addition to New Year's Day, Republic Day (26 January), Independence Day (15 August), Mahatma Gandhi's birthday (2 October) and Christmas day there are around fifty other national, religious and regional holidays. In most institutions and at work, the English calendar is followed. The cow is considered a sacred animal. Except for beef and pork, most other meat products are served in hotels and restaurants and people may often eat fish, mutton or goat. However, India is predominantly a vegetarian country. Indians mainly wear their regional dresses. However, as indicated above, at work men generally put on trousers and shirts and women wear salwar-kameez, saree or trousers and shirts. Men prefer to wear leather shoes and women sandals at work. The proportion of women in the workplace is increasing rapidly. In rural areas the traditional extended family system is still intact. However, in the urban areas this has given way to the nuclear family.

Due to its cultural and regional diversity, Indian food is rich in variety and taste. Nevertheless, the most common dish in north-east and south India is rice and fish, whereas north, central and western India is dominated by chapati or roti (like a round bread), dal (lentil) and vegetarian eating habits. People along the coasts also consume large quantities of fish and other seafood. Most fruits and vegetables are available in India and consumed in large quantities. The majority of the population is vegetarian, and the killing of the cow is not acceptable in India. Drinks are offered during parties, weddings and other social occasions. Finally, the tiger is considered the national animal and the peacock is the national bird of India.

Key issues

- India is perhaps the most diverse country in the world. Given the significant regional variations, it is difficult to say if there is one coherent national culture of India and if there is one clear set of institutional factors that determine management systems suitable for the Indian context. Depending on where an organization is operating, one needs to understand the socio-cultural context of that area and accordingly develop their management systems.
- Indian managers see a strong impact of power distance on their functioning. This element operates through the misuse of power due to different pressures (such as political, caste, group and bureaucratic) and within logic of 'power myopia', which influences their thinking about most management functions (Budhwar and Sparrow, 2002b). As a result, Indian managers tend to rely on the use of power in superior–subordinate relationships in their organizations and are not actively inclined to consultative or participative styles. However, there is clear evidence that these habits and practices are changing, perhaps due to the influx of MNCs.
- A combination of the Indian national culture, stereotypes toward females and the nature of the job, decides the emphasis on masculinity or femininity in Indian organizations. This also influences managerial thinking regarding recruitment, transfers and appraisal functions. However, this glass ceiling is slowly being shattered as more and more females are entering the work force and moving to higher levels of Indian management hierarchies (see Budhwar *et al.*, 2005).
- The specific factors shaping management policies and practices also vary significantly within India (e.g., impact of unions, specific legislation, business customs and norms, availability of skills, competition, benefits available to foreign investors, etc.). Foreign investors need to understand such subtle variations in order to initiate operations at a relevant place and also to better manage different operations in India.
- Despite the evidence of the prevalence of modern/Western management systems in the Indian context, it is important to remember that the majority of management systems of businesses in India still have strong ingredients of the established Indian socio-cultural and institutional set-up (for example, social contacts and relationships are still very important to successfully run businesses in India). Decision makers should not ignore the importance of such aspects while managing businesses in

India. It will be sensible to develop motivational, communication, leadership and related tools with a mixture of both indigenous and foreign aspects.

- Given the significant cultural, economic, political, physical/natural, etc., variations both between India and other countries and also within India, expatriates going to India would need sufficient time to adjust there, also given the uncertainties that are a part of daily Indian life. Mechanisms for in-country support (such as in the form of support from locals, introduction to existing networks) would also be useful.
- With a good parliamentary position there is high likelihood that the incumbent government can complete its full five-year tenure, thus providing much-needed political stability at the national level. Nevertheless, foreign investors should conduct proper political risk analysis and due diligence in order to avoid any unpleasant surprises.
- Traditionally, Indian organizations have practised internal labour markets (ILMs) based on social contacts and relationships. However, in the present context, Indian organizations need to build strong ILMs (which should focus solely on performance and should be less influenced by social, economic, religious and political factors). There are some indications that such developments are taking place in the form of increased emphasis on training and development, preference for talent in the recruitment and performance-based compensation (see Budhwar and Khatri, 2001). However, a lot more needs to be done in this regard to reap the true benefits of such systems.

References

Bass, B. and Burger, C. (1979) *Assessment of Managers: An International Comparison.* New York: Free Press.

Basu, D. D. (1998) *Constitutional Law of India.* New Delhi: Prentice-Hall of India.

Bjorkman, I. and Budhwar, P. (2007) When in Rome . . .? Human resource management and the performance of foreign firms operating in India. *Employee Relations*, 29 (6): 595–610.

Budhwar, P. (2001) Doing business in India. *Thunderbird International Business Review*, 43 (4): 549–68.

Budhwar, P. (2003) Culture and management in India. In M. Warner (ed.) *Management and Culture and Management in Asia.* London: Curzon Press, 66–81.

Budhwar, P. and Bhatnagar, J. (eds) (2009) *The Changing Face of People Management in India.* London: Routledge.

Budhwar, P. and Khatri, P. (2001) HRM in context: the applicability of HRM models in India. *International Journal of Cross-cultural Management*, 1 (3): 333–56.

Budhwar, P. and Sparrow, P. (1998) Factors determining cross-national human resource management practices: a study of India and Britain. *Management International Review*, 38, special issue 2: 105–21.

Budhwar, P. and Sparrow, P. (2002a) An integrative framework for determining cross-national human resource management practices. *Human Resource Management Review*, 12 (3): 377–403.

Budhwar, P. and Sparrow, P. (2002b) Strategic HRM through the cultural looking glass: mapping cognitions of British and Indian HRM managers. *Organization Studies*, 23 (4): 599–638.

Budhwar, L., Reeves, D. and Farrell, P. (2000) Life goals as a function of social class and child rearing practices: a study of India. *International Journal of Intercultural Relations*, 24: 227–45.

Budhwar, P., Saini, D. and Bhatnagar, J. (2005) Women in management in the new economic environment: the case of India. *Asia Pacific Business Review*, 11 (2): 179–93.

Budhwar, P., Varma, A., Singh, V. and Dhar, R. (2006) HRM systems of Indian call centres: an exploratory study. *International Journal of Human Resource Management*, 17 (5): 881–97.

Chatterjee, B. (1992) *Japanese Management and the Indian Experience*. New Delhi: Sterling Publishers.

Daftur, C. N. (1993) Should we apply foreign management theories to Indian systems? *Industrial Relations News and Views*, 5 (3): 8–12.

Datt, R. and Sundharam, K. P. H. (2007) *Indian Economy*. New Delhi: Chand.

Devi, R. D. (1991) Women in modern sector employment in India. *Economic Bulletin for Asia and the Pacific*, June–December: 53–65.

Garg, P. and Parikh, I. (1986) Managers and corporate cultures: the case of Indian organizations. *Management International Review*, 26: 50–62.

Hofstede, G. (1991) *Culture and Organisations: Software of the Mind*. London: McGraw-Hill.

Husain, A. S. (1992) *The National Culture of India*. New Delhi: National Book Trust.

Jain, H. C. (1991) Is there a coherent human resource management system in India? *International Journal of Manpower*, 12 (1): 10–17.

Jain, H. C. and Venkata Ratnam, C. S. (1994) Affirmative action in employment for the scheduled castes and the scheduled tribes in India. *International Journal of Manpower*, 15 (7): 6–25.

Jones, S. (1989) Merchants of the Raj. *Management Accounting*, September: 32–5.

Kakar, S. (1971) Authority pattern and subordinate behaviours in Indian organisation. *Administrative Science Quarterly*, 16: 298–307.

Kanungo, R. N. and Jaeger, A. M. (1990) Introduction. The need for indigenous management in developing countries. In A. M. Jaeger and R. N. Kanungo (eds) *Management in Developing Countries*, London: Routledge, 1–19.

Kanungo, R. N. and Mendonca, M. (1994) Culture and performance improvement. *Productivity*, 35 (3): 447–53.

Kennedy, P. (1993) *Preparing for the Twenty-first Century*. London: Fortune Press.

Krishna, A. and Monappa, A. (1994) Economic Restructuring and Human Resource Management. *Indian Journal of Industrial Relations*, 29 (4): 490–501.

Mankidy, J. (1993) Emerging patterns of industrial relations in India. *Management and Labour Studies*, 18 (4), 199–206.

Mankidy, J. (1995) Changing perspectives of workers participation in India with particular reference to banking industry. *British Journal of Industrial Relations*, 33 (3): 443–58.

Neelankavil, J. P., Mathur, A. and Zang, Y. (2000) Determinants of managerial performance: a cross-cultural comparison of the perceptions of middle-level managers in four countries. *Journal of International Business Studies*, 31 (1): 121–40.

Sahay, S. and Walsham, G. (1997) Social structure and managerial agency in India. *Organisation Studies*, 18: 415–44.

Sharma, I. J. (1984) The culture context of Indian managers. *Management and Labour Studies*, 9 (2): 72–80.

Saini, D. and Budhwar, P. (2007) Human resource management in India. In R.Schuler and S. Jackson (eds) *Strategic Human Resource Management*. Oxford: Blackwell, 287–312.

Saini, D. and Budhwar, P. (2008) Managing the human resource in Indian SMEs: the role of indigenous realities in organizational working. *Journal of World Business*, 43: 417–34.

Silveria, D. M. (1988) *Human Resource Development: The Indian Experience.* New Delhi: New India Publications.

Sinha, J. B. P. (1990) *Work Culture in Indian Context.* New Delhi: Sage.

Sinha, J. B. P. and Sinha, D. (1990) Role of social values in Indian organizations. *International Journal of Psychology*, 25: 705–15.

Sinha, J. B. P. and Kanungo, R. (1997) Context sensitivity and balancing in Indian organization behavior. *International Journal of Psychology*, 32: 93–105.

Sparrow, P. R. and Budhwar, P. (1997) Competition and change: mapping the Indian HRM recipe against worldwide patterns. *Journal of World Business*, 32 (3): 224–42.

Tayeb, M. (1987) Contingency theory and culture: a study of matched English and the Indian manufacturing firms. *Organisation Studies*, 8: 241–61.

Thomas, A. S. and Philips, A. (1994) India: management in an ancient and modern civilisation. *International Studies of Management and Organisation*, 24 (1–2): 91–115.

Tripathi, R. C. (1990) Interplay of values in the functioning of Indian organizations. *International Journal of Psychology*, 25: 715–34.

5 Dynamics of corruption and cronyism

Naresh Khatri

The purpose of this chapter is to paint a broad picture of corruption and cronyism in India. Although common Indians face and talk about corruption every day, systematic research and writing on the topic is limited. Corruption and cronyism have affected the Indian economic growth and well-being of its large population. Thus, it is fitting to examine the major factors that underlie cronyism and corruption in India. Such information would be useful for decision makers. This chapter is divided into three parts. In the first part, the concepts of corruption and cronyism are defined and distinguished from each other. The second part of the chapter discusses the dynamics of corruption and cronyism in India. This part constitutes the bulk of the chapter and is divided into many sections and subsections. The last part of the chapter derives implications for managers and policy makers.

Definition of corruption and cronyism

One of the most common definitions of corruption is the use of public office for private gain (Caiden, 2001; Larmour and Grabosky, 2001; White, 2001). In virtually every society, historians and anthropologists have found that public affairs are distinguished by their exceptional privileges and trappings, and activities most prone to corruption include bidding on public contracts, the use of public funds, the handling of property, tax assessment and collection, zoning and land use, the legislative and elective processes, law enforcement, and the administration of public services prone to political exploitation (Caiden, 2001; White, 2001).

The definition of corruption as the use of public office for private gain fits the needs of public administrators, economists and political scientists well, but it is unnecessarily restrictive for scholars and practitioners of management. The corrupt exchanges can take place not only between a public agent and a private agent, but also between one private agent and another private agent or between one public agent and another public agent.

Webster's Dictionary defines corruption as "bribery or similar dishonest dealings". Corruption breaks the social norm and thus is unethical (Luo, 2000). It involves an explicit, reciprocal, short-term, and date-bound transaction.

A corrupt exchange is basically a "commodity" and is devoid of any relationship between the agents. Larmour and Grabosky (2001) note that, although there is a lack of general agreement about the corruptness of various forms of exchanges, the situations of direct financial gain and illegality are clearly corrupt.

Cronyism usually gets lumped with corruption but has its own dynamics and patterns. The fundamental distinction between cronyism and corruption is that cronyism is based on a tie or a connection or a relationship between actors and involves implicit, unspecified, and reciprocal transactions with no stipulation of a time period during which favors must be returned (Khatri, Tsang, and Begley, 2006). Unlike corrupt exchanges, cronyistic exchanges, more often than not, are based on trust, loyalty, and long-standing friendship.

A review of literature on corruption suggests that most of the so-called "corrupt" acts or exchanges are actually acts or exchanges of cronyism. This occurs because corrupt acts or exchanges often involve collaborators (Krug and Hendrischke, 2003). When collaborators in corrupt exchanges come in frequent contact and engage in repeated exchanges, they may develop trust and long-term friendship. Corruption is by far more commonly used term than cronyism in the Indian parlance, although cronyism appears to be far more pervasive in India and underlies even the acts of corruption. The two terms of corruption and cronyism are used interchangeably in this chapter, although the emphasis is on the systematic features of these phenomena, thus making the treatment closer to cronyism than corruption.

Corruption comes in many forms. There are endemic, pervasive forms and isolated, infrequent forms, and then there are mutually reinforcing networks of complex, indirect, and subtle transactions on the one hand, and isolated, simple, direct, and bilateral transactions, on the other. Cronyism is likely to be the underlying force in corrupt exchanges that are endemic and pervasive and those that are based on mutually reinforcing networks of complex, indirect, and subtle transactions. Thus, to understand certain acts of so-called corruption, we may need to understand cronyism.

The most basic definition or meaning of the word "cronyism" is preferential treatment shown to old friends and associates, without regard to their qualifications (Khatri and Tsang, 2003). Cronyism can occur in two basic forms: instrumental and relational (Khatri and Tsang, 2003; Khatri, Tsang, and Begley, 2006). Instrumental cronyism is motivated primarily by task, utilitarian, and self-interest considerations. Although the value and time period for exchange of favors are implicit, the exchange of favors usually takes place in a relatively short time and value of favors exchanged tends to be more or less similar. Relational cronyism, on the other hand, has relationship, affection, and loyalty at its core. It is long-term in its orientation, i.e., the exchange of favors in relational cronyism takes place over a long period of time and value of favors exchanged can differ greatly depending on the relative status or position of the giver and taker.

Since seeking and maximizing self-interest is socially acceptable in the West, instrumental cronyism as a way to achieve one's goal is not disdained or considered unethical as much as in the East. In fact, much literature on social networking in the West advocates networking precisely to achieve one's self interest (e.g., promotion, pay raises, lucrative positions). On the other hand, relational cronyism is less acceptable in Western culture and may be perceived as "cronyism," an unethical behavior. In Asia and other non-Western countries, relational cronyism is not only socially acceptable but also desirable. In contrast, instrumental cronyism may be perceived as corrupt, unethical behavior. For example, Luo (2000) notes that Western businesses overemphasize the gift-giving and wining and dining in business relationships, thereby coming close to "crass bribery" or being perceived as only "meet and wine" friends.

Dynamics of corruption and cronyism

This part of the chapter forms its core and looks at a number of issues that need to be understood before one can grasp thoroughly the dynamics of corruption and cronyism in the Indian context. Initially, the variants of corruption and cronyism in Asia are discussed. Doing so situates corruption in India vis-à-vis other Asian countries. This section also includes an explanation of some unique varieties of Indian corruption. Next, I explore if there is a connection between economic growth and corruption, followed by a section that examines if there is any relationship between democracy and corruption. The impact of national culture on corruption and cronyism is then discussed, followed by delineation of the three key Indian contextual factors, the Indian political culture, the Indian civil services, and the oligarchic family control of Indian business, that have perpetuated high levels of corruption and cronyism in India.

Nature of corruption and cronyism

Corruption is too vague a term and covers too much ground to be a useful tool for analyzing and predicting acts of malfeasance. Different kinds of acts under the general rubric of corruption show different dynamics, so linking them all together unnecessarily limits our analytic powers (Johnston, 2008). Appropriate reforms require an understanding of the deeper, long-term forces shaping and sustaining corruption, their links to observable local characteristics and contrasts, and careful thought as to how corruption control might function in a given context (Johnston, 2008). Indeed, that sort of deeper analysis is essential if we are to sort out important commonalities and contrasts among cases from more superficial similarities and differences.

Based on *participation* (in the way people pursue, use, and exchange wealth and power) and *institutions* (economic, political, and social laws, systems, institutions), Johnston (2008) identified four syndromes of "Asian corruption" that capture important variations that can be traced to trends in the development of specific societies. The four syndromes are not about just more versus less corruption, but rather are contrasts in kinds of corruption problems. To search for syndromes of corruption is, in effect, to ask what are the underlying developmental processes and problems of which a society's corruption is symptomatic. Specifically, Johnston proposes the following syndromes of corruption: (1) *influence market* corruption, which is typical of well developed economies, such as Japan, Germany, and the United States, (2) *elite cartel corruption*, which is found in Hong Kong, Korea, and Singapore, (3) *oligarch and clan corruption*, which is reminiscent of corruption in India, Malaysia, Sri Lanka, and Thailand, and (4) *official mogul corruption*, which is commonly observed in China, the Philippines, Pakistan, Indonesia, and Myanmar. These four syndromes are next briefly discussed.

Influence market corruption deals with access to decision makers and policy implementers within strong state institutions; often politicians serve as middlemen, trading connections for contributions both legal and otherwise. Matured market democracies offer extensive political and economic opportunities, and generally have strong, legitimate institutions. While they are often held up as reform ideals, many of these countries have not solved corruption problems. Rather, they have fitted their rules to economic realities as well as persuaded people to follow the law, in the process becoming quite accommodating to the interests of wealthy. The social costs and inefficiencies do result from this type of corruption but are limited in their adverse impact. These systems have sufficient safeguards to prevent excessive corruption and the associated dysfunctions.

In *elite cartel corruption*, politics and markets are more competitive, but institutions are relatively weak. Here, networks of elites collude, using corrupt incentives and exchanges to shore up their positions. Power and its links to wealth are in flux, creating new opportunities and risks for elites; much corruption may be defensive in nature as elites protect their economic, political, or policy advantages. Those involved can have a variety of power bases, such as businesses, the military, the bureaucracy, a political party, or ethnic or regional social ties, and corrupt linkages may integrate elites in both the public and private sectors (Johnston, 2008). This corruption occurs at high echelons and common people do not encounter it. Korea and Singapore are examples of this kind of corruption and cronyism. Singapore is usually rated in the "top five" clean countries. However, Singapore seems to have a high degree of very concentrated corruption that has been aligned to a significant extent to its economic growth (Khatri, 2004). Politicians and influential party members sit on the boards of companies and are instrumental in getting resources and preferential treatment. The corrupt exchanges are made very predictable and government does not need to resort to coercion. These exchanges do not come to light because of government's complete control of media.

The *oligarchic/clan corruption* consists of disorderly, sometimes violent scramble among contending oligarchs/clans seeking to parlay personal resources (e.g., a mass following, a business, a bureaucratic chief, judicial or organized crime connections, or a powerful family) into wealth and power. Unlike the elite cartels syndrome, in which, relatively established elites collude within a moderately strong institutional framework, oligarchs/clans contend as free agents in a climate of pervasive insecurity. Inability to enforce contracts or defend property through courts and law enforcement increases the incentive to resort to violence, making military and police services, and mafia protection, all the more marketable (Johnston, 2008). Anti-corruption efforts in such settings will often be smokescreens for continued abuse or ways to put key competitors behind bars. Privatization can become a legalized carve-up of state resources or outright theft.

In the *official mogul corruption*, institutions are weak, politics remains un-democratic or is opening up only slowly, but the economy is being liberalized at least to a degree. Civil society is weak or non-existent. Opportunities for enrichment abound but politics and power are personal, and often used with impunity. Here, economic moguls are top political figures or their clients; they face few constraints from the state framework or from competitors (Johnston, 2008). Military leaders are useful partners, and in some cases are dominant, in such regimes, often using past corruption as a pretext for taking power. Development of civil society is inhibited by both corruption and the political hegemony underlying it, and people will thus have little recourse in case of official abuse.

Johnston (2008) classified India under oligarchs and clans corruption. While this is true, it seems that India is evolving into an elite cartel corruption, the type of corruption currently prevalent in Hong Kong, Singapore, and South Korea, which is less detrimental to economic growth.

There is another meaningful typology of corruption in the Indian society. According to this typology, the corruption is characterized according to the rich and poor (*Economic Times*, 2008a). The rich and educated, who have wealth but no values, pay bribes to subvert the system or escape the laws. Companies too are amongst the bribe-givers, though many of them keep their hands (account books) clean by paying a "consultant" to dispense not advice, but money. Corporate corruption is often the result of a maze of laws, inten-tional bureaucratic delays, and the requirement of dozens of approvals from multiple agencies for a simple task. Corporations use bribes even to score over competition and unfairly win contracts.

On the other hand, there are those who give bribes because they have no choice: the poor and the powerless, for example, have little choice when corrupt officials demand a bribe for a service they control – issuing driving licenses, ration cards, or land-ownership deeds. Corruption thus further exacerbates social and economic inequalities, with the poor having to pay bribes for services that are meant to be free, while the rich get what is not rightfully theirs (*Economic Times*, 2008a). In effect, the well-off get a high rate of return on their bribes, while the poor get a negative one. This kind of corruption has evolved in the context of the Indian political culture (discussed more in a later section on the Indian political culture and corruption).

The rich and poor corruption is also known as elite and petty corruption (Desai and Olofsgard, 2008). In elite exchange, India is notorious for its influence-peddling politicians, money-seeking bureaucrats, and bribe-dispensing entrepreneurs. Older firms, state-owned firms, and foreign firms are better protected from cronyism and corruption arising from the elite exchange. Petty corruption is endemic at the lower, clerical levels of adminis-tration – precisely the point at which the ordinary citizen comes into daily contact with officialdom (Thakur, 2000). People are forced to pay bribes for securing virtually any service connected with the government, even that which is theirs by right and law. The petty corruption does not cost as much in terms of money but it extracts very high costs in terms of inefficiencies, delays, and frustration in common people. Cronyism is usually common at the upper echelons of the society and administrative corruption at the lower strata of the society.

There is a further variety of corruption according to whether it is legal or illegal. In developed countries outright bribery may be less prevalent, companies can sometimes benefit from "legal corruption" by achieving undue influence over regulation and policy making. In such an environment, lax oversight and corporate scandals can be expected. Corruption ought to also encompass some acts that may be legal in a strict narrow sense, but where the rules of the game and the state laws, policies, regulations and institutions may have been shaped in part by undue influence of certain vested interests for their own private benefit. Kaufman used World Economic Forum data to rank countries in terms of the prevalence of such "legal corruption" as well as traditional corruption measure (*Economic Times*, 2009). A very different picture emerges. The United States was found to be rated very poorly in terms of prevalence of legal corruption – about the same as India and South Korea.

Economic performance and corruption

An interesting question that puzzles scholars is whether corruption and cronyism can coexist with fast economic growth. There are several examples that suggest that it is possible to grow rapidly despite pervasive corruption and cronyism in the system, although it depends on whether a system is fol-lowing a liberal economic strategy or a statist-nationalist strategy (Lankester, 2004). A liberal economic strategy means one where the state relies primarily, but not exclusively, on markets and on the private sector to generate growth; where exports and inward investment are encouraged; where the state intervenes selectively to correct market failures but sees its main role as providing public goods such as health, education, training and infrastructure, and a supportive macro-economic policy. A statist-nationalist strategy means one where the state plays a much more interventionist role in allocating resources and organizing production; relies on markets and the private sectors to a far lesser extent; stresses import substitution and self-reliance rather than export growth; and discourages inward investment.

China and India both suffered from stagnant economies when they pursued the statist-nationalist economic strategy. However, since liberalization both countries have experienced explosive growth despite the fact that the Corruption Perception Indices by the Transparency International still rank them high in corruption. Lankester (2004) makes a compelling case in support of the above argument. According to the author, in a period of thirty years, from 1960 to 1990, Indonesia pursued a liberal economic strategy, whereas India mostly followed a statist-nationalist strategy. It was this difference in strategy that led to Indonesia's spectacular economic success over the three decades and a very dismal economic performance of India over the same period. During this time, Indonesia was as corrupt as India, perhaps more so.

From the 1960s to the mid-1980s, India had one of the most controlled economies in the world outside the communist bloc. There were administrative controls on prices, on industrial investment, on bank lending, and the capital markets, on imports and even on some exports. The state reserved for itself the ownership of many key industries; other industries were reserved for small-scale enterprises; domestic industry was heavily protected; competing imports were mostly banned; and inward investments were discriminated against. Large private businesses were prevented from expanding. The public sector provided plenty of jobs but placed a heavy burden on the rest of the economy.

In India, to a large extent, the statist-nationalist philosophy reflected mainstream thinking amongst economists in the 1960s, as it did amongst development economists in many countries – especially in Latin America. It also coincided with India's early post-independence interest in Soviet planning models and with socialist thinking in the Congress Party (Lankester, 2004).

There are other striking examples of economies that suggest that the same magnitude of corruption but of different varieties have significantly different impact on a country's economic growth. For example, both South Korea and Philippines are plagued with corruption. Whereas South Korea grew at a tremendous pace, the Philippines did not. This may be attributed both to the type of economic system as well as the type of corruption. South Korea has followed a liberal economic strategy and it has had elite cartel corruption, which is less harmful to the economic growth than the combination of statist-national economic strategy and the official mogul corruption prevalent in the Philippines (Kang, 2002).

Democracy and corruption

The arguments pointing to the efficacy of elections in a democracy to curb corruption are intuitively appealing. The lower the cost to citizens of expelling non-performing officials, the more one would expect officials to act in the interests of citizens. In practice, however, electoral markets are often highly imperfect, disrupting electoral accountability and the ability of the citizens to sanction governments that allow poor governance outcomes to persist (Keefer, 2006). One key political market imperfection is uninformed citizens. If citizens cannot draw a connection between public policy and their own welfare, neither elections nor other, non-electoral means of expelling politicians easily limit abuses by government officials. The dominance of the Congress Party and its dynastic rule beginning since the independence of the country in 1947 to until mid-1985 resulted in a culture of cronyism and patronage, because the party faced no credible threat from the opposition parties.

Democracy and elections in the absence of an informed and educated citizenry seem no better than dictatorship since elections fail to overthrow the corrupt politicians who keep blinding citizenry with populous economic policies. Public welfare is enhanced when leaders depend on a large coalition to keep them in office (de Mesquita *et al.*, 2001). Under these conditions, those motivated to stay in power have no choice but to promote the public's welfare. To do otherwise is to risk being ousted from the office. Since the mid-1980s there has been gradual erosion of the Congress Party and a credible political challenge has emerged to the party. The emergence of many strong coalitions has resulted in political checks and balances. Keefer (2006) argues that, in both China and India, political checks and balances preceded their fast growth. In China, political checks and balances evolved entirely within the Chinese Communist Party.

Many scholars and businessmen believe that China is a more attractive place to do business partly because it has greater political stability and much greater control of the Communist Party which allows it to make decisions to help China grow at a much faster place. This may have been true before India liberalized its economy. Now India's democracy is one of its most significant advantages over China, along with free and vibrant press. Indian democracy has faced all sorts of upheavals and it has shown its resiliency. In fact, the Indian democracy has strengthened over the years as the Congress Party has lost its dominance in late 1990s and early 2000s (Cohen, 2001; Keefer, 2006; Luce, 2008). The combination of liberal economy and democracy is a very potent one and difficult for China to emulate. It can be argued that China has matured more than India in an economic sense but India is way ahead of China in political maturity.

Role of societal culture in corruption/cronyism

The key to recognizing corruption in a given society is to know something about how that society works (Hooker, 2003). Although societal culture has been shown to be a key variable in understanding human behavior (Hofstede, 2001), policy-making institutions such as the World Bank and IMF are still dominated by economics and other related fields such as finance and political science. Only recently scholars have begun to realize that, perhaps, culture has a greater explanatory power than macroeconomic and financial variables (Steidlmeier, 1999; Waldron, 2002). For example, Waldron (2002) found that the majority of the financial executives from across East and South East Asia, the region most affected by the Asian economic crisis of 1997, did not endorse much of what had been accepted as common wisdom (macro-economic explanations) about the causes of the crisis. On the contrary, nearly two-thirds of the financial executives either agreed or strongly agreed that relationship-based lending (cronyism) had been largely overlooked as a major factor contributing to the East Asian economic crisis. In general terms, "*cultural logic* underscores the numerous socio-cultural values and beliefs that are embedded within organizations and function as a sort of internal gyroscope, which governs the social behavior of people" (Steidlmeier, 1999:121).

Khatri *et al.* (2006) proposed four types of cronyism across the two major cultural dimensions of verticalness–horizontalness and individualism–collectivism (see Figure 5.1). Vertical cultures assume that people are different from one another, take hierarchy as given, and accent status differences as well as respect for authority. Horizontal cultures value equality, see people as similar to one another, therefore interchangeable, and minimize status and authority distinctions. In individualist cultures, social behavior is driven by individual beliefs, values, attitudes, and interests, and personal goals take priority over group goals. Individualists seek task achievement at the expense of relationships. On the other hand, the behavior of collectivists is driven by social norms, duties, and obligations, and collectivists tend to subordinate personal goals to group goals. Collectivists value harmonious relationships even at the expense of task accomplishment. Indian culture is high on verticalness and collectivism, thus making it prone to a high level of cronyism since vertical collectivist cultures are suggested to have the highest level of cronyism, followed by vertical individualist, horizontal collectivist, and horizontal individualist cultures, respectively (Khatri *et al.*, 2006). The Corruption Perception Index of the Transparency International corroborates Khatri *et al.*'s typology. Most of the countries on the higher end of the corruption index are vertical collectivists and most of the countries on the lower end of the corruption index are horizontal individualists. A collectivist culture like India values in-group relationships based frequently on kinship or other ascriptive ties. Thus, the members of a particular group feel obliged to take care of one another and feel duty-bound to allocate rewards more generously to in-group than out-group members otherwise they may face group sanctions. In India, strong boundaries between in-groups and out-groups are drawn based on caste, religion, and region.

Khatkhate (2008), in his book *Ruminations of Gadfly*, argues that, in non-corrupt states like Denmark, people in a village hardly know one another, and family ties are weak – members do not even regularly attend family weddings. But people in an Indian village are in close contact with neighbors, and have

	Individualist culture	Collectivist culture
Vertical culture	Vertical individualists (e.g. France, UK, US) Highest level of instrumental cronyism	Vertical collectivists (e.g. Asian, African, Latin American, East European countries; India, Brazil, Egypt, Hungary) Highest level of relational cronyism
Horizontal culture	Horizontal individualists (Scandinavian countries: Sweden, Denmark, Norway) No or low level of instrumental cronyism	Horizontal collectivists (Israeli kibbutz, New Zealand) No or low level of relational cronyism

Figure 5.1 Cultural dimensions and cronyism in India.

strong ties within families and communities. He further notes that people in authority are much more corrupt in India since tradition approves the giving of priority to one's family, caste, and religious group over abstract ideas like the public interest. But in Denmark, public interest is viewed as a top priority, and this notion is facilitated by the lack of strong family and social networks. It is worth noting here that Denmark is a horizontal individualist culture that according to Khatri *et al.*'s classification is expected to show the least amount of corruption. Khatkhate gives examples of Indians who blossomed when they went abroad, but could not have achieved similar success in Indian conditions, marred by cronyism, political interference, and wooden bureaucratic rules. Specifically, he mentions Lakshmi Mittal, who once said that if he had tried to buy an existing steel plant in India, he would have had spent half his life chasing *netas* (politicians) and *babus* (bureaucrats), where he could complete takeovers abroad in a few months.

Kakar (1971) observes that an Indian is less sensitive to the goals of work and productivity that are external to a relationship, and more to the unfolding of emotional affinity. The power play in organizations tends to be very personal, wherein those close to the superior are bestowed with all kinds of (including undue) favors, while those who are not, tend to be distanced and discriminated against. In general, Indians tend to be collectivist and, invariably, people seem to be linked to the rest of social body by a network of highly diversified ties (also see Sparrow and Budhwar, 1997; Budhwar and Sparrow, 2002). This embeddedness, however, rarely goes beyond one's own family, kinship, linguistic, and religious group. Over a period of time, the practice of marrying and fraternization within the same caste has created an intricate framework wherein a sharp distinction has evolved between the in-group (family members and individuals from the same caste) and the out-group (non-family members and those from other castes) (Gopalan and Rivera, 1997). Consequently, Indians show strong favoritism to in-group members and are suspicious and hostile toward out-group members.

Although some think that the Asian countries including India are getting westernized rather rapidly, changes presently taking place in these nations and societies are mostly superficial, cosmetic in nature. For example, Luo (2000) suggests that the establishment of institutional law in economically advanced or more developed Asian societies, such as Japan, South Korea, Hong Kong, Singapore, and Taiwan, has not displaced reliance on personal connections. Maintaining relationships remains the core values of these societies. Waldron (2002: 47) reported that the financial executives in Asian countries hit by the economic crisis expect relationship lending to endure as a fundamental part of the business culture and Boisot and Child (1996) suggest that many Asian societies are not moving toward market capitalism, but rather toward a relationship-based "network capitalism."

Political culture and corruption

The Indian National Congress has ruled India for most of the time since its independence. Administrative systems and social, economic and political institutions that exist in India today show a deep imprint of the Congress Party's philosophy and policies. Thus, in this chapter, most of my discussion pertains to the Congress culture and how it has perpetuated cronyism throughout the Indian administrative and economic system. The discussion is not meant to suggest that other political parties are necessarily any better. They too have similar problems of their own that may be even worse.

> The Indian state was partly a creation of Nehru. But Nehru's motivations were ideological and they were in tune with broader international fashion at the time. Sixty years later, the persistence of the unreformed state can no longer be attributed to ideology. We have to look deeper to discover why India's state is still permitted to operate in its radical form. Some of the reasons are to be found in the habits and character of the Congress Party.
>
> (Luce, 2008: 197)

Indian leaders need to rebuild the archaic and inefficient process by which policy is made at the center. At present, decisions are excessively centralized, parliamentary consultation is weak, the talents of outsiders are rarely utilized, and coordination among differing Ministries and bureaucracies is poor (Luce, 2008).

A good example of cronyism rampant in the central government was reported in the *Economic Times* (2007). The government recently got all the independent directors – including directors elected by minority shareholders – of public sector banks to step down and appointed party workers and loyalists in their place. These supposedly "independent" directors include at least five secretaries of the All India Congress Committee, as well as many senior members from the All India Mahila Congress and Sewa Dal. In general, institutional directors who are appointed by the central government, sit as mute witnesses to various acts of corporate malfeasance and misgovernance, stirring only when they receive directions from the government. And, the government officials routinely use these directors as pawns in a complex game of favoritism and cronyism (*Economic Times*, 2007).

The political culture both at the center and in the states is all about preferential access to a whole range of public goods, from free first-class plane and rail tickets, the opportunity to jump queues, the ability to pull strings, and the availability of free services for which the poor have to pay. If you are rich and important, you rarely pay. If you are poor, you usually pay through the nose, and there is no guarantee you will get what you pay for (Luce, 2008).

Indian civil services and corruption

India has long practiced economic planning or command capitalism through extensive state regulative controls of industry and cumbersome licensing schemes, partly due to political and bureaucratic corruption (Das, 2001). *Netas* (politicians) and *babus* (bureaucrats) have run the show and strangulated tremendous human potential, creativity, and entrepreneurship of Indians. Indian politicians do not take kindly to administrative reforms that separate policy making from policy implementation because doing so takes away from them their ability to shower favoritism on their cronies. Similarly, elite civil services have been the vanguard of resistance to any attempt to change the status quo and have been largely successful because of the political leadership's undue dependence on them.

The civil service has been corrupt and served the interests of patrimonial politics (Das, 2001). The present system has worked well only in coordinating rents and getting them shared across both the official and political realms. Day-to-day administration provides ample opportunities for money-making, such as transfers and postings of civil servants, awarding of major contracts and concessions, and the provision of goods and services free or below market prices (Das, 2001). As the implementing body for all government policies, state laws and regulations, the civil service is at the heart of the governance problems in India (Das, 2001; Nikomborirak, 2007).

Oligarchic family control and corruption

Firms controlled by oligarchic families are generally adept rent-seekers who thrive in societies with low trust levels and corruption (Fogel, 2006). Oligarchic family control is more prevalent in the large corporate sectors of countries like India whose bureaucracies are less efficient, whose governments direct more economic activities, whose political rent-seeking opportunities are more lucrative, and whose financial markets are less functional. Most of these conditions of rent seeking have existed in India since independence and continue to do so.

India has the second-largest number of billionaires per trillion US dollars of GDP, after Russia (*Economic Times*, 2008b). While Russia has eighty-seven billionaires for the US$ 1.3 trillion of GDP it generates. India has fifty-five for the US$ 1.1 trillion of GDP. Germany has the same number as India with four times its GDP. The common perception that these are software billionaires is not correct. Three factors – land, natural resources, and government contracts are the predominant resources of the wealth of Indian billionaires and all of these factors come from the government. Too many people in India have become rich based on their proximity to the government.

The countries with more extensive family control over their large corporate sectors tend to have worse socio-economic outcomes. Highly concentrated economic power that has existed in India perpetuates poor institutions, which are bad for growth. A mutually reinforcing relationship exists in which poor institutions lead to the rise of concentrated economic power and the oligarchies in turn use their economic might to reap political advantages and shape institutional development most favorable to their interests (Fogel, 2006).

Corruption and red-tapism, partly a consequence of oligarchic control, are the major barriers to growth of entrepreneurship in India, a government study has found. The study on entrepreneurship, conducted by National Knowledge Commission and reported in the *Economic Times* (2008b) is based on interviews of 155 entrepreneurs from across the country. Entrepreneurs were found to face difficulty and delays in meeting various government requirements such as registration of company, obtaining licenses, and registering the property. The study also quoted the World Bank report *Doing Business in South Asia 2007* to point out the inordinate delay of thirty-five to fifty-two days to start a business in India. The official costs of starting a business were noted to be high and the process quite complex involving no less than thirteen procedures (*Economic Times*, 2008c).

While in the pre-reforms era, corruption used to be about sale of permits, reforms have created new sources of rents for the establishment. Land can be expropriated from those who do not have connection or formal title. Public land can always be disposed off to favored parties. Contracts can be assigned to chosen friends despite a sham of public bidding. The rents are shared by the politicians and corrupt businessmen (*Economic Times*, 2008b).

Deterioration of institutions

At the time of independence, India inherited a fairly corruption-free, robust administrative system. Individuals heading various central government bodies (for example, the chief of the army staff, the judges to the Supreme Court and high courts, vice-chancellors of universities, etc.) were chosen based on merit. Nehru, the first Prime Minister of India from 1947 to 1964, did not interfere in important appointments and the Indian administrative system remained a decent one. Since then, because of the interference of government in appointments, the Indian administrative system and institutions have unraveled. Now most central government departments and institutions and state government departments have become politicized and corrupt. Almost the entire nation seems to be gradually becoming more and more disorderly and lawless.

The Indian judicial system was free from political interference for many decades after independence, but has become deeply politicized and corrupt over time. According to a Transparency International's 2006 survey, 77 percent of the Indian respondents described the judicial system as corrupt. About 36 percent of the people paid bribes to judiciary. The average amount of money paid by a household in India to judiciary was the highest as compared to other sectors. In February 2006, twenty-six Supreme Court judges faced a backlog of more than 30,000 pending cases; over 3 million cases were pending in the high courts. At the current rate of resolution it will take 350 years for the country's 670 judges.

The same is true of the accounting practices in Indian companies. India inherited the British accounting system and it can be said that Indian accounting practices were good for a long time. But they too have deteriorated, as evident from the recent scandal involving Satyam.

Conclusions and key issues

What does it all mean for firms that want to do business in India? India's major undoing, more than anything else, was to rely on the socialist philosophy and its statist-nationalist economic strategy. Lack of economic freedom has been suggested to account for 71 percent of corruption in a society (Wikipedia, 2009). There are so many examples of Asian countries that have prospered economically despite ubiquitous cronyism and corruption. But there is none that has grown rapidly using the statist-nationalist economy. Even the 'Indian pseudo-intellectuals' who backed the socialist economic model in the past have understood the root cause of India's economic problems. Now, finally, the genie is out of the bottle and the Indian bandwagon is rolling; it is as hard to stop now as it was to start. Scott Bryman, the outgoing president and chief executive of General Electric India, who had lived in New Delhi for fourteen years, noted that the endemic culture of bribery, corruption, kickbacks, nepotism, and cronyism that he saw when he had first arrived has significantly dissipated (Haniffa, 2007). Further, he summarily dismissed the political risk in terms of investment, saying, "India has shown over the last six elections its resilience in terms of who's in power . . . Nobody in India is arguing that you should turn the clock back on liberalization . . . The important thing is privatizing and airports."

There are many strong forces propelling India forward. First, the liberal economy is allowing Indian entrepreneurs to flex their muscles. Although presently the wealth is concentrated in a few hands, over time, new entrepreneurs, the likes of Narayanan Murthy of Infosys, will keep appearing on the horizon. Indian people have been strangulated for too long. They are hungry and they are restless. They have waited for too long and seen many economies go past them. Second, India's democracy has matured and shown tremendous resilience. It is as vibrant a democracy as there can be. Democracy in combination with its liberal economic strategy and its massive size make India a place to be. India's free and vigorous press is its third major strength. It will be a big force in bringing more transparency and curbing corruption and cronyism in India. It has shown its caliber by bringing to light so many high profile corruption scandals, which might not have been possible in most other countries. The fourth Indian strength lies in Indian people and professionals. Indian institutions and systems are already compatible with the Western economies and there is a large pool of English-educated people. Indian professionals and businessmen have already proven their acumen and brilliance all over the globe. As a British historian, E. P. Thompson, rightly noted, "There is not a thought that is being thought in the West or the East that is not active in some Indian mind."

There are historical forces that should not be underestimated that may resist the forces of change and once more put India off-track. Indian politicians (*netas*) and bureaucrats (*babus*) in tandem have perpetuated a highly cronyistic system. A recent survey ranked India's "suffocating bureaucracy" as the worst in Asia and suggested that it wields tremendous power at both the national and state levels (*Times of India*, 2009). The survey also noted that the Indian civil service is extremely resistant to reform. The elite civil servants have become used to power and are not likely to give it up so easily. The answer to neutralize both *netas* and *babus* lies in a bigger and relatively unfettered private sector that can become an engine of Indian growth and prosperity. *Netas* and *babus* can keep getting their rents in the government/public sector. The other major negative force to contend with is the concentration of wealth in the hands of a few families. These families would want to protect their empires from the upstarts. They would want to continue to plunder rents in collaboration with politicians and bureaucrats. Thus, they would keep putting hurdles in the way of meaningful institutional reforms. Still another major obstacle in the way of India's growth and prosperity is the caste-based social system. The political parties keep reinforcing the caste system and as a result India remains a divided society.

Beyond providing an understanding of the dynamics of cronyism and corruption in India in this chapter, there are two specific points that international managers and companies may take note of.

- First, an international manager or company in doing business in India has to ultimately operate in a state. The state government in India has sufficient autonomy and legal rights. Thus, it is important for the international managers and companies to fully understand the make-up of the government in the state, and try and predict how long it is likely to remain in power. Further, it is critical to find if the state government belongs to the same or different political party as the central government. For example, if the state government belongs to the same party as the central government then one has not to worry about the state government as much because all important decisions can be influenced through Delhi; the state government officials obey the order of the central government.

- The second important point to note is that India's other major problem (apart from political instability and corruption) lies in its weak infrastructure. However, India has improved significantly in this aspect as well in the last ten years, although it has a long way to go and infrastructure will continue to hold India back for many more years.

- As noted earlier, corruption in India is of two types – elite and petty. Indian society is very hierarchic and elitist. As a result, elites including international managers and companies are not affected by day-to-day corruption that common Indians face. International managers and companies get into trouble only by showing arrogance and lacking cultural sensitivities but not because they are strangers or outsiders.

- The experience in overcoming corruption in other countries and societies suggest that the way to ensure better behavior is not to introduce more regulations, but to do as much as possible to promote transparency; transparency is the most powerful weapon against corruption and cronyism. "Sunshine is the best disinfectant" (*Economic Times*, 2009). Corruption feeds on control.

- The permit-license raj of the old socialist system spawned an inefficient regulatory regime, crippling high compliance and transaction costs, a corrupt bureaucratic system, and a rent-seeking political system. Free and vibrant press and gradual evolution of simple laws that strengthen transparency will be the key to reduce corruption and cronyism. Further, it goes without saying that more education and a more civil society lead to improved laws and institutions.

References

Bjorkman, I. and Kock, S. (1995) Social relationships and business networks: the case of Western companies in China. *International Business Review*, 4 (40): 519–35.

Boisot, M. and Child, J. (1996) From fiefs to clans and network capitalism: explaining China's emerging economic order. *Administrative Science Quarterly*, 41: 600–29.

Budhwar, P. and Sparrow, P. (2002) Strategic HRM through the cultural looking glass: mapping cognitions of British and Indian HRM managers. *Organization Studies*, 23 (4): 599–638.

Caiden, G. E. (2001) Corruption and governance. In G. E. Caiden, O. P. Dwivedi and J. Jabbra (eds) *Where Corruption Lives*. Bloomfield CT: Kumarian Press, 15–37.

Cohen, S. P. (2001) *India: Emerging Power*, Washington DC: Brookings Institution Press.

Das, S. K. (2001) *Public Office, Private Interest: Bureaucracy and Corruption in India.* New Delhi: Oxford University Press.

de Mesquita, B. B., Morrow, J. D., Siverson, R. and Smith, A. (2001) Political competition and economic growth. *Journal of Democracy*, 12 (1): 58–72.

Desai, R. M. and Olofsgard, A. (2008) Do Politically Connected Firms undermine their own Competitiveness? Evidence from Developing Countries. Brookings Global Economy and Development Working Paper No. 18. Available at SSRN: http://ssrn.com/abstract=110014.

Economic Times (2009) Corporate fraud scandals can detonate anywhere. 9 January.

Economic Times (2008a) Conquering corruption. 9 July.

Economic Times (2008b) Political influence in businesses a concern. 12 September.

Economic Times (2008c) Corruption, red-tapism affect entrepreneurship in India: study. 7 July.

Economic Times (2008d) Why does corrupt India grow fast? 13 April.

Economic Times (2007) Good biz, poor governance. 14 May.

Fogel, K. (2006) Oligarchic family control, social economic outcomes, and the quality of government. *Journal of International Business Studies*, 37: 603–22.

Gopalan, S. and Rivera, J. B. (1997) Gaining a perspective on Indian value orientations: implications for expatriate managers. *International Journal of Organizational Analysis*, 5 (2): 156–79.

Haniffa, A. (2007) Bribery, corruption down in India: outgoing GE India chief, *rediff.com*, 22 May.

Hofstede, G. (2001) *Culture's Consequences: Comparing Values, Behaviors, Institutions and Organizations across Nations.* Thousand Oaks CA: Sage.

Hooker, J. (2003) A cross-cultural view of corruption, working paper. Graduate School of Industrial Administration, Carnegie Mellon University.

Johnston, M. (2008) Japan, Korea, the Philippines, China: four syndromes of corruption. *Crime, Law, and Social Change*, 49: 205–23.

Kakar, S. (1971) Authority patterns and subordinate behavior in Indian organizations. *Administrative Science Quarterly*, 16: 298–307.

Kang, D. C. (2002) *Crony Capitalism: Corruption and Development in South Korea and Philippines.* Cambridge: Cambridge University Press.

Keefer, P. (2006) *Governance and Economic Growth in China and India.* Washington DC: World Bank Development Research Group.

Khatkhate, D. (2008) *Ruminations of a Gadfly: Persons, Places, Perceptions.* New Delhi: Academic Foundation.

Khatri N. (2004) HRM in Singapore. In P. Budhwar (ed.), *HRM in Asia and the Pacific Rim.* London: Taylor & Francis, 221–38.

Khatri, N. and Tsang, E. W. K. (2003) Antecedents and consequences of cronyism in organizations. *Journal of Business Ethics*, 43: 289–303.

Khatri, N., Tsang, E. W. K. and Begley, T. (2006) Cronyism: a cross-cultural analysis. *Journal of International Business Studies*, 37 (1): 61–75.

Krug, B. and Hendrischke, H. (2003) The economics of corruption and cronyism: an institutional approach to the reform of governance. In J. B. Kidd and F.-J. Richter (eds) *Corruption and Governance in Asia.* Basingstoke: Palgrave Macmillan, 131–48.

Lankester, T. (2004) 'Asian drama': the pursuit of modernization in India and Indonesia. *Asian Affairs*, 35: 291–304.

Larmour, P. and Grabosky, P. (2001) Corruption in Australia: its prevention and control. In G. E. Caiden, O. P. Dwivedi, and J. Jabbra (eds) *Where Corruption Lives*. Bloomfield CT: Kumarian Press, 175–88.

Luce, E. (2008) *In Spite of the Gods: The Rise of Modern India*. New York: Anchor Books.

Luo, Y. (2000) *Guanxi and Business*. Singapore: World Scientific.

Nef, J. (2001) Government corruption in Latin America. In G. E. Caiden, O. P. Dwivedi and J. Jabbra (eds) *Where Corruption Lives*. Bloomfield CT: Kumarian Press, 159–73.

Nikomborirak, D. (2007) Civil service reforms and the quest for better governance: the Thai experience. *TDRI Quarterly Review*, 22 (1): 3–8.

Pagano, M. S. (2002) Crises, cronyism, and credit. *Financial Review*, 37: 227–56.

Sparrow, P. R. and Budhwar, P. (1997) Competition and change: mapping the Indian HRM recipe against worldwide patterns. *Journal of World Business*, 32 (3): 224–42.

Steidlmeier, P. (1999) Gift giving, bribery, and corruption: ethical management of business relationships in China. *Journal of Business Ethics*, 20 (2): 121–32.

Thakur, R. (2000) Corruption undermines India. *Japan Times*, Tokyo, 1 July.

Times of India (2009) Indian bureaucracy ranked worst in Asia: survey. 3 June.

Trompenaars, F. (1993) *Riding the Wave of Culture*. London: Nicholas Brearley.

Waldron, D. G. (2002) A study of managerial perceptions of relationship-based lending and the East Asian economic crisis. *Multinational Business Review*, 10 (2): 42–51.

White, R. D., Jr (2001) Corruption in the United States. In G. E. Caiden, O. P. Dwivedi and J. Jabbra (eds) *Where Corruption Lives*. Bloomfield CT: Kumarian Press, 39–55.

Wikipedia (2009) Political corruption. http://en.wikipedia.org/wiki/political_corruption (downloaded 20 March 2009).

6 Infrastructure

Devendra Kodwani

The Indian population is expected to touch 1.5 billion by 2050. The government and people of India aspire to grow rapidly. This presents enormous opportunities to meet the demand of people across a range of goods and services. The government of India and the governments at the state level are aware of the fact that the opportunities created by opening up of Indian economy can not be converted into reality in absence of good quality infrastructure services such as transport, communication networks, energy and water. On the one hand there are opportunities to meet demand for goods and services which requires good quality infrastructure support. On the other hand there is a strong need to develop road networks, generate and distribute electricity, utilize gas and petroleum resources, develop and connect ports and airports and railways for seamless transport of goods. Thus infrastructure services present an enormous scope for business over the next two to three decades. The Indian government's recent recognition to the need for bringing up these facilities to world class standards is supported by putting in place the emphasis on development of infrastructure. Good beginning has been made in development of road networks. The exploration of natural gas has expanded and the private sector has also been invited to participate in these efforts. The communications access has improved many fold and the costs have been reduced. All these are good signs for doing business in India. But a lot needs to be done at the policy level and in terms of ensuring that private domestic and foreign businesses have access to infrastructure services to make contribution to India's economic development.

This chapter has three main objectives. First, to discuss the status of and expected developments in infrastructure services that support business in India. Second, to argue why multinational and other business enterprises should consider investing in Indian infrastructure sectors. Finally, to discuss the issues that investors in infrastructure should understand while implementing their business plans in infrastructure services. In other words this chapter provides two perspectives on the infrastructure services in India – it looks at infrastructure as business opportunity from investors' perspective and then it considers issues faced by users of infrastructure services. Given the nature of issues and size of opportunities involved in provision of infrastructure there is relatively more space devoted to expected developments in infrastructure services which should be of interest to both the users of services as well as potential investors.

The chapter is organized as follows. In the next section it is made clear what infrastructure means in the Indian policy framework. The meaning of infrastructure services is explained and services are grouped into categories, namely *energy*, *telecommunications* and *transport*. This is followed by a discussion of business opportunities and challenges faced in each of the groups. An important mechanism to involve private sector in the Indian infrastructure has been the use of public–private partnership (PPP) mode. Salient features and uses of PPP in India are discussed. Users' perspective is discussed in the following section before concluding the chapter with some useful tips for both the users and investors in the Indian infrastructure and references to some useful resources.

Infrastructure services in the Indian economy: the big picture

Box 6.1 shows what the central government's advisory committee on infrastructure considers to be infrastructure industries. To simplify the presentation and understanding, the list of industries is reclassified into three groups, namely *energy* industries, comprising electricity (conventional and renewable sources included) and oil and gas (exploration, refinery and distribution included), *telecommunications* and *transport*, comprising roads,

---

Box 6.1 Industries recognised as infrastructure in India

- Electricity (including generation, transmission and distribution) and repair and maintenance of power stations
- Non-conventional energy (including wind energy and solar energy)
- Water supply and sanitation (including solid waste management, drainage and sewerage) and street lighting
- Telecommunications
- Roads and bridges
- Ports
- Inland waterways
- Airports
- Railways (including rolling stock and mass transit system)
- Irrigation (including watershed development)
- Storage
- Oil and gas pipeline networks

Source: Government of India, Planning Commission, Secretariat for Committee on Infrastructure (New Delhi, 2008).

ports, airports and railways. We leave out water supply and irrigation from the scope of this chapter. The main reason for this is that water supply and irrigation are two of the most sensitive political issues where the policy framework for involvement of private sector or that of multinationals is hardly evolved. So even though water and sewerage are potentially major industries requiring investment and development of markets at present there is little indication that private sector will be allowed in near future. The scope of discussion in this chapter is therefore restricted to the three groups of industries as described above.

According to the Planning Commission, the Indian central government's think tank, power sector alone presents an opportunity of investment to the tune of US$ 130 billion over the five-year period to 2012 (Table 6.1). Ports, roads, airports, telecoms, and oil and gas present similarly significant investment opportunities. According to one estimate, the investment in infrastructure needs to grow to 9 per cent of GDP to support the economic growth rate of 9 per cent (Rastogi, 2008). It is clear from Table 6.1 that India offers great opportunities for business in infrastructure services. A climate conducive for business requires legal and other institutional framework to ensure contract enforcement, appropriate labour laws and infrastructure services supporting business. Specifically in infrastructure industries there has been concerted effort to improve the business environment through regulatory and legislative changes. Substantial progress made in policy reforms has opened up various infrastructure services for both domestic and multinational enterprises to invest in India. Table 6.2 lists the amount of ownership permissible and the modes of entry into India for different sectors.

The efforts to increase the share of private participation in infrastructure in India have been showing results (see Figure 6.1). A chief mode of private sector investment in infrastructure has been through public–private partnership agreements which are discussed later in the chapter. An outstanding example

Table 6.1 Investment required for Indian infrastructure, 2007–12 (US$ billion)

Industry	Investment
Power	130
Railways	66
Highways	49
Ports	11
Civil aviation	9
Others	55
Total	320

Note: Calculated at Rs 45.30 = US$ 1, at 2005–06 prices.

Source: Ministry of Finance, *Report of the Committee on Infrastructure Financing*, New Delhi: Government of India, 2007.

Table 6.2 Infrastructure industries: caps on foreign investment and entry routes

Sector	Ownership limit (%)	Entry route	Remarks
Power	100	Automatic	Includes generation (except nuclear power, where FDI is prohibited), transmission and distribution of power
Telecoms			
Basic, cellular and value-added services	74	FIPB beyond 49%	
ISP with gateways	74	FIPB beyond 49%	Subject to licensing and security
ISP without gateways	100	FIPB beyond 49%	requirements; FDI cap of 74% for
E-mail, voice mail	100	FIPB beyond 49%	global mobile personal
Radio paging	74	FIPB beyond 49%	communications by satellite
End-to-end bandwidth	74	FIPB beyond 49%	
Infrastructure providers providing dark fibre	100	FIPB beyond 49%	
Telecom manufacturing	100	Automatic	
Roads	100	Automatic	Includes construction and maintenance of roads, highways, bridges and tunnels
Ports	100	Automatic	Applies to construction and maintenance of ports
Civil aviation			
Airports	100	Automatic	FIPB beyond 74% for existing airport
Domestic airlines	49	Automatic	Subject to no direct or indirect equity participation by foreign airlines. FDI up to 100% allowed for NRIs
Cargo, chartered and non-scheduled airlines	74	Automatic	Investment up to 100% allowed for non-resident Indians
Ground handling services	74	Automatic	Investment up to 100% allowed
MRO, flying training and technical institutes	100	Automatic	for non-resident Indians
Petroleum and natural gas			
Petroleum refining	100	Automatic	
Petroleum product pipelines	100	Automatic	
Petroleum product marketing	100	Automatic	Subject to minimum investment of US$ 450 million in exploration and production or refining or pipelines or terminals
Petroleum refining, public-sector units	49	FIPB	
Other			
Mass rapid transport system	100	Automatic	Includes associated real estate development in all metropolitan cities
EOU/SEZ/Industrial park construction	100	Automatic	100% allowed in industrial park subject to minimum of ten units and no unit occupies more than 50% of allocable area. Minimum industrial area of 66%
Satellite establishment and operation	74	FIPB	

Notes: FDI Foreign direct investment. FIPB Foreign Investment Promotion Board.

Source: http://www.investmentcommission.in/sector.htm#a (accessed 10 February 2009).

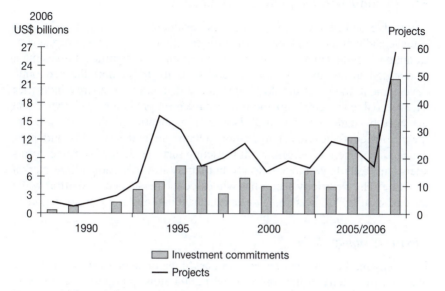

Figure 6.1 Increasing trends in private participation in Indian infrastructure.

Source: World Bank and PPIAFF, PPI Project Database, p. 4, www.pppinindia.com/pdf/gridlines.
pdf, March 2008 (accessed 28 July 2009)

of how better infrastructure services can enhance the competitive advantage
of other businesses is provided by improvement in access to and cost of
telecommunication in India. This has enabled major IT companies such as IBM
and Microsoft to create research bases in India apart from various IT-enabled
services that have contributed to global business productivity. Recognising
the growing need for transport and the expanding road networks most of the
global auto companies from Japan, Europe and the USA have set up manufacturing facilities in India.

Key messages from this section are summarized below. In the following
sections we discuss sector specific business climates starting with the energy
sector in the following section.

- Indian infrastructure offers tremendous opportunities for growing
  businesses in India.
- Government policy framework is distinctly supportive of private and
  multinational investors.
- The trend in private sector investment in infrastructure industries has been
  growing and is likely to continue in the same direction.
- The benefits of improved infrastructure in roads, telecommunications and
  liberalized markets in energy have begun to make India a major destination
  for doing business.

Energy industries: suppliers' perspective

Affordable and secure energy supply is absolutely necessary if India is to achieve and maintain high economic growth rate. Low energy per capita consumption in India (Figure 6.2) suggests that rapid and significant investment is required in energy industries to add capacity to support the economic development and meet the domestic energy demand. The energy industries such as coal, gas, petroleum and power have been predominantly owned and managed by state-owned entities. However, as mentioned above the government considers the electricity supply chain, oil and gas grids and non-conventional energy sources as infrastructure services. In the last fifteen years energy markets have moved slowly but surely towards competitive market structure. The electricity sector has witnessed the most concerted effort while the coal industry has been more or less stagnant in terms of government policy.

Electricity supply chain

Electricity markets and policy have witnessed major changes since 1991. The National Electricity Policy announced in 2005 aims to provide electricity to all households in India and remove the peak demand supply gap. However, in the last two decades the demand for electricity has been growing at a much higher rate than the supply of electricity creating a demand supply gap. The present market structure is characterized by government-owned utilities dominating in all three segments (generation, transmission and distribution) of the industry. The government's policy objective of ensuring electricity access for all Indians by 2012 means the need to substantially improve the reliability and quantity of power supply for all Indians and also importantly to make power supply commercially viable (Government of India, 2007). The government's approach to achieve these objectives is depicted in Figure 6.3.

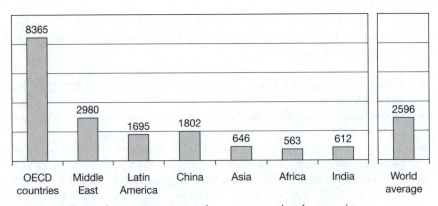

Figure 6.2 Per capita energy consumption: a cross-national comparison.

Source: Key World Energy Statistics (2007)

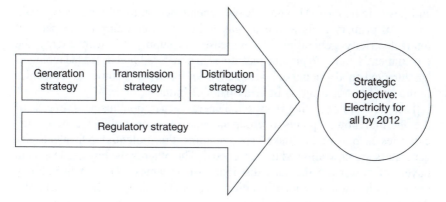

Figure 6.3 Strategies to achieve electricity supply objectives.

Power generation strategy focuses on cost of generation and capacity addition. The entry of private and foreign direct investment is permitted and up to 100 per cent foreign ownership is permissible (see Table 6.3). There are also fiscal incentives such as income tax holidays and waiver of import duties on equipments for large power plants. All this would make power generation business a highly attractive proposition. A look at the private sector participation in the generation shows that private sector participation in generation is

Table 6.3 Major players in petroleum and natural gas in Indian markets

Company	Revenue FY 07 ($ billion)	Upstream	Midstream: pipelines	Downstream	
				Refining	Retail outlets
Public sector					
IOC	50.8	✓	✓	✓	✓
BPCL	26.9		✓	✓	✓
HPCL	22.1		✓	✓	✓
ONGC	15.2	✓	✓	✓	✓
Domestic private players					
Reliance industries	27.2	✓	✓	✓	✓
International private players (FY 06)					
Shell	355.8				✓
British Gas (Centrica)	32.9	✓			✓
Cairn Energy	0.29	✓			

Sources: BP Statistical Review of World Energy, 2007, Capitaline Fortune, Ministry of Petroleum and Natural Gas, Directorate General of Hydrocarbons, and BP Statistical Review of World Energy.

still low (Figure 6.4). Also note heavy dependence on fossil fuels as the main source of primary fuels with coal, gas and diesel accounting for 63 per cent total electricity generation. To increase the supply of clean energy the government's policy to provide incentives to non-fossil fuel based technologies has attracted good amount of investment from foreign and domestic companies in the wind power projects in many parts of India.

There are two operating risks in the energy generation business. In case of the thermal power plants overdependence on monopolistic state-owned collieries is one of the risks. To overcome this potential risk electricity generators are now allowed to import coal. The other is the buyers. The main buyers of power are the state distribution companies who remain publicly owned with few exceptions in cities such as Mumbai, Delhi, Kolkata and Ahmedabad. Most state-owned distribution companies are loss making. The state governments have recognised this as potential barrier for private sector to enter generation business and have therefore, tried to reduce the risk by providing guarantees regarding the obligations of state-owned distribution companies. Any power producer therefore, needs to consider these challenges and ensure that the power purchase agreements provide necessary protection against this risk.

For transmission segment the central government's focus is on developing the transmission network for inter-state transmission of power to enable development of competitive wholesale electricity markets. Geographical spread and increasing demand for electricity mean significant investment is required in the transmission networks. So far this segment has been owned and managed by a central government-owned National Grid Corporation. The Central Electricity Regulatory Commission has put in place a regulatory

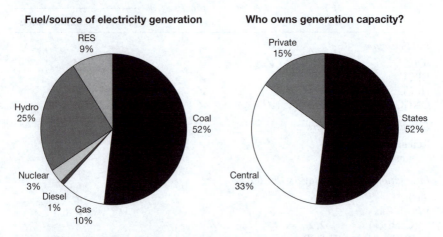

Figure 6.4 Fuel mix and ownership structure of electricity generation in India, year end 2008.

Note: RES Renewable Energy Sources.
Source: Based on data from Ministry of Power, Government of India, 2008

framework to facilitate competition in use of transmission networks and supply in India. To facilitate development of trading in electricity the Indian Energy Exchange (IEX) and Power Exchange India Ltd (PXIL) have been set up in 2008.

The distribution segment of electricity markets is again mostly dominated by the state-owned enterprises. The distributors are responsible for delivering the electricity to the consumers. This has made distribution business most controlled by the regulators who decide the prices they can charge. Despite the restructuring of the electricity sector and setting up of independent regulatory bodies the state governments have not given up effective control of the prices charged by the distributors. The regulatory bodies have recommending powers to determine the tariff to be charged from consumers but the final prices are still decided by the distribution companies in consultation with the state government. This is perhaps the most thorny and important issue in terms of viability of electricity industry. The subsidy and transmission and distribution losses are two issues that cannot be resolved without political commitment. Since the viability of generation and transmission also depends on the soundness of the distribution companies it is clearly the most important part of the electricity industry. The main challenges to the commercial viability of distribution are three fold. One is to reduce the transmission and distribution losses which are up to 40 per cent in some cases. Second is the need to ensure subsidies from the state governments are recovered in time. Third is the need to reduce the large gap between the prices and costs of supplying to some consumer segments. The central and state governments have tried to help meet these challenges. The state-owned electricity supply boards have been restructured and corporatized to enhance transparency and accountability. The electricity regulatory commissions have been striving through their price control orders to rationalize the pricing. The price regulation by the commissions also provides incentives for reducing transmission and distribution losses and increasing investment in network expansion and maintenance.

Petroleum and natural gas

The petroleum and natural gas supply industry comprising transport, refining and marketing of petroleum products constituted about 15 per cent of India's gross domestic product with revenue of US$ 130 billion in 2007 (Government of India, 2008). According to the government estimates, an investment of US$ 35–40 billion by 2012 is required in petroleum and natural gas industries. The crude oil refining capacity is set to grow at 10 per cent per annum till 2012 and the gas demand is set to grow at 11.7 per cent per annum during the period between 2008 and 2012 (Government of India, 2008). Thus opportunities lie in oil refining, gas exploration and the gas distribution networks in the cities, and for building liquid cargo terminals at major ports for import of crude oil and gas.

At present most of the refining, exploration, gas pipelines and marketing distribution facilities are owned by the public sector enterprises. However, in the recent past a private sector domestic company, Reliance Industries, has changed the character of the industry by setting up the largest refinery in the country with a capacity of 27 million metric tonnes (t) per annum (MMTPA) in Jamnagar.

The policy for oil and gas industries has been substantially liberalized with 100 per cent private and FDI allowed across the range of value chain. Table 6.3 shows the market structure and major players in petroleum and natural gas industries in India. Major multinational firms now operate in Indian oil and gas industries. Petrol and diesel prices still are determined by the government but competition based on service quality has been increasing in the distribution segment of this industry. To further streamline the regulatory and market structure in oil and gas the government of India has set up the petroleum and natural gas regulatory board.

Business environment in petroleum sector is conducive for investment but the rationalization of pricing policies in retailing is still a big expectation given the politically sensitive nature of the subsidies involved. Gas exploration and laying of gas distribution networks is likely to remain big investment opportunity for private investors. In conclusion, the following key messages are worth noting regarding the energy industries in India, which are important for her economic development.

Electricity

- The electricity markets are now segmented into Generation, Transmission and Distribution.
- Generation markets are opened up for inter-state supply, creating opportunity for competitive markets.
- A meaningful regulatory system is in place in most of the states.
- Regulators' aim to ensure rationalization of prices to meet the costs and allow reasonable returns to investors.
- The managers of the electric utilities will need to be able to operate in an evolving regulatory system.

Petroleum and natural gas

- Oil and gas exploration policy liberalized.
- FDI permitted in most of the supply chain.
- Regulatory board set up.

Telecoms: connecting India and investing in the convergence revolution

India is the fifth largest telecom services market in the world with US$ 23 billion in revenues in 2007. Much of India's success in export of IT-enabled services has been made possible by the telecommunication revolution that has taken place in India over the last decade. Figure 6.5 shows the dramatic growth in the tele-density (number of landline phones for every 100 people) in urban areas in India. However, it is also seen that there is a big difference between the urban and rural tele-density. This shows the need for expanding the telecom networks beyond major cities and towns into villages.

The Indian telecoms market has recorded a phenomenal growth in terms of new connections, diversity of services and development of very competitive markets in basic telephone and cellular phone business. As of March 2009 there were 37.96 million wire-line connections and 391.76 million had access to cellular (wireless) phones (TRAI, 2009). Nearly 75 per cent of connections are provided by private sector companies which include multinational companies such as Vodafone and Hutchison. Although in absolute numbers this looks big, Indian telephone demand is still likely to grow substantially over coming decades. Combined with basic telephone services, there is going to be big demand for network expansion and modernization as the demand for broadband increases. The convergence of voice-video communication and broadcasting is likely to increase and create demand for supporting technologies and services.

The main features of the entry routes and private sector participation were listed in Table 6.3 earlier. Broadly the private and foreign investment in basic telephone services and the telecom equipment manufacture is encouraged by the government. The business model is getting license from the government to offer telecommunication services in a regulated environment. The Telecom Regulatory Authority of India (TRAI) regulates the prices, quality standards and encourages competition in the sector. The government's telecom policy

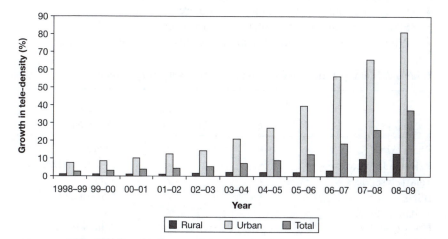

Figure 6.5 Increasing tele-density in India.

Source: Government of India report on Private Participation in Infrastructure, Committee on Infrastructure, June 2009. Available online, www.infrastructure.gov.in (accessed 27 July 2009)

and relatively more effective telecom regulatory policy have been successful in ensuring the transition from a state-owned monopolist market in telecommunications to a competitive one. Table 6.4 provides the details of market players and services they offer. As is seen apart from the main public sector enterprise BSNL, there are few major national and international players in the market competing for a rapidly growing market.

The market structure of the telecommunications sector in India is competitive and regulated. Generally the regulatory environment has been consistent with the policy objective of maintaining arm's-length relation with the industry and the government and thereby encouraging competition in the market. The revenue streams are not distorted by the subsidies although there is universal service obligation applicable to basic telephone service providers. Overall the industry is poised for sustained growth but at somewhat lower rates than the extraordinary growth rates of 40 per cent observed in last six years. Very high growth rates observed in the recent past just reflect huge unmet demand and a low base from where the markets started to grow. A thriving telecommunications industry is successfully removing a big barrier in transmission of the knowledge and information in Indian economy that is crucial for markets to identify and meet the demand of various goods and services. The following key messages emerging from the above discussion of telecommunications show a promising start and a bright future for Indian telecommunications.

- Sources of sustained demand.
- Telecommunications are backbone of knowledge-based industries which are going to grow in India.
- Expansion and modernization of networks.
- Broadcasting and entertainment industries.
- Increasing role of Internet based commerce.
- Stable and transparent regulatory environment.
- Private sector and multinational companies encouraged to invest.

Table 6.4 Major players in the telecommunications industry in India, 2008

Company	Services				
	Cellular	Basic	NLD[a]	ILD[b]	Promoter
Bharti Airtel	•	•	•	•	Bharti
Reliance Inforcomm	•	•	•	•	Reliance ADA
Tata Teleservices	•	•	•	•	Tata
BSNL	•	•	•		Government
Vodafone Essar	•		c		Essar
IDEA Cellular	•		c		Aditya Birla

Notes: [a] National Long Distance. [b] International Long Distance. [c] Launch planned.

Sources: TRAI, DoT, TSMG analysis, in Government of India, Investment Commission Report, New Delhi (2008: 32).

Transport: removing bottlenecks and supporting trade

While telecommunications support the flow of information of knowledge, the equivalent of optical fibre optics in real economy are the roadways, railways, waterways and airways. These networks are required to support transport of goods from, into and within India's vast lands and present the opportunities to invest in long-term projects of developing roads, ports and airports. Bringing down the costs, improving efficiency and quality of transport infrastructure is a key policy objective that the government of India is pursuing vigorously. We consider below the scope and business environment in each of these infrastructure services starting with roads.

Roads

The inland transport is mostly through the road and rail network. India has the second largest road network in the world, with 3.3 million km and 70 per cent of freight and 85 per cent of passenger traffic carried through roads (Government of India (a)). The size of the total road network is large but only 66,000 km (2 per cent) of the roads are highways and expressways, which carry only 40 per cent of the road traffic. The government of India is conscious of this fact and has therefore set the following ambitious targets for expanding the national highways network over the next five years (Government of India (b)):

- Developing 1,000 km of expressways.
- Developing 8,737 km of roads, including 3,846 km of national highways, in the north-east.
- Four-laning 20,000 km of national highway.
- Four-laning 6,736 km on north–south and east–west corridors.
- Six-laning 6,500 km of the Golden Quadrilateral and selected national highways.
- Widening 20,000 km of national highways to two lanes.

At present the government of India spends about $4 billion annually on road development but, as pointed out in Table 6.2, the scope of investment in highway roads alone is to the tune of US$ 49 billion. So how is this opportunity to be viewed from a business perspective? Does the investment in road projects offer returns that would commensurate with the risks in road projects? What are the strategic considerations that a management must make if it were entering the road sector? The important business issues are modes of entry in the market, the extent of private ownership allowed and the business models that will work for road development and operating business.

The government of India has taken a clear policy stand on the involvement of the private sector in the road sector by allowing 100 per cent private and foreign investment in the road projects. Overall, in infrastructure services public–private partnership framework (see Box 6.2 for salient features of the

---

Box 6.2 Key features of public–private partnerships in India

PPP has been used as a organizational vehicle by the central and state governments to involve the private sector to implement large projects in sectors such as roads, ports, airports and urban infrastructure. In the past these projects were implemented by state agencies only. But to benefit from competitive markets and to invite private capital PPPs have been adopted in a big way. Because of the following feature of PPP agreements state has to follow due diligence and go through a systematic process of opportunity identification and approval process as depicted in Figure 6.6.

- PPP involves transfer of public assets, including land (e.g. an existing road or airport facility).
- Delegation of governmental authority to collect and appropriate user charges that are levied by force of law and must therefore be 'reasonable'.
- Provision of services to users in a monopoly or semi-monopoly situation, which imposes a special obligation on the government to ensure adequate service quality.
- Sharing of risks and contingent liabilities by the government, e.g. when claims are made under the respective agreements or when the Central Government has to provide a backup guarantee for non-performance by the entity granting the concession.

Source: Adapted from Department of Economic Affairs, Ministry of Finance, Government of India, Guidelines for Formulation, Appraisal and Approval: Central Sector PPP Projects (New Delhi, 2008). Available online at http://www.pppinindia.com/pdf/guidelines_approval_central_sector_ppp_projects_english.pdf (accessed 1 August 2009).

PPP framework) has been used to encourage private investment in this sector. There has been significant increase in the private sector investment in the road sector with as many as forty contracts coming to financial closure in 2006. Of the total private investment in infrastructure projects during 2001–06 the share of investment in the transport sector has increased from 18 per cent to 34 per cent (Harris, 2008). The main business model used involves award of a construction contract to private companies who are contracted to build, operate and transfer (BOT) under what has been called public–private partnership schemes. In road development projects the business risks arise in terms of uncertain traffic, time and cost over runs.

However, the PPP policy and institutional framework has been prepared to mitigate these risks and support the private sector investors. For example, some state governments have tried to mitigate these risks for state and city road projects by agreeing to Build, Operate and Transfer with fixed annual payments

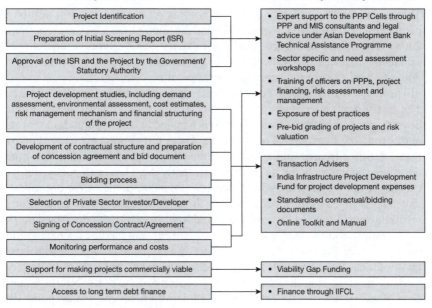

PPP Projects-Process | **Initiatives by Ministry of Finance**

Figure 6.6 PPP projects process management.

Source: Public Private Partnerships: Creating Enabling Environment for States, Department of Economic Affairs, Ministry of Finance, Government of India, New Delhi, 2008 p. 2, www.pppin india.com/pdf/creating_enabling_environment_state_projects-english.pdf (accessed 1 August 2009)

to the developer thereby the state absorbing the traffic risks. For timely completion of the projects the government has taken several policy measures and has set up purpose oriented financial and other implementation agencies to facilitate development of infrastructure through PPP. These measures include detailed guidelines for project preparation, financial assistance for feasibility study of opportunities, financial assistance in form of Viability Funding Gap in case the project's financial viability is affected by universal service obligations, and debt and equity funding facilities from India Infrastructure Project Development Fund and India Infrastructure Finance Companies. There is a comprehensive one point source of information in Ministry of Finance to deal with all PPP related matters and a dedicated government of India website www.pppindia.com that provides access to all the government guidelines, procedures and documents to save time and cost for the interested parties. Potential investors must keep in mind the fact that policies to involve private sector in road constructions and operation projects may vary from state to state particularly with respect to land acquisition. Again, there is now a move to develop a national policy on the land acquisition and resettlement issues but so far it is not there.

Ports

The cargo handling capacity of Indian ports is set to rise from 700 million t per annum to 1.5 billion t in year 2013 and 2 billion t by 2020 (Business Line, 2008). To expand the cargo handling capacity and to improve operational efficiency requires investment which government is keen to attract from domestic and foreign investors and port operating companies.

There are twelve major ports in India that are managed by Port Trusts. The tariffs for major ports are fixed by Tariff Authority for Major Ports. Seventy per cent of the volume of cargo is handled by major ports. Minor ports numbering 187 manage rest of the cargo. These minor ports are controlled by State Maritime Boards. Indian ports handle all types of cargo and some of the ports have container handling facilities. Recently there has been policy shift to encourage private participation in port development. Some of the big investments on BOT basis have been made by Maersk (Mumbai port), Dubai Ports International (Mumbai, Chennai, Vizag and Kochi), P&O (Mundra Adani port).

The policy allows 100 per cent FDI and 100 per cent income tax exemption for a period of ten years. The government has prepared a National Maritime Development Policy where in it has identified several projects to be implemented for enhancing the efficiency and capacity of the ports. Nearly 64 per cent of proposed investment of US$ 13.5 billion on the major ports till 2011–12 is envisaged to be financed from private sources. A major vehicle for channelling the private investment is expected to be PPP. Bulk of developments of minor ports in coastal states of Gujarat, Andhra Pradesh and Tamil Nadu is envisaged to be financed from private sources again using PPP as organizational vehicle.

Productivity of the current infrastructure at ports is far from satisfactory. But there is a determination in the government policy announcements to reduce the waiting period for ships before they are allotted a berth to dock. To achieve the target of providing berth on demand as it is possible in Singapore requires construction of new berths including those suitable to handle large container ships, investing in mechanization of port operations and computerization of procedures. In addition investment is required for construction of storage space and providing road and rail connectivity to hinterland.

Railways

The issue of connecting ports with hinterland illustrates the need for an integrated view of infrastructure services and that is what the recent government policy framework on infrastructure development aims at. Indian railways are the second largest rail system in the world, with the route length of 63,221 km. Cargo movement through containers is key link to improving the logistics efficiency. Fourteen private companies have been granted licences to run container trains. There are plans to create dedicated rail network for cargo movement. Dedicated Freight Corridor Corporation of India, a special purpose entity for development of a dedicated rail network for cargo movement has been set up (Planning Commission, 2009). Along the dedicated freight corridors the special economic zones are being developed where multi-modal logistics parks will be developed. Private sector companies have opportunities to participate in all these projects to enhance the quality and quantity of transport capacity of Indian railway network system. Again the way forward indicated by the government policy is to encourage use of PPP type of contracts which have been discussed above in detail.

Airports

There are 454 airports and airstrips in India and sixteen designated international airports. Passenger traffic and air cargo businesses are expected to grow with the economic development. Government plans envision need from handling traffic of 280 million passengers by year 2020 from the current level of about 100 million passengers. Air cargo traffic is likely to touch 3.3 million t by 2010 (Government of India (c)). This therefore requires investments to the tune of US$ 30 billion in development of airport infrastructure. Most of the airports in India are owned by central government through a public enterprise Airport Authority of India. But there have been few major privatization decisions whereby international airports at Delhi, Mumbai and Bangaluru are now privately managed. This development is significant as it has enabled bringing the best global practices in the airport services and providing performance benchmarks for other airports.

Opportunities are more likely to be in greenfield projects and in acquiring airports through privatization transactions. The business model to be used is going to be PPP in most cases.

Conclusion on transport infrastructure

The transport infrastructure presents a variety of opportunities for building and operating roads, ports, railways and airports projects. In all these transport sectors the government policy is quite market-friendly and business models likely to be used are one or other form of BOT operated through PPP. The external environment challenges are stability of political commitment, appropriate regulation and availability of finance. Of these, the last one is likely to be a challenge because Indian capital markets and banking institutions are small when compared to the funds required for infrastructure development. For example, there are only eleven Indian banks with an equity base of more than US$ 1 billion (Business World, 2009). But since Indian financial and capital markets are well developed and foreign investment framework is clearly laid out the projects can be financed by international consortium partners. Below is a summary on the Indian transport sector.

● Roads, railways, ports, and airports all need to expand the capacity and improve the quality of services.

- Investment in transport projects is of long term nature with typical project life being twenty to thirty years.
- Supportive institutional framework.
- Fiscal benefits include tax holidays.
- 100 per cent foreign direct investment allowed.
- Government conscious of risks involved and willing to share the operating risks.
- Viability Gap Funding and other financial support.

Infrastructure services: users' perspective

So far the focus of the chapter has been the business opportunities provided by the infrastructure industries in India. However, there is also a need to provide some discussion for business enterprises who wish to set up business in India. The foregoing discussion has clearly shown that there is gap in the demand for and supply of most infrastructure services. This has been partly due to underinvestment by the state-owned enterprises in the infrastructure, on the other hand, this gap seems to have widened in the recent years due to a rapid increase in the demand for infrastructure services driven by a growing economy.

Electricity

Cost and continuous supply of electricity is central to successful industrialization and the Indian government is keen to ensure that business activities are not hampered by inadequacy of supply or high cost of electricity. In the preceding section various aspects of electricity supply chain were discussed and the steps that government has taken to increase the supply of electricity. However, here we note two specific aspects of policy that are user oriented. First is to create a competitive market for electricity consumers. Second is to allow captive power generation facility.

The Electricity Act provides for competitive markets in case of large consumers whose demand exceeds 1 MW. Such consumers can source their electricity from any supplier rather than from the regional monopolies. This not only could be cost effective but will also help in securing continuity of supply. This policy measure thus empowers the large electricity consumers.

In addition to above, the businesses with continuous and large quantity demand for power can set up their own captive power plants. The past few years have seen a large number of cement and steel manufacturers setting up their own power plants. Together these two measures provide an alternative strategy for the business users of electricity to meet their demand for electricity in India.

Petroleum and natural gas

A key issue for businesses that use natural gas and other petroleum products is to recognise that oil and gas still remain effectively government administered industries and therefore, competitive pricing may not evolve in four or five years. But over the next five to ten years it can be expected that gas markets at least will become competitive because of increasing domestic supply of gas and entry of private players in the exploration and distribution. This augurs well for Indian power generators and others who rely on gas based technologies.

Telecommunications

Compared to other infrastructure services in India, business users of telecommunications services comprising basic telephone services, mobile telephones or Internet and broadband connectivity would feel most satisfied. In terms of quality, access and cost Indian telecommunications services are globally competitive. But as noted above much of the growth has been in urban areas. Most of the software and IT exporting businesses have developed clusters of companies around few major cities in India. This has introduced a geographical imbalance in the growth of telecommunication networks. This further influences the choice of industrial locations where IT and Internet are likely to be key requirements.

India has got a growing talent base in computer, video game production, animation and music that can play a vital role in export of services to global entertainment and leisure industries. Telecom industry will need to provide affordable access to high bandwidth Internet connectivity to such users who at the moment are restricted to only few pockets in the country.

Transport

Users of transport services face capacity constraints in all modes of transport. But the situation is changing quite fast in roads, railways, airports and ports. Bulk users of railway containers now have the choice of using services provided by private container train operators. The development of dedicated freight corridors will further ease pressure on Indian railway transport system. Most international airports are upgrading their infrastructure and in the past few years international airports at New Delhi, Mumbai have been redeveloped and new airports have been developed at Hyderabad and Bangaluru. A private sector new port has been developed in Gujarat with container berths. Other ports are also upgrading their facilities. It can be argued reasonably that transport costs in India will decrease and service quality will improve significantly over the next few years. Below the key messages from the user's perspective are presented.

- Large electricity users in India now have the opportunity to choose their suppliers and even set up their own captive power plants to secure the supply of electricity.
- Gas markets are liberalized and getting more competitive, which should benefit the users of gas.

- World-class telecommunication facilities exist in big cities and surrounding satellite towns like Gurgaon near New Delhi.
- Big improvements in the capacity and quality of transport infrastructure services are under way.

Summary and key issues

This chapter has argued that India's economic development critically depends on adequate and efficient infrastructure services. At present the infrastructure services in most industries such as energy, telecommunications and transport need substantial improvements and capacity expansion. But at the same time this situation also offers significant business opportunities for investment in infrastructure.

Understand institutional and market environment. From the investor's perspective doing business in India means the same thing as doing business anywhere, i.e. dealing with people and organizations in a given institutional environment. But since institutional environment varies among countries and India being a federal country it varies across the states, it creates an external business environment that needs understanding of the local institutions, legislations and market structure.

- The market structure in energy supply chain is dominated by the public sector.
- There are policy intentions and instruments in place to create competitive markets in generation and supply of electricity.
- There has been significant liberalization of the petroleum exploration and refining markets.
- The petrol and diesel retail markets for private sector will remain a challenging opportunity till the issue of subsidies on petrol and diesel is resolved at the political level.
- In telecommunications, the institutional structure, regulation and markets seem to be working well and the scene is set for increasing competition.
- Regulatory framework has been set up to facilitate competition, rationalization of tariffs and to provide consumer protection in most of the infrastructure industries.

Understand opportunities

- Opportunities in the infrastructure industries are very large.
- Opportunities are in long term projects typically with projects lasting for twenty to thirty years.
- Most opportunities require large capitals costs.
- Public–private partnerships are going to be the preferred mode of joint ventures between government and the private sector.

- Significant long term tax benefits and other incentives on offer.
- Although telecommunications have reached most urban parts of India, there still remain opportunities for expanding the access and tele-density.
- In addition there are opportunity to upgrade telecommunication networks so that they can handle increasing traffic on the Internet and also to be able to manage convergence of telecommunication, media and entertainment industries.
- The strategic challenges in telecommunications are more conventional business challenges such as offering value for money to customers, quality of services and differentiation to achieve economies of scope and scale that this sector offers.

Managing challenges. The policy framework in most of these sectors is still evolving and is directed towards encouragement of private investment. It was argued that the two biggest challenges for any investors in this sector are in the external environment for business.

- First is mobilizing the finance for huge projects. India's own capital markets and banking industry are unlikely to be in position to supply the required finance. This means mobilizing funds from international investors.
- Second, in some sectors, such as road development, the government of India has to reform the administrative procedures for land acquisition which is a tricky political problem. But the good news is that the government is serious about this reform and in a short period of time appropriate legislation will be passed.
- Many states have created an institutional framework to support private sector interested in investing in infrastructure services.

References

Business Line (2008) Cargo traffic by sea poised for major growth, 4 April 2008, http://www.businessline.in/cgi-bin/print.pl?file = 2008040450120700.htm&date = 2008/04/04/&prd = bl& (accessed 6 August 2009).

Business World (2009) Where are the funds to finance India's infrastructure projects? 9 January 2009, http://www.businessworld.in/index.php/Infrastructure/_Dreams-Suspended.html.

Government of India (a) website http://www.pppinindia.com/opportunities-roads.asp (accessed 6 August 2009).

Government of India (b) website http://www.pppinindia.com/sector-highways.asp (accessed 18 February 2009).

Government of India (c) website http://www.pppinindia.com/sector-airports.asp (accessed 15 February 2009).

Government of India (2008) *Opportunities in the World's Largest Democracy*, Investment Commission Report, New Delhi.

Government of India (2007) *National Electricity Policy*, New Delhi, http://cea.nic.in/planning/national_Electricity_policy.htm (accessed 6 August 2009).

Harris, C. (2008) India leads developing nations in private sector investment, Gridlines, http://www.pppinindia.com/pdf/gridlines.pdf (accessed 6 August 2009).

Planning Commission (2009) *Private Participation in Infrastructure*, Government of India, New Delhi, http://infrastructure.gov.in/pdf/Infrastructure.pdf (accessed 1 August 2009).

Rastogi, A. (2008) The infrastructure sector in India. In A. Rastogi, P. Kalra and A. Pandey (eds) *India: Infrastructure Report.* New Delhi: Oxford University Press.

Rastogi A., Kalra, P. and Pandey, A., eds (2008) *India Infrastructure Report.* New Delhi: Oxford University Press.

TRAI (2009) Telecom Regulatory Authority of India press release dated 13 July, http://www.trai.gov.in/WriteReadData/trai/upload/PressReleases/692/pr13july09no59.pdf (accessed 31 July 2009).

Part II

Conducting business in India

7 Entry modes and dynamics

Vikas Kumar and Olga Annushkina

India is one of the fastest-growing emerging economies in the world and an important receipient of foreign capital in Asia. Although the absolute amount of foreign direct investments (FDI) entering India is substantially less than that entering China, the other major emerging economy, its rate of growth far exceeds that for China (UNCTAD 2008). Import flows into the country are also characterized by a similar trend. While India's absolute imports are far less than that of China's, its rate of growth is substantially higher (UNCTAD 2008). Tables 7.1 and 7.2 provide details in this regard. The statistics are reflective of the critical significance that India commands, vis-à-vis its Asian counterparts, for the international expansion of foreign multinational enterprises' (MNEs). In this chapter, we discuss the dynamics associated with entry mode options available to foreign MNEs that wish to enter the Indian market. We substantiate our discussion with case studies of two Italian companies (Lavazza and Fiat) that have entered the Indian market in very different fashions, illustrating the inherent complexity in designing entry strategies and the importance of accounting for industry and institutional factors in such an endeavour.

Studies on entry modes into the Indian market are important for practitioners and business scholars for at least three reasons. First, India is a classic example of an emerging economy undergoing institutional transition, with steady introduction of liberal trade and FDI policies since the early 1990s (Budhwar, 2001; Zattoni, Pedersen and Kumar, 2009). The economic reforms undertaken in 1991 marked a waterhed event in India's economic transformation (Chittoor, Sarkar, Ray and Aulakh, 2009) but were only the beginning of structural changes being instituted in the product, capital and labour markets. Since 1991, further reforms have been made, albeit in an uneven manner, in dismantling state monopolies, reducing and/or eliminating tariff and non-tariff barriers to imports, liberalizing financial markets, and consistently raising the upper limit of foreign participation through foreign direct investments in almost all economic sectors (Bhaumik, Gangopadhyay and Krishnan, 2008). The dynamism brought about by the evolving institutional context of India makes it imperative to constantly re-evaluate the entry options available to foreign MNEs.

Table 7.1 Inward foreign direct investment in India (US$ million)

Country	1990–2000 annual average	2004	2005	2006	2007	CAGR 2004–07 (%)
China	30.104	60.630	72.406	72.715	83.521	11
Hong Kong	13.841	34.032	33.618	45.054	59.899	21
Singapore	9.204	19.828	13.930	24.743	24.137	7
India	1.705	5.771	7.606	19.662	22.950	58
Thailand	3.198	5.862	8.048	9.010	9.575	18

Source: World Investment Report, 2008, p. 255, UNCTAD fact-sheets on India, China, Hong Kong (China), Singapore, Thailand.

Table 7.2 Import flows into India (US$ million)

Country	1980	1990	2000	2004	2005	2006	CAGR 2004–07 (%)
China	19.505	53.810	225.175	561.422	660.218	791.793	19
Hong Kong	22.399	82.490	213.328	271.458	299.967	334.691	11
Singapore	24.013	60.959	134.633	172.697	200.197	238.797	18
India	14.822	23.991	50.336	99.835	134.690	185.095	36
Thailand	9.213	33.414	61.924	94.407	118.143	130.605	18

Source: UNCTAD Handbook of Statistics, 2008 (online: www.unctad.org).

Second, India's economy has posted an average growth rate of more than 7 per cent since 1994, and is predicted to continue at this high pace of growth in the foreseeable future. More important, this growth has been fuelled by domestic consumption (Kumar, 2006) and by home-grown entrepreneurs (Huang and Khanna, 2003), in complete contrast to the external (foreign) demand-driven economy of other emerging economies such as China. Although the relatively more favourable inward FDI policy of China vis-à-vis that of India has allowed quick development of a number of Chinese sectors, the long-term sustainability of such a strategy is questionable (Huang and Khanna, 2003). India, with its strong 300 million odd middle class consumers and a sizeable pool of young talented workforce proficient with the English language, poses as a very attractive market as well as an efficient manufacturing base of knowledge-based industries for foreign MNEs. It is not surprising that in spite of the problems of weak infrastructure, fractured polity, widespread poverty, high corruption and bureaucracy that plague the Indian economy, AT Kearney's FDI Confidence Index placed India as the second most attractive FDI destination in 2005. In terms of Offshore Location Attractiveness Index, it placed India at the top.

Finally, India represents the world's largest functioning democracy and a significant military power that is non-political (MacDonald, 2006). Terrorism, ethnic violence, corruption and religious differences are evident in India's social and political spectrum, however, none of these issues of grave concern pose any threat to the foundations of democracy that is deeply rooted in the Indian psyche. Unlike in its neighbouring countries, chances of a military coup or takeover by a communist regime are highly unlikely. Given the huge market potential and the steadily improving investment climate of India, foreign MNE interest in entering and operating in India is only natural. Choosing the right entry mode option is the first necessary step for a successful long-term operation in an international market.

Background information

Entry modes differ greatly in advantages and drawbacks and the choice of an appropriate entry mode is a function of the trade-off between control and cost of resource commitment (Anderson and Gatignon, 1986). The entry mode options available to a firm include exporting, licensing, joint-venture (JV) and wholly owned subsidiary (greenfield or acquisition). Exporting and licensing (and similar other contractual agreements) are non-equity-based entry modes, whereas, JV and wholly owned subsidiary are equity-based entry modes (Pan and Tse, 2000). Factors that determine choice of an entry mode can be classified into ownership advantages of a firm, location advantages of a market, and internalization advantages of integrating transactions (Agarwal and Ramaswami, 1992). Ownership advantages include those emanating from intangible assets such as technology or brand and from the firm's ability to develop differentiated products. Location advantages emanate from higher market potential and lower investment risks of the host market that create higher earning potential for the entrant firm. Internalization advantages emanate from external uncertainty in the marketplace and bounded rationality on part of managers that make contract based transactions more expensive. Institutional environment of the host market plays an important role in determining its location advantages and level of uncertainty, and consequently affects entry mode choice.

Firms with high ownership advantages and/or entering into host markets with high location advantages typically go for high control modes such as majority-owned JV and wholly owned subsidiary. Although high control modes have higher costs, they are better suited to protect the assets and specialized skills of the firm. In addition, a high control mode has better long-term profit potential of benefiting from economies of scale in host markets with high location advantages. Microsoft, Intel and Texas Instruments, firms in knowledge-intensive informational technology industry with high ownership advantages, have set up research laboratories in India through wholly owned subsidiaries. The highly skilled and relatively cheap labour force of India serves as a significant locational advantage to foreign firms entering India, particularly those operating in knowledge-intensive industries. A potential drawback of entry and operation through a high control mode is the high exit costs in situations of political turmoil or sudden policy reversal by host country government. Both, IBM and Coca-Cola had to make costly exits from the Indian market in the late 1970s in wake of increasing government pressure to take on local partners and dilute equity in their Indian operations. In situations of high external uncertainty, firms typically go for the highest control modes such as wholly owned subsidiary or the lowest control mode such as exporting. Both these entry mode options allow the firm to avoid transactions and thereby circumvent external uncertainty as well as retain control over their assets and skills.

High control entry modes such as JVs and acquisitions provide access to resources held by local firms, and greenfield operations allow the entrant to buy or contract for local market resources such as real estate and human capital (Meyer, Estrin, Bhaumik and Peng, 2009). General Electric (GE), one of the largest investors in India, entered the country through a range of JVs with local Indian companies such as Godrej (for refrigerators and washing machines), Indian petrochemicals (for plastics), and Wipro (for lamps). The JV option of entry provided GE with easy access to market knowledge and distribution channels held by the local partner. However, there is always potential for conflict arising due to different cultural backgrounds of respective management teams that are involved in a JV. An acquisition based entry and subsequent operation overcomes this potential drawback to a large extent. Coca-Cola for its re-entry into the Indian market in 1992–93 chose to acquire Parle Exports, a major player in the Indian soft drinks industry with 60 per cent market share. Besides access to local distribution infrastructure, the acquisition allowed Coca-Cola in quickly responding to the threat posed by entry of Pepsi, a global rival, into the Indian market in the late 1980s. Nevertheless, acquisition requires an astute understanding of acquired resources in order to efficiently integrate them with the existing ones. This post merger/acquisition integration process might become challenging for companies that are either inexperienced internationally or have limited managerial capabilities in dealing with new foreign entities. Foreign market entry through a greenfield venture, on the other hand, can largely avoid such a challenge. Many companies including Pizza Hut, KFC, Kellogg's, Johnson & Johnson, and DuPont have entered the Indian market by establishing a greenfield venture. A key advantage to companies adopting such an entry mode is their complete control and flexibility in conducting their operations. Especially in emerging markets like India where few local companies might have a brand identity as powerful as that in developed markets, Western consumer product companies with high brand values might prefer going along doing business alone instead of looking for strategic partners.

High control entry modes are typically common with firms that have sufficient international presence and experience of operating in a multitude of institutional environments. On the other hand, for firms that are relatively new to the international marketplace, exporting and contractual agreements are used often to enter foreign markets. In sum, firms usually have a number of entry modes to choose from, the choice largely depending on the control–cost trade-off. We summarize the various entry mode options a firm may have for specific business activities that it wants to conduct in a foreign market in Table 7.3.

Along with the decision on the specific mode of entry, firms also need to decide what particular firm-activity it wants to conduct in the foreign market. The firm-activity it wants to transfer abroad denotes the primary motivation of the firm – market, efficiency, asset or resource – to internationalize. Traditional international business theories (Dunning, 1988; Johanson and Vahlne, 1977) as well as empirical evidence suggest that firms initiate internationalization by entering with simple tasks via non-equity contract-based means. For example they would sell their products in the international market through export contracts with external agents. With passing of time, firms gain experience and knowledge and may engage in setting up a branch office with little investment to setting up a JV and/or wholly owned subsidiary with relatively higher investment. Also, the firm may now be transferng more complex activities such as production and R&D to the foreign market. Broadly speaking, the firm will have the following three entry mode options (Dematté and Peretti, 2003):

1   Contract-based entry modes: export or sourcing contract, offshoring-outsourcing, licensing or franchising and other.
2   Intermediate solution between a contract-based and equity-based entry modes: creation of a representative or a branch office, which does not involve a registration of a separate legal entity.
3   Equity-based entry modes: joint ventures, acquisitions or greenfield.

Evolving entry modes

The range of entry modes – from exporting, licensing, JVs, and wholly owned subsidiary operations – are all available to firms to enter and operate in the Indian market. However, as noted earlier, the institutional environment of the location, India, has an impact on the scale and scope of the different entry modes. More specifically, there are quantitative and qualitative restrictions on foreign businesses entering India arising primarily from the regulatory institutional environment. The other components of the institutional environment – normative and cognitive components – do not pose any significant and easily observable limitation on foreign entrants. Since the major economic reforms undertaken in 1991, India has made significant strides in liberalizing its economy, with a particular emphasis on FDI and trade policy. This has led to increased integration with the global economy through increased inward and outward foreign investments and trade. However, there still exist a number of restrictions on FDI and trade inflow into India. Figure 7.1 is a snapshot of India's imports in 2007, which is reflective of the heavy bias towards

Table 7.3 Entry mode options for specific firm activity

A. Firm activity transferred to foreign market	B. Form of presence			
	Contract-based presence	Representative or branch office	JV	Subsidiary
Sales and marketing	E.g. export contracts stipulated via agents	E.g. a branch office that co-ordinates export activities	E.g. a JV with a local distributor	E.g. a fully owned commercial subsidiary
After-sales	E.g. contract with a service company	E.g. a branch office that co-ordinates a local service provider	E.g. a JV with a local service company	E.g. a fully owned subsidiary that provides after-sales services
R&D	E.g. technical collaboration (contract-based) with a local R&D centre	E.g. a branch office that co-ordinates collaboration with a local R&D centre	E.g. a JV with a local R&D centre	E.g. a fully owned R&D laboratory
Production	E.g. sourcing contracts (importing from India)	E.g. a branch office that co-ordinates local suppliers and follows logistics	E.g. a JV with a local manufacturer	E.g. a fully owned factory

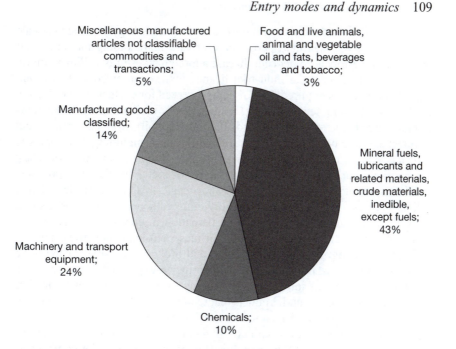

Figure 7.1 Indian import structure, 2007 (US$ 201.4 million).
Source: UN ComTrade data

commodities and other primary goods (over 40 per cent of the total) and lack of manufactured goods. This is partly due to the restrictive import policies instituted by the Indian government, the huge domestic demand created by the increasing populaton, and partly due to India's emerging position as a global manufacturing hub for a range of products and services.

Prior to 1991, foreign firms were only allowed a maximum of 40 per cent shareholding in their Indian subsidiaries (Chibber and Majumdar, 2005). The 51 per cent foreign shareholding instituted after the 1991 reforms allows foreign investors effective control over operations, asset, income partitioning as well as giving them greater flexibility in implementing strategic changes and transfering skills and resources to and from the subsidiary unit in India. As part of the 1991 reforms, the number of public sectors, exculsive only for the state, was reduced from seventeen to seven: arms, ammunition, defense equipment; atomic energy; coal and lignite; mineral oils; mining of ferrous and certain non-ferrous metals, gold, and diamonds; atomic minerals; and railway transport (Majumdar, 2009). This list has been further reduced and only three sectors – atomic energy, atomic minerals and railway transport – remain closed to private investment. Then there are certain sectors for which industrial licensing is compulsory: distillation and brewing of alcoholic drinks; production of cigars and cigarettes; electronic aerospace and defence equipment; industrial explosives; hazardous chemicals; drugs and pharmaceuticals.

In addition, a limited number of industrial sectors are categorized 'small-scale sector', where the maxmum permissible private shareholding including that by foreign investors is 24 per cent. In case a foreign investor is willing to invest more than 24 per cent, an industrial licence with a compulsory 50 per cent export obligation is required. List of items reserved for exclusive manufacture by the small scale sector, as of October 2008, include some food items (pickles and chutney, bread, mustard oil, groundnut oil); wooden furniture and fixtures; exercise books and registers; some injection-moulding thermoplastic products; some consumer products (wax candles, laundry soap, safety matches, fire works, agarbatties, glass bangles); some metal mechanical products (padlocks, stainless steel utensils, domestic utensils in aluminuim, steel chairs, rolling shutters, steel almirahs, etc.).[1] Furthermore, there are certain procedural as well as capital limits on foreign participation in companies operating in financial services, telecommunications, airlines, petroleum industries, housing and real estate, agriculture, print media, and broadcasting. FDI in the trade sector is limited to wholesale trading, bulk imports, export activities, domestic trading of products of joint ventures, trading of high-tech products, medial and diagnostic products and products that require specialist after-sales service.

Foreign participation in e-commerce activities is restricted to business-to-business (B2B) transactions with an obligatory divestment of 26 per cent of equity stake in favour of domestic investors in five years if the company is also listed elsewhere in the world. The Indian retail sector is one of the latest areas of business to be opened for foreign investors. However, the 51 per cent shareholding is allowed only in single-product retailing.[2] For larger discount retailers like Wal-mart, the only option was to enter the Indian market through a JV. Wal-mart formed a fifty–fifty JV with Bharti Enterprises, a local Indian conglomerate with business interests in telecommunications, agriculture, insurance and retail.[3] The JV firm has been allowed to operate only as a wholesale intermediary that between farmers, manufacturers and retailers. On a whole, inspite of limitations on FDI, in 2004–07 the inflow of foreign capital to India showed the strongest double-digit growth among the largest emerging economies in Asia (see Table 7.1).

Next, we discuss the entry strategy of two Italian companies, Lavazza and Fiat, into the Indian market. This discussion will add to our understanding of entry into India in the following two ways. First, Italian firms that consider entering the Indian market have to manage considerable information asymmetry and transaction costs due to institutional and economic differences, but also due to absence of any long-lasting historical or political ties between the two countries. Majority of studies on entry into India are based on companies from the US and UK, which though institutionally and culturally quite distant from India share ties through the presence of large diaspora, erstwhile colonial rule and use of English as the business language. In this respect Italy can be considered a more distant market and thus generating potential to enrich entry strategy discussion with studies based on Italian companies in India. Second, entry by Italian companies into the Indian market is a relatively new phenomenon and understanding the process is likely to provide more recent and relevant insights given the changing institutional environment of India.

Italian companies entering India

According to the Italian Institute of Foreign Commerce (ICE), there are seventy-eight Italian entities present in India and registered at ICE offices as of December 2005 (for details see www.ice.it). More than 40 per cent operate through representative or branch offices (low control–low cost approach) for primarily commercial and market research activities. However, 52 per cent of them operate either as a JV or a wholly owned subsidiary (high control–high cost approach). Only nine out of the seventy-eight have a production unit in India.

While it is difficult to infer much from the statistics in Table 7.4, the figures suggest that Italian firms tend to opt for the high control–high cost modes of entry (JV and subsidiary) in a larger number of cases. Within this category there is almost an equal split between JVs and subsidiary (acquisitions and greenfield). This is consistent with what Chandrasekaran and Ryans (1996) found in their study on US firms entering the Indian market. Out of the thirty market enteries they considered, sixteen were in the form of JVs between US and some local Indian player. This is indicative of the need of some local market resources by a majority of foreign entrants who wish to operate in India. In only one case, that of Coca-Cola's entry into India in the late 1980s, was acquisition used as an entry mode. Among some of the high-profile enteries of Italian companies into India, Fiat's entry evolved from initially a licence to a greenfield venture and finally establishing a JV, Piaggio's entry evolved from licensing to greenfield, whereas Luxottica and Lavazza entered the Indian market through acquisitions of local Indian companies. Acquisition is somewhat uncommon as means to enter the Indian market because regulations still discourage complete buy-outs of local companies. This makes exploring the underlying issues in the context of acquisition as an entry mode for the Indian market relatively more interesting. Below, we discuss the case of Lavazza's entry into the Indian market.

Table 7.4 Italian companies operating in India, registered by December 2005 at the Institute of Foreign Commerce

Form of presence	No.	%
Representative office, branch office, liaison office	33	42
Joint venture	22	28
Subsidiary	19	24
Other	4	6
Total	78	100

Source: www.ice.it.

Lavazza's entry into India

Lavazza, specializing in espresso coffee, is one the biggest leaders in the Italian coffee market. It started its activities back in 1895, in Turin, a city in northern Italy. In the 1970s, in order to offset the effects of the economic recession, Lavazza started its export activities, first to other European countries and later to the rest of the world. The first foreign subsidiary was set up in 1982–83, in France, followed by a branch office in Germany in 1987. Later in 1988 the company founded Premium Coffees in New York and Lavazza Kaffee in Vienna. In 1989, Lavazza diversified its product portfolio by introducing Espresso Point Lavazza, or automatic distributors, in addition to the existing two product lines, coffee sold to bars and coffee sold to retailers. Lavazza Coffees in London and a training centre in Frankfurt were established in 1990. In 1992 the company made its first acquisition abroad, of a French producer and distributor, Holper. In Italy, Lavazza acquired Coinca, an old Piedmont producer of blends for coffee bars, caffé Bourbon (from Nestlé) and Suerte (from Star, a famous Italian food-processing company). Having already attained a solid 44 per cent market share in Italy and established strong positions with European retailers, Lavazza started its geographical expansion into non-European markets after the mid-1990s. Lavazza entered Portugal and Brazil in 2001 and 2005, respectively.

On 10 March 2007 Lavazza celebrated its official entry into the Indian market with the acquisition of the Barista and Fresh & Honest coffee chains. India, one of the largest producers of coffee in the world, has a long history of coffee consumption. Traditionally, the fresh coffee beans were roasted at home, pounded into coffee powder, which was then mixed with hot water, milk and sugar and served hot. After the arrival of foreign firms into the Indian coffee market, consumption habits have shifted towards instant coffee and espresso. While instant coffee became readily available in coffee shops and restaurants and has also entered the Indian household, espresso is primarily available only at five-star hotels and few coffee chains. Since the mid-1990s, the demand for coffee in India has significantly grown, partly due to an increase in out-of-home consumption, which had became a status statement for young and ambitious Indians working for local and foreign blue-chip companies.

Barista, at the time of acquisition, accounted for around 150 shops in India, most of which were concentrated in New Delhi, Mumbai and Bangalore. Soon after the acquisition, Lavazza announced its intention to expand the number of shops to 400 by 2010, leveraging on the premium positioning of Barista in the Indian retail coffee market. Fresh & Honest, a leader in office coffee service, at the time of acquisition was present in twenty-two cities spread all over India, selling 300,000 cups per day[4] or 800,000 tons of coffee per annum.

The choice of acquisition to enter the Indian market, as per the company management, was motivated by at least three important factors. First, Lavazza's management believed that the Indian coffee market is bound for a phenomenal growth. This was based on the macroeconomic growth of the country as well as on changing consumption habits of Indian consumers. In order to capitalize on this growth momentum, Lavazza had to act in a timely and swift manner. Illy, its major competitor back home in Italy, was already present in India, where it operated through the Fresh & Honest coffee machines. For Lavazza, Illy's presence in India posed a constant threat as well as served as a motivation to enter the Indian market, whenever it decided to do so, in a rather rapid fashion. Growing organically through a greenfield venture would have been extremely challenging, owing to financial and managerial requirements to operate in a new environment where coffee consumption outside of home was still relatively underdeveloped. A greenfield venture would have required far greater commitment by Lavazza's managers in order to fully understand the Indian consumers and their coffee-buying behaviour. Also, greenfield venture would have enticed other foreign players like Illy to go ahead with their own expansion in the Indian market. Given that Lavazza was not the first foreign coffee company in India, major expansion by others could have had a potentially stifling effect on Lavazza's business in India.

Second, at the time Lavazza was on its internationalization drive beyond Europe and was seriously contemplating about entry into India, an extremely viable target in form of one of the biggest retail coffee chains (Barista) and coffee machine operators (Fresh & Honest) in India was available for sale on the market. The two businesses were complementary. Barista, said to have revenues of Rs 45 crore (or Rs 450 million, equal to approximately €7 million), served out-of-home coffee whereas Fresh & Honest operated coffee-selling machines in offices of major foreign and domestic companies in large metropolitan cities of India. Barista had around 150 stores and Fresh & Honest served through approximately 2,500 selling points in offices all over India. Both, Barista and Fresh & Honest belonged to the same business group, which helped in speeding up the negotiations for the acquisition. Sterling, which was a diversified conglomerate with business interest in Internet services, broadcasting, agriculture and wellness, was reconfiguring its business units and planned to exit the coffee market completely to concentrate on the bio-energy sector. Sterling Group and Lavazza agreed to a sale price of US$ 125 million, or approximately €94 million,[5] for the complete take-over of the two businesses (Barista and Fresh & Honest).

Third, Lavazza fully realized the need for enormous resources, especially the distribution capability and brand awareness, to have any chances of a long-term successful operation in the Indian market. These resources could have been obtained only through some form of local participation in the form of JV or acquisition. Lavazza as a brand was unknown to the Indian consumers. On the other hand, Barista had established a strong brand image in the premium segment of out-of-home coffee market. Barista stores were seen as high-end places for couples and women to meet and talk while tasting high quality coffee. Lavazza capitalized on this strong brand to make a swift and widespread entry by a full take-over of Barista. Fresh & Honest, although a smaller brand, was very well distributed across the major cities of India through a strong distribution network. Lavazza realized the importance of possessing an already existing distribution network in the Indian market context, which is plagued by a very weak infrastructure, making it difficult to create a distribution network from ground-up. A JV might have been an alternative, however, finding a partner with all the necessary resources was less likely. As such, Lavazza did not waste time in deciding to go for an all out buy-out of Barista and Fresh & Honest, business entities that possessed those necessary resources.

Discussion. Acquisition: the right entry mode?

Given the above factors, acquisition seemed like a good entry mode strategy for Lavazza. However, an important question pertains to the price of approximately €94 million that Lavazza paid for the two businesses it acquired. Was the acquisition too costly for Lavazza? Going by the revenues that Barista and Fresh & Honest were making at the time of the acquisition, €94 million seemed like a substantially high value. But Lavazza's strategy of entering India was with an objective of eventually entering Indian households through sales of its espresso packages from retail stores in India. India's retail store industry is extremely fragmented with hardly any large retail chain. Indian retail market consists of 6–10 million small 'Mom and Pop' shops, small grocery stores managed by families, and some domestic retail chains that had insufficient coverage to reach out to all potential customers. However, the retail sector like many other economic sectors in India was soon expected to undergo reforms allowing private and foreign participation in a significant manner. Once the regulations were passed, India was likely to witness phenomenal changes in the way products would be sold, through large and organized retail chains many of them with foreign collaborators. Lavazza's major source of income worldwide was from espresso coffee packages sold at retail stores. A very small portion of the total income derived from owning retail coffee shops. In the case of India, the institutional environment did not allow the flourishing of a strong retail industry with large incumbents. Hence, for Lavazza selling its products through the multitude of small retail stores, which could have been served through simple exports, was never a feasible entry mode option. Nevertheless, Lavazza firmly believed that the retail sector would slowly but surely evolve, with all the liberalization policies being introduced, and it had to be fully prepared for that moment. When the time of large-scale domestic and foreign retailers arrived Lavazza could start selling its coffee packs to a much larger consumer base. Entry into India through acquisition of Barista and Fresh & Honest was only the first step for the long-term sustainability of its business in India. This would give them a head-start to familiarize their name with the Indian consumers giving them a sizeable captive market when they start selling their products through retail stores.

   The acquisition marked the first step of Lavazza's entry into India, and thus the post-acquisition integration process was of critical importance for the overall success of its India venture. The integration process went along rather smoothly. Italian and Indian cultures looked compatible and cultural issues did not create any major sources of friction between the management teams at Lavazza's Italian headquarters and those based in India. In fact, Lavazza's top management was pleasantly surprised by the level of qualification of Indian managers, who often had a degree from an American or European university. Most of the managers who worked for Barista and Fresh & Honest decided to continue with the company after acquisition. The quality of the equipment and skills that Lavazza acquired took some of their managers by surprise. Not only were Fresh & Honest machines imported from Switzerland, some of the engineers that operated the machinery were as skilled and competent as Italian ones. During the first twelve months of the post-acquisition period, Lavazza spent a lot of resources on cross-integration of the local management. Indian managers spent months in Italy, learning the company's values and tricks of the trade regarding high-end Italian coffee, while Italian managers spent months in India, learning about the new market and about 15,000 newly acquired Indian employees of Lavazza.

   The brand identity of Barista was strong enough for Lavazza to make any significant alteration. Thus, Lavazza gave the existing Indian management major responsibility and associated authority and flexibility in managing the coffee shops. The overall friendly atmosphere in the shops was maintained. The focus of Lavazza's efforts was to continue maintaining the brand identity of Barista and Fresh & Honest. Lavazza would bring its strong marketing skills and financial resources in order to give these brands their 'second life'. The overall idea was to integrate the two brands, linking them with Lavazza's name ('by Lavazza'), in order to conquer most of the 'out of home' coffee-consuming customers. In the offices of IBM, Infosys, Microsoft and the like, young Indian yuppies would drink 'Fresh & Honest by Lavazza', and on the way home or while meeting their friends, they would go to 'Barista by Lavazza'. Integrating the two brands also meant organizational changes. Prior to the acquisition, Barista and Fresh & Honest had almost entirely separate operations, including two marketing departments with little in terms of common strategy making.

   Has the acquisition strategy of entry and operating in the Indian market worked for Lavazza so far? While it is too early to make any conclusive analysis, there have been some signs of success. Lavazza, through this acquisition, not only has some early-mover advantage, it has been able to eliminate a major competitor, Illy, from India. As noted earlier, Illy operated through Fresh & Honest. It was only natural for Lavazza to stop the contract with Illy once it had full control of Fresh & Honest. As such, the full control through the acquisition route of entry allowed Lavazza to take decisive action in a short span of time against one of its major competitors. Acquisition of the two business units involved a huge influx of resources, financial as well as marketing, by Lavazza headquarters to the Indian subsidiary. Such huge investments are a cause for concern for the management, particularly in emerging markets as they have weak property protection and governance mechanisms. India, with its institutional evolution, offered a relatively high level of transparency of its legal context and also provided sufficient property rights protection. As such, Lavazza's commitment of resources in the acquisition of Barista and Fresh & Honest has not been undermined due to a lack of institutional protection. One of the main assumptions that Lavazza made while planning the rapid entry into India was that the retail sector would soon be liberalized to foreign players that will be instrumental in changing the entire structure of the retail market. The Indian government has allowed foreign players to participate in the Indian retail sector and the effect can already be seen in the rapid expansion of a number of domestic retail chains in the country. If this trend continues, Lavazza will be in a good position to launch its product through the organized retail chains of foreign and domestic companies as it already has the competencies to work with large distributors in other international markets.

The acquisition posed challenges for Lavazza, given the investment it made and the exposure it received in the Indian market, in a rather short period of time. The average stay inside the Barista coffee shop was approximately thirty minutes and the price for one cappuccino was Rs 35 (€0.56). Therefore, one of the challenges the company faced right from the start was to increase the average spending per customer. This was tricky as the pricing was already on a higher side with little room for further increase. The Indian legislation did not permit much sale of merchandise, as that would classify Lavazza's coffee shops as retail stores making it incompatible with foreign ownership regulations at the time of entry. Although, Lavazza became the owners of Barista and Fresh & Honest overnight through this acquisition, Indian consumers who visited the stores were obviously unaware of the Lavazza name. Rebranding Barista and Fresh & Honest so as to make Lavazza closer to the Indian consumer required astute strategizing. Lavazza slowly started branding its name along with that of Barista and Fresh & Honest. It realized that a complete overhaul of the brand would have been a disaster. Coca-cola, after acquiring the local Indian brand Thums-up, in the initial few years, tried to downplay the Thums-up brand and promote its own. However, this strategy backfired and the Coca-cola management decided to give greater attention to maintaining the brand identity of Thums-up and capitalize on that. Aware of the subtle difficulties in re-branding an already existing strong brand, Lavazza moved ahead with far greater caution.

The Indian market, after the acquisition, remained under attentive control of Lavazza headquarters, who periodically evaluated not only such market trends as Lavazza's brand equity, individual store performance, product line performance, price elasticity of demand (also in terms of packaging, since for the Indian market small packages generally increased the accessibility of products to a larger share of population), but also such macroeconomic indicators as GDP and GDP per capita, inflation, and the like. India, according to Lavazza management, still had to resolve three major problems that constrained its growth, namely infrastructure, energy and portable water. However, the main strength of the Indian economy was its ability to produce for the home market and to be able to sell in the home market too. This was in contrast to some other emerging markets such as Russia and China that largely depend on foreign demand for internal growth of production. With the completion of the Indian acquisition, Lavazza continued its expansion into other emerging markets, leveraging on the acquired expertise and skills and entered Brazil late 2007 by building a new factory.

Fiat's entry into India

Fiat (Fabbrica Italiana Automobili Torino), an Italian flagship car manufacturer, was found in 1899 in Turin (Piedmont region, northern Italy). Mr. Agnelli, the founder of the company, saw the company's future in mass car production based on the premise that increasing economic activity would lead to higher wage rates across the board, making consumption of cars necessary and also affordable. Fiat's small cars became very popular in Italy and later in Europe. In 1936 Fiat launched its most famous model, the 500, also known as the Topolino ('Little mouse' in Italian), the world smallest economy car. This model was discontinued in 1995 to give way for the Fiat 600 and Fiat 500 that were launched in 1960 and 1962, respectively. Fiat's internationalization drive began with setting up of manufacturing facilities in South Africa, Turkey, Yugoslavia, Argentina, Brazil and Mexico. However, the US remained too prohibitively competitive for Fiat to make any plans of taking on the Big Three American automobile giants in their home market.

The year 1966 saw a change in Fiat's management, with an inclination towards the American style of managing operations. Old managers were fired and assembly-line production was introduced. In 1978, Fiat acquired Lancia, a top-end car manufacturer, and a year later its auto brands (Fiat, Lancia, Autobianchi, Abarth and Ferrari) were spun off into a separate company, Fiat Auto. In 1986 Fiat Auto acquired its largest national competitor, Alfa Romeo. A few years later, after the acquisition of Maserati, Fiat Auto had gathered virtually all the current Italian car brands. Its brand portfolio would be eventually reorganized around two luxury brands (Ferrari and Maserati) and three mass-market brands (Fiat, Alfa Romeo and Lancia). The Fiat brand was used for economy segment cars, Alfa Romeo for sporty 'technological masterpieces' that still belonged to the mass market, and Lancia for stylish, understating upper middle-class customers. With regard to international diversification, Fiat Auto had established production facilities in Russia, Poland, France, Turkey, Brazil, South Africa, China and India.[6]

Fiat's first experiences in the Indian market go back to as early as the beginning of 1900s, when it signed a distribution agreement with Bombay Motor Cars Agency. In 1959, Fiat stipulated a licensing agreement with Premier Automobiles Ltd (PAL) for the production of the Fiat 500 and, later, of the Fiat 1100.[7] The licensing agreement expired in 1972, but PAL continued to produce Fiat models, using the brand PAL Padmini. A subsequent agreement with PAL was signed in 1981. Given the restrictive FDI policies and the immature car market of India, the licensing arrangement that Fiat used to access the Indian market seemed reasonable based on the cost–control trade-off.

When in 1990s India substantially alleviated FDI regulations, Fiat found its Indian subsidiary, Fiat India Auto Ltd (FIAL) and subsequently built a new, wholly owned factory in Ranjangaon (Maharashtra) with the planned production capacity of 100,000 cars to be achieved by 1999. Fiat's idea was to strengthen its position in all emerging markets through a 'World Car Project' where India would serve as the production site. Fiat, thus, attempted to strengthen its partnership with PAL. The latter would assemble the Fiat Uno model from 'completely knocked down' (CKD) kits in its Kurla facility close to Mumbai (Maharashtra). However, the optimism of the mid-1990s did not translate into reality for Fiat. PAL did not agree to Fiat's proposal for the assembly of the Uno and Fiat had to renegotiate the nature of its contractual alliance. Fiat had to create a joint venture with PAL, Ind Auto Ltd (IAL) with a 51 per cent equity capital contribution. This shift in the contractual alliance from licensing to JV was partly due to PAL's reluctance to operate the Kurla production facility without any significant capital investment by Fiat. By 1998 Fiat increased its participation in IAL to 76 per cent, in 2000 to 95 per cent and in 2004 to 99 per cent (by 2006 Fiat owned 100 per cent of the venture, and renamed it Fiat India Private Ltd). One big implication of this new venture creation by Fiat was freezing the wholly owned greenfield project in Ranjangaon. The sales results that followed were not sufficient to justify the investment, and Fiat was almost ready to call its Indian venture a failure. However, Fiat was able to secure a new partner in Tata Motors, a much bigger and more widely known company compared with PAL. With this new alliance partner Fiat was able to relaunch its Ranjangaon production facility and decided to close down the Kurla factory. With all the changes Fiat had to bring about in its Indian operations, it seems to be far from being categorized as successful. The only highlight of Fiat's India strategy is in its continued survival in the country.

Concluding remarks and key issues

The above discussion on the two Italian companies' India entry brings about very interesting and somewhat contrasting takeaways. We summarize the key lessons below:

- Despite the opening up of the Indian economy to foreign investment, there remain substantial restrictions on the overall scope and scale of participation that foreign companies can achieve. For example, foreign participation in e-commerce is restricted to B2B transactions only.
- Constantly changing institutional environment, including regulations pertaining to foreign investment in India, poses severe challenges to foreign companies strategizing on entering the country. On the other hand, it also opens up new opportunities to exploit. Lavazza was able to exploit the new relaxed acquisition rules in order to enter and gain market share in India in a very short span of time. Fiat on the other hand struggled to gain market share despite its long presence in the Indian market.
- Finding a local partner for entry into India can be complicated, but is key to success in the long run. Lavazza acted swiftly in acquiring Barista, the local partner, in making its India foray. Barista was an established brand, had a reasonable market presence and was up for sale, factors making it the right platform for a foreign company to enter a difficult market like India by capitalizing on the acquired resources – brand, distribution, market share. Fiat's experience with its Indian partners, for the most part, was characterized by lack of commitment and willingness to work together.
- Entry strategy serves as only the first, yet an important, step in the overall success of the venture in the new foreign market. It needs to be constantly evaluated for future entry and operation in the foreign market. Fiat's licensing agreement to access the Indian market was a risk-averse strategy. In the context of changing institutional environment in India and an influx of foreign car manufacturers, Fiat might have been better off by being proactive in making a larger commitment in the Indian market. Lavazza took the gamble by investing heavily in order to be prepared for reaching out to a larger market with the rapidly maturing retail sector in India.
- Risky and emerging markets require innovative approaches to market entry. Lavazza, prior to its entry into India, was not very familiar with the business of operating coffee shops. However, it saw an opportunity in making such an innovative foray to be able to sell its main product, the coffee packets, through retail shops in India as and when it matures. Fiat on the other hand adopted the conventional cautious approach of entry, potentially losing out on the growing car market in India.
- Flexibility in entry and operation can be a very useful tool, especially in emerging markets like India marked by external shocks. Fiat has been able to survive, despite all its problems, due to its flexibility in partnering with different local players in India. Lavazza is fairly new to the Indian market; however, having a flexible approach can be handy in situations of sudden government policy changes. Exiting the market only to re-enter at an opportune moment, as what IBM and Coca-cola did for their Indian operations, should also be part of the strategic options for the firm.

Notes

1   http://www.laghu-udyog.com/publications/reserveditems/reserved.pdf.
2   http://theindiaeconomy.blogspot.com/2008/05/fdi-policy-of-india.html.
3   'Wal-mart in India Fact Sheet', September 2008, www.walmartfacts.com.
4   www.megamondo.com, 'Accordo per la catena Barista e Fresh & Honest café', 9
    October 2007.
5   http://www.vccircle.com.
6   OICA statistics, http://oica.net.
7   www.ibef.org.

References

Agarwal, S. and Ramaswami, S. N. (1992) Choice of Foreign Market Entry Mode: Impact of Ownership, Location and Internalization Factors. *Journal of International Business Studies*, 23 (1): 1–27.

Anderson, E. and Gatignon, H. (1986) Modes of Foreign Entry: A Transaction Cost Analysis and Propositions. *Journal of International Business Studies*, 17 (3): 1–26.

Bhaumik, S. K., Gangopadhyay, S. and Krishnan, S. (2008) Policy, Economic Federalism and Product Market Entry: The Indian Experience. *The European Journal of Development Research*, 20 (1): 1–30.

Budhwar, P. (2001) Doing Business in India. *Thunderbird International Business Review*, 43 (4): 549–68.

Chandrasekaran, A. and Ryans, J. K. (1996) US Foreign Direct Investment in India: Emerging Trends in MNC Entry Strategies. *International Executive*, 38 (5): 599–612.

Chibber, P. K. and Majumdar, S. K. (2005) Property Rights and the Control of Strategy: Foreign Ownership Rules and Domestic Firm Globalization in Indian Industry. *Law and Policy*, 27 (1): 52–80.

Chittoor, R., Sarkar, M. B., Ray, S. and Aulakh, P. S. (2009) Third World Copycats to Emerging Multinationals: Institutional Changes and Organizational Transformation in the Indian Pharmaceutical Industry. *Organization Science*, 20 (1): 187–205.

Dematté, C. and Peretti, F. (2003) *Strategie di internazionalizzazione*. Milan: EGEA.

Dunning, J. H. (1988) *Explaining International Production*. London and Boston MA: Unwin Hyman.

Huang, Y. and Khanna, T. (2003) Can India Overtake China? *Foreign Policy*, July–August: 74–81.

Johanson, J., and Vahlne, J.-E. (1977) The internationalization process of the firm: a model of knowledge development and increasing foreign market commitments. *Journal of International Business Studies*, 8: 23–32.

Kumar, N. (2006) Reforms, Global Integration and Economic Development: Prospects and Challenges for India. *Public Policy Research*, September–December: 138–46.

MacDonald, S. B. (2006) A Tale of Two Indias. *Society*, July–August: 72–7.

Majumdar, S. K. (2009) Crowding out! The Role of State Companies and the Dynamics of Industrial Competitiveness in India. *Industrial and Corporate Change*, 18 (1): 165–207.

Meyer, K. E, Estrin, S., Bhaumik, S. K., and Peng, M. W. (2009) Institutions, Resources, and Entry Strategies in Emerging Economies. *Strategic Management Journal*, 30 (1): 61–80.

Pan, Y. and Tse, D. K. (2000) The Hierarchical Model of Market Entry Modes. *Journal of International Business Studies*, 31 (4): 535–54.

Root, F. R., (1998) *Entry Strategies for International Markets.* Lexington MA.: Lexington Books.

UNCTAD (2008) *World Investment Report, 2008.* Geneva: United Nations.

Zattoni, A., Pedersen, T. and Kumar, V. (2009) The Performance of Group Affiliated Firms during Institutional Transition: A Longitudinal Study of Indian Firms. *Corporate Governance: An International Review*, 17 (4) 510–523.

8 Markets, consumers and consumption patterns

Ravi Shankar and Debdeep De

Marketing and distribution strategies in India have gone through substantial changes as the concept of consumerism has gradually started seeping in. The Indian market has become increasingly attractive for global marketers, an amount sufficient to sustain purchases of foreign consumer products. Foreign marketers in diverse sectors, from automobiles and consumer electronics to soft drinks and fast food, have entered the Indian market and are competing with domestic marketers. An essential requirement for marketing success in India is access to local channels of distribution. Most products sold in India in a tiered distribution system: distributor, wholesaler, and dealer/retailer. Most channel intermediaries are small and relatively unsophisticated operators, unlike the large chains commonly seen in the west. They are often family-run businesses bound in a cultural tradition where bargaining and negotiation are common business practices. To remain competitive in the attractive Indian market, foreign suppliers must be able to effectively manage their relationships with local intermediaries. The key to this would be using the right influence strategies which would help the supplier attain its business goals, but which would also keep the intermediaries satisfied, motivated, and performing.

A source firm directs influence strategies towards a consumer, with an intention to cause a change in the latter's behaviour (Frazier and Summers, 1984). The vastly different cultural environment in India means that influence strategies commonly used in the West may not be effective in the Indian market and local adaptations need to be made. In this chapter we undertake the patterns of suppliers' strategies to influence Indian dealers and the immense opportunities existing in the Indian retail with a diversified consumer basket.

Prior to the economic liberalization in the 1990s, the economy of India was a seller's market in most instances. The usually asymmetrical power structures in Indian distribution channels in a seller's market meant that suppliers were more likely to employ direct influence strategies (requests, promises, threats, and legal pleas) and, in particular, the coercive ones among them (threats and legal pleas) which did not seek to alter dealers' perceptions but just told them what to do. The market conditions are quite different now with more competition and dealers being able to choose from among many suppliers in most industries. Thus, the balance of power in distribution channels has become more symmetrical.

Legal pleas are not likely to be used widely in a relatively traditional culture of India where relationships are governed more by social norms than the word of law (Terpstra and David, 1991). The high-context nature of the Indian culture (Hall, 1976) does not place a high value on formalized expressions since the meanings of words used in communication tend to be more subjective and amenable to different interpretations. Businesses in high-context cultures do not emphasize rules and regulations to the extent that businesses in low-context cultures do (Terpstra and David, 1991). The threat strategy is likely to be used even less because it is intimidatory by definition, and the relatively more symmetrical power balance situation in Indian marketing channels mean that dealers are probably not going to take obvious threats from suppliers lying down. Favours in exchange of desired actions are common and often expected in many traditional societies such as India. In economically less affluent environments, the promise of some reward is usually highly effective in getting others to perform desired acts (Kinsey, 1987).

The present chapter attempts to analyse the birth of the retail industry in India as an emerging trend of the changing consumer patterns of the Indians and tries to identify the strategies to be undertaken by the foreign investors to penetrate the Indian market. The chapter is divided into the following sections. The next section provides the introduction of the Indian market which is quite diverse in nature. The second talks about the demographic profile of the Indian consumers. The third discusses the changing consumption pattern of the Indian consumers and highlights the major consumption trends by which the Indian consumer stands different. The fourth talks about the changing pattern of the Indian distribution system from a strategic perspective in response to the growth of the retail sector. This is followed by the fifth, which illustrates the birth of the retail sector in India and identifies the different patterns of the segments of retail prevailing in India. The sixth section discusses the growth prospects of the retail sector in India as a reflection of the change in consumerism in India and is followed by the seventh section, which discusses the policy issues in the Indian retail sector. The final section provides the summary.

Demographic profile of the Indian consumer

As the Indian economy is moving into the higher growth path, the rapid changes in income level and consumption patterns have been the subject of interest, debates and analysis. Rising per capita income, increased literacy and rapid urbanization have caused rapid growth and change in demand patterns. The rising aspiration levels, increase in spending power has led to a change in the consumption pattern.

Essential items such as food, beverages, rent and fuel accounted for 82 per cent of consumption in 1950–51, and 78 per cent after twenty years, a shift of about 4 per cent. By 1990–91, these items accounted for 64 per cent of consumption, a shift of fourteen points, a much larger shift as an under penetrated economy gathered pace. During the last seventeen years, the trend has accelerated further and today essential items account for fewer than 40 per cent, still high by developed country standards but significantly down from earlier periods. India is beginning to see the first signs of a long-term consumption boom as a result of rising disposable incomes, higher life expectancy, rapid urbanization and changing lifestyles.

With the global crisis in the second half the financial year 2008–09 the industrial output experienced decline towards the end of 2009. The global demand conditions may improve and economic growth is expected in 2010. The budget for the current year has allocated a significant level of resources to rural development. The deceleration in industrial growth has been sharp in the fiscal year 2008–09 and the output performance of the sector has remained weak in the first two months of the first quarter of the current fiscal. The services sector GDP has recorded a growth of 9.7 per cent even as agriculture and industry recorded steep decline in growth. However, within the services, the sectors that are closely associated with the industrial activity have seen significant decline in growth rates in the second half of 2009 (see Table 8.1 for details).

In spite of these facts India still remains a destination market. The different factors which indulge in the producers to target the Indian market among others includes low cost material and labour.

Table 8.1 Assessing the macroeconomic scenario, 2009–10 (real GDP at factor cost)

	Projections in April 2009–10		Current projections 2009–10
	Base scenario	Alternative scenario	
	% change year on year		
Agriculture	2.5	2.5	1.0
Industry	6.0	6.3	6.7
Service	7.9	8.5	9.4
Total	6.5	6.9	7.2
Goods exports ($ value)	9.1	9.1	12.0
Goods imports ($ value)	5.0	10.0	5.5
Inflation (WPI-based)	5.2	5.2	3.7
	As % of GDP at current prices		
Fiscal deficit (centre)	4.4	4.5	6.2
Current account deficit	2.9	3.5	2.4

Source: NCAER (2009).

Urban versus rural households

India's economic growth has accelerated significantly over the last two decades and so too the spending power of its citizens. The real average disposable income has soared and a new middle class has emerged. Yet much remains unknown about how India's consumer has evolved. There are large differences in income, expenditure and savings patterns between rural and urban India. Urban households earn around 85 per cent more than rural ones, spend three-fourths more and, as a result, save nearly double that of rural households. Much of this can be explained by differences in profession and education. Even for the same profession and levels of education, urban earnings are higher. A survey conducted by NCAER in 2005 – *The Great Indian Middle Class* – defines the middle class as those households with an annual income of Rs 2–10 lakh at 2001–02 prices. The lowest income quintile accounts for 22.4 per cent of the population and just 6 per cent of income. But India is changing rapidly – the middle class, which accounted for 2.7 per cent of the population in 1995, now accounts for 8.3 per cent. However, regional disparities are a matter of concern. Two-thirds of the poor reside in the ten low-income states. The findings of the Max New York Life NCAER India Financial Protection Survey released in 2008 reveal there are 205.9 million households in the country, of which 30 per cent (61.4 million) live in urban areas and the rest (144.5 million) in rural areas (for more details see Table 8.2).

Given that urban families are marginally smaller than rural ones, the share of India's urban population is slightly lower – at around 28.6 per cent. While the average family size in the country is five members, less than 1 per cent of Indian households are single-member ones and around 10 per cent have more than seven members. Since only 17 per cent of women work, the average number of workers per household is 1.4 (1.34 in urban areas and 1.43 in rural ones). And around 28 per cent of the country's population is engaged in a financially remunerative job of some sort. Indeed, 68.8 per cent of households have just a single earning member while 23.7 per cent have two earning members and 7.5 per cent have more than two earning members (for other details see Table 8.3).

Table 8.2 Estimates of Indian households and population

Variable	Rural	Urban	All India
Households (million)	144.5	61.4	205.9
Population (million)	732	295	1,027
Household size	5.08	4.81	5.00
No. of earners per household	1.43	1.34	1.40

Source: Max-NCAER India Financial Protection Survey, 2008.

Table 8.3 Average household size, urban and rural (million)

States	Household	Individuals	Average household size
All India	226	852	3.8
Andhra Pradesh	20	65	3.3
Assam	6	22	3.7
Bihar	17	64	3.8
Jharkhand	6	21	3.7
Chandigarh	0.2	1	3.4
Delhi	4	14	3.9
Goa	4.4	1	3.9
Gujarat	0	44	3.5
Haryana	12	19	3.8
Himachal Pradesh	5	5	3.9
Jammu and Kashmir	1.4	1	3.7
Karnataka	0	46	4.2
Kerala	12	28	3.7
Madhyra Pradesh	8	49	3.6
Chhattisgarh	13	17	37
Maharashtra	5	86	3.5
Orissa	23	31	3.7
Punjab	9	22	3.3
Rajasthan	5	46	4.2
Tamil Nadu	11	57	4.2
Uttar Pradesh	17	130	3.4
Uttaranchal	30	7	4.4
West Bengal	2	68	3.9
	18.807		3.667942787

Source: Indian Readership Survey, 2009.

Literacy

At the all-India level, households analysed on the parameter of highest literacy amongst their members, it was revealed that 19 per cent have members who have passed middle school (eighth class), nearly a fourth (23 per cent) of households have at least one member who has completed high school (tenth class), and 18 per cent have done higher secondary (twelfth class). At the all-India level, 17 per cent of all households have at least one graduate member; it is 30 per cent for urban areas and 11 per cent for rural areas.

Income–expenditure profile

Household incomes have grown by about Rs 580,000 crores during the two years to reach a level of Rs 3.61 million crores. However, dramatically different shifts have occurred in the higher and the lower-income categories. Whereas the proportion of households earning less than Rs 75,000 p.a. has reduced by 2.6 per cent and the proportion earning between Rs 75,000 and Rs 150,000 p.a. has reduced by 2.5 per cent, the proportion earning over Rs 10 lakhs p.a. has increased by 2.7 per cent and the proportion earning over Rs 3 per annum has increased by 3 per cent. The three higher-income categories have all seen an increase in proportion while all the three lower-income categories have seen a decrease in proportion. There have been very significant shifts in consumer spending patterns in the short interval between 2006 and 2008. While the consumer market has grown by 19 per cent during the interval, the key difference has been a decline in proportion spent on basic food (cereals and bread, pulses, sugar and gur, oils and oilseeds, fruits and vegetables, potato and other tubers, milk and milk products, meat, egg and fish, coffee, tea and cocoa, spices, other food, beverages, pan and other intoxicants, tobacco and its products) and the gains have been made in the category of miscellaneous goods and services which includes among others hotels and restaurants, utilities, rent, medical expenses, recreation, personal transport and education. The expenditure on food has grown by just 5 per cent whereas the expenditure on the latter category has grown by as much as 29 per cent, well above the average expenditure growth. In fact, every other category has declined in proportion, except the durables, which has remained stable (see Figure 8.1).

Social trends

Social trends of a country have impact on retailing in a country. India is a country that is vast geographically and diverse culturally. This has taken its toll on retailing with retailers having to adapt to the local cultures of the area in which they have established or plan to establish. This is a major reason for many or most retailing chains restricting their operations to a certain part of the country. But the trends now are slowly moving towards cultural integration where people of all states and diametrically opposite cultures tend to try out foods and materials of other states and communities. This movement towards social integration would make it very feasible in the near future for retailing chains and erstwhile local chains to spread across the country.

In the same country prevalence of different societal class as depicted in the figure reveals that the Indian consumer is very different in terms the societal structure cut across the country. Traditionally Indian women are expected to look after the household activities as a housewife. Increased income levels and more women willing to make use of their education by working has increasingly affected the shopping pattern that is moving towards fulfilling

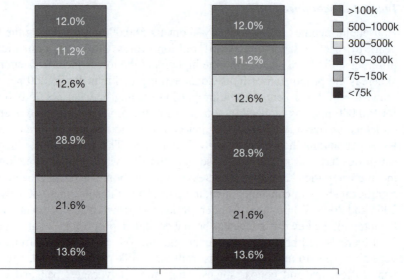

Figure 8.1 Changing pattern in income among Indian households.
Source: Market Skyline of India, 2008–09

the need of convenience shopping in the form of supermarket (now graduating to hyper format) home deliveries. Indian consumer is quality and price conscious and this awareness would drive the retailers to rework their supply chain relationships.

Income by occupation

Labourers constitute the largest segment of the population, heading a little over 31 per cent of the country's households; self-employed agriculturists are the next largest segment (30.3 per cent), salaried members account for a little over 18 per cent and the non-agricultural self-employed members account for 17.5 per cent of the country's households. The figures differ for rural and urban areas – while the salaried account for just 10.5 per cent of rural households, in urban areas they account for 36.9 per cent.

Changing trends in consumption

With changing lifestyle there has been a shift in consumption habits from carbohydrate-based staples towards protein-rich foods. The area under cultivation for cereals has stagnated over the past forty years, with a negative growth rate of 0.07 per cent, which explains the decline of its share in the consumption basket. Fruits, vegetables and meat-based products on the other hand have shown consistent growth thereby increasing their share in the basket. Rise in household incomes and affordability, aided by increasing urbanization (28 per cent of the total population was urban in 2006 in contrast to 17 per cent in 1951) has played a significant role in this shift in consumption. Personal consumption expenditure on food items has seen a decline from 73 per cent in 1971–72 to 54 per cent in 2004 in rural India. Among urban households, this expenditure has declined to 42 per cent, thereby underlining the trend that with increase in per capita income, per capita expenditure is spread among other commodities besides food.

The report on India Shopping Trends 2008 by the Knowledge Company, Technopak, highlights the following shopping behaviour:

- Patronage of traditional formats is universal across product categories shopped for.
- Purchases from modern format outlets in the recent past have been high – significant proportions emerge for purchases made from supermarkets, hypermarkets, departmental stores and even the new pharmacy and wellness stores.
- Most shoppers have made purchases from multiple format types in the last one year.

With a large middle class, rapid increases in purchasing power and the greater availability of more and more consumer goods, the shift towards consumerism has gained momentum and companies are adopting aggressive advertising and marketing techniques. International brands already present in the market include Benetton, Lacoste, Levi Strauss, Crocodile, Dockers, Lee, Wrangler, Nike, Reebok, Adidas, Zegna, Marks & Spencer, etc.

Indian consumption patterns are also slowly converging with global norms. The Indian consumer is now spending more on consumer durables, apparel, entertainment, vacations and lifestyle-related activities. According to industry estimate festive-season sales account for around one-third of the total sales of Rs 35,000 crore domestic consumer durables. The domestic consumer product markets have become intensely competitive both in the durables and non-durables (FMCG) segments. In an environment where supply is no longer a constraint, consumers are demanding more and better products at much lower prices. Table 8.4 explains the penetration of consumer durables in 2008.

If we take a closer look at the rural and urban consumption pattern we can observe from Figure 8.2 that the consumption pattern of the rural and the urban households is converging. Thus the major shift in the consumption pattern can be summarized as:

- People are spending proportionately less on food items and more on transport, which is a combination of running their own vehicles as well as making use of transport services. They are travelling more and also incurring higher costs due to fuel price inflation, and better quality of civic transport.

Table 8.4 Penetration of consumer durables (%)

	All	Urban	Rural
All households (million)	223	67	156
Bicycle ownership	52	49	53
Television ownership	46	76	34
Music system (two-in-one Walkman, radio, CD, etc.) ownership	22	29	19
Refrigerator ownership	13	32	5
Telephone (landline, terrestrial, wireless line) ownership	12	21	7
Motor cycle ownership	10	18	7
Aircooler ownership	7	17	3
DVD player ownership	6	15	2
Washing machine ownership	4	13	1
Still camera ownership	3	9	1
Scooter ownership	3	8	1
Moped ownership	2	5	1
Computer at home ownership	2	5	0.3
Car, van, Jeep ownership or use	2	5	1
Air conditioner ownership	1	3	0.0
Internet access at home (through PC, television ownership)	1	3	0.1
Digital camera ownership	1	2	0.1
Microwave oven ownership	1	2	0.0
Vacuum cleaner ownership	0.5	2	0.0
Printer ownership	0.3	1	0.1
Video-recorder/player ownership	0.3	1	0.1
Cooking range ownership	0.3	1	0.0
Video-camera/camcorder ownership	0.2	0.5	0.03

- People are spending more on health and well-being (included in the fastest-growing category, miscellaneous goods and services). The cost of medical care has gone up, while there has been an increase in life expectancy, which in turn means people live longer, with greater need for medical care.
- They are also spending more on fuel and power at home. The cost of energy has gone up (and will continue to grow) along with greater consumption of electrical goods.

On the other hand, apart from low penetration, even the per capita consumption in most of the FMCG categories (including the high-penetration categories) in India is low as compared with both the developed markets and other emerging economies. Though India has reduced poverty significantly

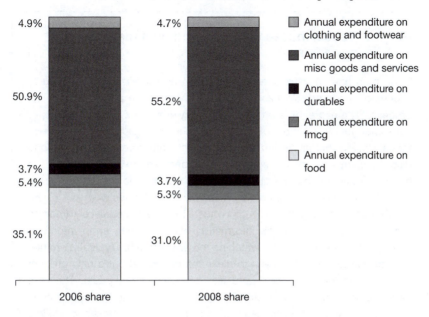

Figure 8.2 Consumption pattern of Indian households.
Source: Market Skyline of India, 2008–09

during the last decade, there are still over 110 million households who live on less than Rs 75,000 per annum. However, the good news is that this segment is shrinking dramatically in urban India and at a slightly slower pace in rural India.

Strategic change in the marketing distribution system

Traditionally the supplier–retailer relation in India comprised several layers such as the national distributor, the regional wholesaler and the end retailer. However, this scenario is fast changing with the concept of organized retail creeping in and increasing its presence in the country where the relationship is directly with the manufacturer. However, this new model has been affecting the relationships that the manufacturer enjoys with the traditional system which is still the most dominant in the entire retail sector, which is characterised by low cost of establishment, transport and overheads. The issue of differential pricing and the growing dissatisfaction among the traditional retailers is being addressed by the manufacturers. The supplier–retailer relationship would come under severe pressure as each party would try to squeeze maximum margins out of the other.

With a large middle class, rapid increases in purchasing power and the greater availability of more and more consumer goods, the shift towards consumerism has gained momentum and companies are adopting aggressive advertising and

Box 8.1 Gender-based differences: Indian men are different

While men have always been a part (albeit an unwilling one) of grocery shopping, modern retail has made them more active participants in the process. There are differences in the way men and women shop for consumer goods in a modern retail store, Men are explorers in the modern format, losing themselves to the allure of colours, interesting packs and display, whereas women are focused shoppers who explore with one eye on the list and the budget cut-off. Men have a very flexible notion of the budget, since it is not their primary responsibility, whereas women are ever watchful of exceeding the budget too much. Men shop 'cognitively' (reading product literature and pack information) while women shop intuitively (through their senses and by watching other shoppers). Typically, women tend to use touch as a means to glean information about a new product (pressing, shaking the pack) and also smell (sniff the pack). They are oblivious or dismissive of pack information. Appreciating the difference in the cognitive and intuitive modes of shopping allows marketers and retailers to present new products appropriately. For example, some retailers use open samples of new products for women shoppers to touch, smell and feel, whereas some manufacturers use 'tactile-loaded' descriptors of products on their packs for women to sensorily process the information. Modern format offers New Age men who are no longer just curious about macho products such as shaving aids or lighting products. They are also inquisitive about products that are overtly targeted at women. Personal care is one big domain for exploration. In a recent study of toiletries, women shopped for basic toiletries such as soap and shampoo in a pragmatic and matter-of-fact manner, whereas men spent double the time shopping. They also checked out new launches, compared price points and even sneaked an occasional sniff or spray of some of the products such as deodorants. Thus men are no longer interested in a product just because it is not specifically targeted at men, nor are they automatically rejecting a product because it is targeted overtly at women. Their needs have become more complex and so have their shopping rituals. It is time manufacturers and retailers took notice of these needs and serviced them through better offerings as well as well thought out shop presence and display.

Source: *Business World*, 2009.

marketing techniques. India is growing less conservative, but sensitivity to religious beliefs and customs is required. Advertising in only English is acceptable, but the use of Hindi or any regional language along with English is both desirable and effective in marketing consumer goods (see Table 8.5).

Due to the increased level of competition, both dealers and manufacturers have created business directories in which products and services are categorized and widely advertised. A wide variety of magazines also plays a pivotal role in advertising and marketing. Large hoardings and neon-sign

Table 8.5 India's leading magazines ('000)

Publications	Genre	IRS R2 2006	IRS R1 2009	% difference
		All Fig '000s		
India Today (Eng.)	General interest	3137	1955	−38
Readers Digest	General interest	2046	1327	−35
Outlook	General interest	1093	533	−51
The Week	General interest	673	322	−52
Frontline	General interest	321	118	−63
Time	General interest	185	57	−69
Wisdom (Eng.)	General interest	807	455	−44
Sahara Time	General interest	52		−100
Business Today	Business magazine	600	287	−52
Business India	Business magazine	428	222	−48
Business World	Business magazine	286	165	−42
Outlook Money	Business magazine	160	84	−48
Capital Market	Business magazine	77		−100
Dalal Street Inv. Journal	Business magazine	68		−100
Outlook Business	Business magazine		166	–
Business and Economy	Business magazine		82	–
Filmfare	Entertainment	1270	490	−61
Stardust (Eng.)	Entertainment	879	388	−56
Cine Blitz	Entertainment	231	50	−78
Showtime	Entertainment	80		−100
Femina	Women	574	309	−46
Women's Era	Women	454	200	−56
Femina Girl	Women		103	–
Savvy	Women	112	26	−77

Source: Indian Readership Survey, 2009.

advertising are widely used. Doordarshan is the national television, with many channels. Amongst the more popular channels are the Star TV, CNN, MTV, Discovery and BBC. There are several major national English-language newspapers and many weekly, fortnightly and monthly magazines. Prominent amongst these are the *Times of India, Indian Express, Hindustan Times, The Hindu, Economic Times* (newspapers) and *Business Today* and *India Today* (magazines). In most hotels and bookshops one can find most of the foreign newspapers and magazines (especially British and American).

With increased purchasing power, promotional campaigns for consumer products should emphasize quality, price and durability. Most customers have a very positive perception of the quality of foreign-made products and are willing to pay a premium for them. This has been fuelled by the growth of networking sites, which facilitates the product promotion.

Transformation in the supply chain

A successful retailer's winning edge will therefore come from sourcing – how best it can leverage its scale to drive merchandise costs down, increase stock turns and get better credit terms from its vendors. There are obvious and hidden areas where costs can be pruned and the benefits of this lower cost of retailing can be passed on to customers as lower prices, which in turn should fuel demand. For example the food supply chain in India is full of inefficiencies – a result of inadequate infrastructure, too many middlemen, complicated laws and an indifferent attitude. The entire supply chain framework has undergone a huge change with the farm and services emerging to ensure quality and timely supply of produce for the operations.

Innovations in transport logistics

The logistics service providers have been innovating several interesting formats and models for the retail sector. As of now, organized retail chains in India do not, by far, outsource logistical requirements, they develop their own network. This was basically due to the fact that the supply chain was still in its infancy stage, which has begun to mature and the systems are being well defined. As retail chains begin to focus more and more on the retail end, the logistics support would begin to get outsourced. The logistics service providers have begun to come out with innovative customized solutions for the retail chains such as GATI's model for distribution of Alphonso mangoes throughout the country with information technology support.

Online retailing

The single most important evolution that took place along with the retailing revolution was the rise and fall of the dot-com companies. A sudden concept of non-store shopping emerged, which threatened to take away the potential of the store. More importantly, the very nature of the customer segment being addressed was almost the same. The computer-savvy individual was also a sub-segment of the store-frequenting traffic. Internationally, the concept of net shopping is yet to be proven. And the poor financial performance of most of the companies offering virtual shopping has resulted in store-based retailing regaining the upper hand. Other forms of non-store shopping including various formats such as catalogue/mail order shopping, direct selling, and so on, are growing rapidly. However, the size of the direct market industry is too limited to deter the retailers. For all the convenience that it offers, electronic retailing does not suit products where look and see attributes are of importance, as in apparel, or where the value is very high, such as jewellery, or where the performance has to be tested, as of consumer durables. The most critical issue in electronic retailing, especially in a country such as India, relates to payments and the various security issues involved.

However, using the Internet to source products and also check for availability of stock among stores of retail chains has been proven to be effective and cuts down on wastage by a vast amount. It makes logistical support very easy and efficient. The trend in India is such that the use of the electronic medium for business purposes and integrating it into the systems is increasing. This would slowly spread into the retailing sector as well. It has already started in the case of some large retail houses where the affects are here to see. This again would result in the supply chain getting leaner and vertically integrated. Though the initial costs to implement these systems are high, in the long run it results in cost reduction where this privilege can be passed on to the final consumer. India is the second largest wireless network in the world, overtaking the United States and second only to China, adding 8 million subscribers every month (for details see Figure 8.3).

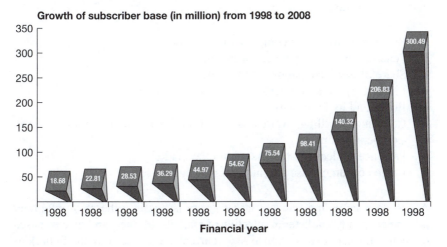

Figure 8.3 Subscriber base of wireless network in India.

Source: TRAI

Emergence of the retail sector

The rapid economic growth and the ongoing consumer boom have contributed greatly to the growth of the retail sector. The reform measures post liberalization of the economy together with the changing demographics has provided a strong growth stimulus to the sector. According to the FICCI–Ernst & Young 2007 report the sector accounts for over 10 per cent of the country's GDP and 8 per cent of total employment. With the fast-growing economy, changing lifestyles, and favourable demographic patterns, Indian retail is expected to grow by 9.5 per cent annually. Furthermore, with organised retail at around 5 per cent share of the overall market, there is a huge potential for growth in the coming years. However, the boom in retailing has been confined primarily to the urban markets in the country. Even there, large chunks are yet to feel the impact of organized retailing. There are two primary reasons for this. First, the modern retailer is yet to feel the saturation effect in the urban market and has, therefore, probably not looked at the other markets as seriously. Second, the modern retailing trend, despite its cost-effectiveness, has come to be identified with lifestyles. In order to appeal to all classes of the society, retail stores would have to identify with different lifestyles. In a sense, this trend is already visible with the emergence of stores with an essentially value-for-money image. The attractiveness of the other stores actually appeals to the existing affluent class as well as those who aspire to be part of this class. Hence, one can assume that the retailing revolution is emerging along the lines of the economic evolution of society.

For marketers, the decision to enter a new market is dependent on a number of factors, which help them select and prioritise markets. The following key factors impact their decisions for gauging market potential and allocating marketing spends.

- Revenue share of the company in the market.
- Penetration of the company in the market.
- Share of new acquisitions in the market.
- Life cycle of the product/service offering in the market.
- Brand and its fit to market.
- Consumer profiling: awareness, intention to buy and ability to purchase.
- Competition intensity.
- Presence of decision makers within the market.
- Large consumer base and increasing affluence levels.

Access to a large and relevant target group is possibly the most important parameter for any marketer in selection of markets. Markets are selected based on their affluence level as well as size (current and expected in the future), as a judicious mix of both would be critical for any market to be seen as high potential (see Table 8.6).

Table 8.6 Retail grocery company shares: percentage value, excluding sales tax, 2004–08

Company	2004	2005	2006	2007	2008
Pantaloon Retail India	0.1	0.2	0.3	0.5	0.9
Spencer's Retail	–	–	0.1	0.2	0.7
Subhiksha Trading Services	0.1	0.1	0.1	0.3	0.6
Aditya Birla Retail	–	–	–	0.1	0.5
Reliance Retail	–	–	0.0	0.3	0.5
REI Agro	–	–	–	0.0	0.2
Mother Dairy Fruit & Vegetable	0.1	0.1	0.1	0.1	0.1
Other	99.7	99.7	99.3	98.4	96.4
Total	100.0	100.0	100.0	100.0	100.0

Source: Euromonitor International estimates.

The retail sector in India is estimated at US$ 280 billion. Organized retail, estimated at US$ 14 billion, accounts for a meagre 5 per cent of the total market in India. Rising disposable incomes (especially among the middle class), increasing consumer base in urban areas, and a potentially strong rural consumer market will fuel this growth in the near future. India has been rated as the most attractive emerging retail market in the world for the third time in succession. The sector is expected to grow rapidly to reach US$ 30 billion by 2010 driven by the increasing number of nuclear families, working women, greater work pressure, easy accessibility and convenience. The growth in the retail sector has driven a mall-building boom across the country, with the total number of malls expected to increase to 600 by 2010 from an estimated 300 by end of 2007. The different retail categories like food and groceries, apparel, consumer durables and pharmaceutical products account for almost 70 per cent of the total retail market in India, with an estimated market size of around US$ 197 billion. The various categories have evolved differently, organized retail in consumer durables and apparel categories has gained higher penetration levels of over 5 per cent and 15 per cent respectively, while the food and groceries retail category penetration stands at around 1 per cent only. Apparel (ready-made garments) constitutes the biggest category within the organised retail pie at 39 per cent followed by food and groceries, and consumer durables. The low penetration levels of organised retail in India provide huge potential for retailers to tap a highly unexplored market.

Food and groceries

Food and groceries account for the largest share of retail spend (approximately 54 per cent) by consumers. However, organized retail in this category is estimated at US$ 1.5 billion, accounting for slightly over 1 per cent of the total market. India is the leading producer of milk and second largest producer of fruits and vegetables in the world. Food and groceries account for a significant part of private consumption in the country. The present situation of organised retail in this category clearly indicates the huge growth opportunity available to the organised players entering the market.

Apparel

The apparel retail market in India is estimated at US$ 19.15 billion. It comprises the sales of ready-made garments in men's wear, women's wear and kids' wear. The market size of the three segments is estimated at US$ 7.92 billion, US$ 6.6 billion and US$ 4.63 billion respectively. Penetration of organized retail in this category is high in the urban centres and is growing steadily in other areas. The growth in this category will be driven by the young, with their frequently changing preferences and the high level of branding and promotional activities done by apparel retailers spread across formats such as department stores, hypermarkets, own retail outlets and franchise stores. The establishment of theme shops and the advent of new kids' apparel brands will also contribute to the growth of this category in India.

Consumer durables

The consumer durables (including consumer electronics) market is estimated at US$ 20 billion. The organized retail market is valued at US$ 1.25 billion, whereas 93.7 per cent of the market is unorganized and is valued at US$ 18.75 billion. The mobile handset market, estimated at US$ 5.85 billion, experienced a growth rate of 75 per cent to 80 per cent in 2006. Computer peripherals, laptops, gaming consoles, camera and hand-held devices have also grown at around 40 per cent to 50 per cent in the same year. These devices have driven growth of the category in recent years. Organized retail enjoys high penetration levels in the urban markets; hence the increase in spends on electronics and household appliances by rural households is expected to be a major driver of growth in the future. Rising incomes and easy access to credit are also expected to contribute to the growth of this category.

Other

Other niche retail categories including jewellery and accessories, footwear, home furnishing, and books and music have also experienced significant growth, being driven primarily by the changes in the lifestyle of consumers and the entry of organised players offering better options. Together, they account for US$ 83.1 billion of the total retail market. With greater adoption of the internet (Figure 8.4), e-retailing is also emerging as an alternative retail channel.

The FICCI–Ernst & Young 2007 report on *Winning with Intelligent Supply Chains* says the retail sector in India is highly fragmented, with over 12 million unorganized retailers across the country (see Figure 8.5). More than

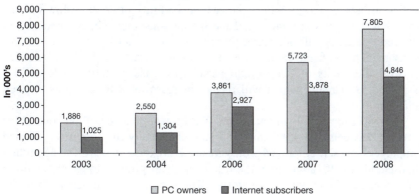

Number of Internet Subscribers in India

Figure 8.4 Internet subscribers in India, 2008.
Source: IAMAI

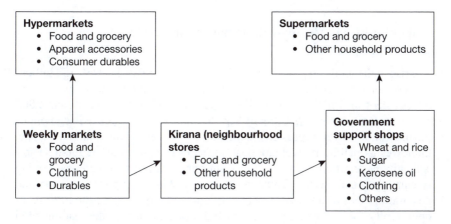

Figure 8.5 The Indian retail landscape.
Source: EY Research

80 per cent of these outlets are small family businesses using household labour. With the entry of modern retailers over the last few years, the share of the organized market has been growing rapidly to reach 5 per cent of the total market.

China and Brazil, India's main emerging market peers, took about ten to fifteen years to reach the current levels of 20 per cent and 38 per cent respectively of organized retail from 5 per cent when they began. India too is moving in the direction towards growth and maturity in the retail sector at a fast pace. The young have been driving growth in the market. The power of youth today is evident in its large numbers, propensity to consume and in its ability to influence larger household decisions. Discussing the major factors/drivers for the growth of retail market in India the first major factor which influences the growth is the easy availability of credit at low interest rates has changed the mind set of the Indian consumer. Though penetration of credit cards is still at around thirteen to fifteen cards per 1,000 persons, consumers prefer using credit cards to carry out transactions. With nationalized and private banks offering credit cards with ease, penetration levels are expected to increase, which will further increase retail transactions through this medium.

The driver for the Indian retail sector has been around 40 million households earning between US$ 4,000 and US$ 10,000 annually and comprises salaried employees and self-employed professionals. It is expected to grow to 65 million households by 2010 and play the role of a major growth driver for retailing of various product retailing categories. Rural India will also benefit from the country's rapid economic growth and will see a significant increase in annual household incomes over this period. The Ernst & Young 2008 report on *The Dhoni Effect: Rise of Small Town India* says that the urban growth story has been driven largely by metros.

Opportunities in the growth of the retail sector: the changing trends

The rise in the food and groceries retail segment is estimated at US$ 152 billion; it accounts for over half the total retail market in India and is growing at 3.5 per cent to 4 per cent annually as per the FICCI–Ernst & Young 2007 report on *Winning with Intelligent Supply Chains*. The organized segment of the market, however, represents just around 1 per cent of the total market, i.e. the lowest penetration level amongst all major categories in the retail sector. This low penetration presents significant opportunity for companies seeking to enter this retail sector. Thus, with a major share of the retail market and penetration rates of just over 1 per cent, food and groceries are the ideal retail opportunity for organized players, as India ranks amongst the leading food production and consumption centres of the world.

Food products are the single largest component of private consumption expenditure, and account for as much as 35 per cent of the total spending. India is the leading producer of pulses and milk and also ranks among the top three producers of rice, wheat, groundnuts, tea, coffee, tobacco, spices, sugar and oilseeds in the world. The country is also a leading exporter of cereals and pulses. Agriculture exports account for about 14.2 per cent of India's total exports. With annual production of around 149 million tonnes, India is the second largest producer of fruit and vegetables. The annual production of fruit is 48.36 million tonnes, while that of vegetables is around 101.43 million tonnes, accounting for 10 per cent and 14 per cent of global production respectively. These large volumes of fruits and vegetables production, together with consistent high year-on-year growth, indicate the huge market oppor-tunity for the food and grocery retailers. This opportunity, however, is more discernible in the urban markets that offer clear arbitrage benefits on procurement, than rural markets where margins are non-existent.

Milk and dairy products is another large consumption category in the Indian food and beverages basket, reinforcing India's position as the leader in milk production. This success can be attributed to various initiatives undertaken as a part of Operation Flood, which lay emphasis on organizing milk producers into co-operatives; building infrastructure for milk procurement, processing and marketing; and providing financial, technical and management assistance to the producers. This category offers huge opportunities to the processing industry, with 35 per cent of milk currently produced undergoing some form of processing.

The shift in consumer expenditure due to a change in lifestyle represents huge business opportunities for aggregators like ITC's e-choupal where they can not only procure basic food produce from farmers now but also act as suppliers and retailers for a range of non-food items that are witnessing an increasing demand in rural markets. Lifestyle changes and multicultural shifts have also resulted in increasing adoption of alternate dietary habits across regions. Southern India, which has traditionally been a rice consumption and production belt, is seeing a steady rise in wheat consumption, the staple of northern India.

Food and grocery purchases from hypermarkets were much lower. However, they all had also purchased from the traditional format outlets, including mandis, the local vegetable market and street hawkers. This was interesting to note as the obstacle here was not lack of awareness or exposure to modern format outlets. The important point to note is that evaluating a supermarket is more a requirement than a specific aspect on which a supermarket can differentiate itself. More importantly, discounts, promotions and loyalty points are vital to consumers. Clearly, there is tremendous potential in this market to develop differentiated offerings on the basis of relationship-based reward programmes and evolving patronage beyond mere convenience-led habituation.

It is widely felt that the key differentiator between the successful and not so successful retailers is primarily in the area of technology. Simultaneously, it will be technology that will help the organized retailer score over the unorganized players, giving both cost and service advantages. Retailing is a technology-intensive industry. Successful retailers today work closely with their vendors to predict consumer demand, shorten lead times, reduce inventory holding and thereby, save cost. Wal-mart pioneered the concept of building a competitive advantage through distribution and information systems in the retailing industry. They introduced two innovative logistics techniques – cross-docking and electronic data interchange. Today, online systems link point-of-sale terminals to the main office where detailed analyses on sales by item, classification, stores or vendor are carried out online. Besides vendors, the focus of the retailing sector is to develop the link with the consumer. Data warehousing is an established concept in the advanced nations. With the help of database retailing, information on existing and potential customers is tracked. Besides knowing what was purchased and by whom, information on softer issues such as demographics and psychographics is captured. Retailing, is at a nascent stage in India. The relatively complicated information systems and underlying technologies are in the process of being established. Most grocery retailers such as Food World have started tracking consumer purchases through CRM. The lifestyle retailers through their affinity clubs and reward clubs are establishing their processes. The traditional retailers will always continue to exist but organized retailers are working towards revamping their business to obtain strategic advantages at various levels – market, cost, knowledge and customer. With differentiating strategies – value for money, shopping experience, variety, quality, discounts and advanced systems and technology in the back end, change in the equilibrium with manufacturers and a thorough understanding of the consumer behaviour – the ground is all set for the organized retailer.

At the beginning of this millennium, sceptics dismissed modern format retail as being at least fifteen years away from seriously impacting shopping behaviour in India. But the proliferation of national chains of grocery stores, theme malls and penetration of these chains to the smaller cities at an accelerated pace has disproved many hypotheses, Retailers have evolved new concepts for the Indian market and are beginning to see positive results, exposure to novel retail formats across malls, grocery outlets and specialty outlets are converging in rapid evolution of consumer expectations.

Policy issues in the retail sector

With retailing in India attracting the attention of global players, the Indian government is paying increasing attention to the country's retail environment, and the impact the opening up of retailing would have on domestic retailers. The Indian government does not allow foreign direct investment in retailing in India, other than for single-brand retailing, in which FDI is allowed up to a maximum of 51 per cent, subject to government approval. Approval for foreign direct investment in single-brand retailing needs to be obtained from the Foreign Investment Promotion Board, working under the Ministry of Finance. For instance, in April 2007 the state government of Uttar Pradesh, in north India, forced retailers such as Reliance Fresh and Spencer's to close shop, stating that growing opposition from smaller traders to such stores was creating a law-and-order problem for the state. However, the prospect of international retail chains like Wal-mart, Carrefour and Ahold entering the country has enthused many suppliers and also consumers who are looking for a wider choice and finer prices product. Foreign direct investment inflows as on January 2009, in single-brand retail trading, stood at approximately US$ 25.18 million, according to the Department of Industrial Policy and Promotion (DIPP).

Government policies on FDI aside, retailing operations in India are mainly governed by the Shop and Establishment Acts of the various states. These prescribe the registration, opening and closing hours, working conditions, holidays, and health and safety measures, with the provisions varying from state to state. Where relevant, local/municipal, employment and contract labour legislation also applies. Retailers private labels fall under the legislation concerning the specific products, such as the Standards of Weights and Measures Act 1976 and Prevention of Food Adulteration Act 1954, which are applicable to packaged food, etc. Small retailers, especially independent stores, are typically part of district/state-level associations. Large retailers, on the other hand, are represented by the Retailers' Association of India, with members such as Pantaloon Retail India, Shoppers' Stop and Subhiksha Trading Services. The Retailers' Association of India was set up in 2004, with a vision to develop, facilitate and propagate practices and processes that will develop Indian retailing.

In India, the concept of bazaar is very significant. In particular, Delhi has dozens of such bazaars, ranging from Old Delhi's Chandni Chowk – a real bazaar in the Middle Eastern sense of the word – to roadside hovels to upscale markets like in South Extension and Greater Kailash. In the Central Market at Lajpat Nagar, a sprawling shopping district in South Delhi, any ready-made suit or a suit piece, or world-class opticals, sandals and shoes, can be purchased at an affordable price. The merchants are competitive with each other as shoppers go from shop to shop, bargaining for a better deal.

Many people argue that thousands of people would become unemployed with Wal-mart's entry. And this is true also because if the customer can get a quality product at a low cost then they will definitely go for that. But there is also a powerful counter-argument which is that in each sector that has been opened to private investment, such as insurance, banking, civil aviation, etc., has grown. In sectors where competition is stronger, FDI has had a much more obvious positive impact. A study of India by the McKinsey Global Institute (2007) showed that the removal of FDI restrictions in the automotive sector unleashed competition and investments, resulting in a threefold increase in productivity that translated into a threefold increase in output due to falling prices. Employment also rose. So, once adjusted for one-time events and government shortcomings, the fundamental picture of FDI would be quite positive.

With an increasing number of retail outlets there has been a steady rise in the number of retail employment opportunities, although most retailers complain about the lack of educated and trained staff. The Minimum Wages Act 1948 is applicable throughout India, with the appropriate central and state governments setting minimum wages. Most retailers conduct their own training programmes to bring the people on the shop floor up to speed in handling retail operations. For instance, Pantaloon runs a Gurukul workshop for the training of its sales employees. Some companies also provide substantial pay hikes, sign-on bonuses and employee stock options to retain employees.

Summary and key issues

Over the last fifty years the Indian market has emerged as one of the most significant markets in terms of increase in purchasing power and a gradual shift towards more aggressive consumerism. The lack of infrastructure, proper banking facilities on one hand, and low literacy rate, low disposable income on the other hand are typically the unique features of the Indian market. The gaps are now being bridged and the Indian market is on the threshold of a boom. The investment in organized retail with the changing consumption patterns are evidence of growth and development in the Indian market. In order to appeal to all classes of society, retail stores would have to identify with different lifestyles. Hence we may find more regional players and it would take an enormously long time before nation-wide successful retail chains emerge. This is the main reason as to why the successful retail chains in the country today operate at regional segments only and are not aiming at nation-wide presence, at least for the time being. To illustrate with examples, the RPG Group's Food World, Nilgiris, Margin Free, Giant and Subhiksha, all of which are more or less spread in the southern region; Sabka Bazaar has a presence only in and around Delhi; names such as Haiko and Radhakrishna Foodland are Mumbai-centric; while Adani is Ahmedabad-centric. India's overall retail sector is expected to rise to US$ 833 billion by 2013 and to US$ 1.3 trillion by 2018, at a compound annual growth rate (CAGR) of 10 per cent. Also, organized retail, which accounts for almost 5 per cent of the market, is expected to grow at a CAGR of 40 per cent from US$ 20 billion in 2007 to US$ 107 billion by 2013 (A. T. Kearney). India has emerged as the third most attractive market destination for apparel retailers with one of the largest numbers of retail outlets in the world. Thus a foreign investor targeting the huge Indian market should have an eye on the following:

- The birth of the retail industry in India is an emerging trend of the changing consumer patterns of the Indians, which has facilitated the foreign investors to penetrate the Indian market.
- Prior to the economic liberalization in the 1990s, the economy of India was a seller's market in most instances. The market conditions are quite different now with more competition and dealers being able to choose from among many suppliers in most industries.
- Rising per capita income, increased literacy and rapid urbanization have caused rapid growth and change in demand patterns. The rising aspiration levels and an increase in spending power has led to a change in the consumption pattern.
- India is beginning to see the first signs of a long-term consumption boom as a result of rising disposable incomes, higher life expectancy, rapid urbanization and changing lifestyles.
- The services sector GDP has recorded growth of 9.7 per cent even as agriculture and industry recorded a steep decline in growth.

- There are large differences in income, expenditure and savings patterns between rural and urban India. Urban households earn around 85 per cent more than rural ones, spend three-quarters more and, as a result, save nearly double that of rural households. This has led to a wide range of dispersion in the taste and preferences of the consumers.
- There are 205.9 million households in the country, of which 30 per cent (61.4 million) live in urban areas and the rest (144.5 million) in rural areas. Given that urban families are marginally smaller than rural ones, the share of India's urban population is slightly lower – at around 28.6 per cent. While the average family size in the country is five members, less than one per cent of Indian households are single-member ones and around 10 per cent have more than seven members. This highlights the family size and the demand emanating from these classes of consumers.
- The Indian audience for advertising are fragmented by so many official languages and television channels along with print publications that it requires careful media planning for advertising campaigns.
- At the all-India level, 17 per cent of all households have at least one graduate member: it is 30 per cent for urban areas and 11 per cent for rural areas, once again revealing the wide spectrum of the consumers.
- The three higher income categories have all seen an increase in proportion while all the three lower income categories have seen a decrease in proportion. There have been very significant shifts in consumer spending patterns.
- Increased income levels and more women willing to make use of their education by joining work has increasingly affected the shopping pattern, which is moving towards fulfilling the need of convenience shopping in the form of supermarket (now graduating to hyper format) home deliveries.
- The Indian consumption patterns are also slowly converging with global norms. The Indian consumer is now spending more on consumer durables, apparel, entertainment, vacations and lifestyle related activities.
- However, this new model has been affecting the relationships that the manufacturer enjoys with the traditional system, which is still the most dominant in the entire retail sector, which is characterized by low cost of establishment, transport and overheads.
- The retail sector in India is estimated at US$ 280 billion. Organized retail, estimated at US$ 14 billion, accounts for a meagre 5 per cent of the total market in India.
- The Indian government does not allow foreign direct investment in retailing in India, other than for single-brand retailing, in which foreign direct investment is allowed up to a maximum of 51 per cent, subject to government approval.

This makes the point very clear that the strategy among most existing retail chains of various formats is to completely saturate the markets where they are already established players and then move on to virtually untouched areas where the challenge of sourcing resources and extending their supply chain model to best suit the size and expanse of the market would be a challenging task. Industry topography in India is such that spreading presence across cities is a tough call. Thus organized retailing chains going national require significant investment and have to be intertwined with complex but proper supply chain and logistics issues to enhance the sector in the country.

References

Business World (India) various issues.

Frazier, G. L. and Summers, J. O. (1984) Interfirm Influence Strategies and their Application within Distribution Channels. *Journal of Marketing*, 48 (3): 43–55.

Hall, E. (1976) *Beyond Culture*. New York: Doubleday.

India Shopping Trends (2008) The Knowledge Company. *Technopak Indian Readership Survey*, 2008.

Internet and Mobile Association of India.

Kinsey B. H. (1987) *Agribusiness and Rural Enterprise*. New York: Croom Helm.

Market Skyline of India 2008–09.

Max–NCAER India (2008)Financial Protection Survey.

National Council of Applied Economic Research (2009) *Household Survey Telecom Regulatory Authority of India*.

Terpstra, V. and David, K. (1991) *The Cultural Environment of International Business*, 3rd edn. Cincinnati OH: South Western Publishing.

McKinsey & Co. (2007) *The Bird of Gold: The Rise of Indian Consumer Market*. McKinsey Global Institute.

Ernst & Young (2008) *The Dhoni Effect*. Ernst & Young.

Winning with Intelligent Supply Chains (2007) FICCI and Ernst & Young.

9 Issues and challenges of managing projects in India

A case study

Prasanta Dey

The success parameters for any project are in time completion, within specific budget and with requisite performance (technical requirement). The main barriers for their achievement are the changes in the project environment. The problem multiples with the size of the project as uncertainties in project outcome increase with size. For example large-scale construction projects are exposed to uncertain environment because of such factors as planning and design complexity, presence of various interest groups (project owner, owner's project group, consultants, contractors, vendors, etc.), resources (materials, equipment, funds etc.) availability, climatic environment, the economic and political environment and statutory regulations (Dey, 2001). Although risk and uncertainty affect all projects, size can be a major cause of risk. Other risk factors include the complexity of the project, the speed of its construction, the location of the project, and its degree of unfamiliarity. Projects are risky as they are planned with many assumptions.

Industrial projects are characterized by technical complexity, environmentally and socially sensitive, capital intensive, involvement of many stakeholders (client, consultants, contractors, suppliers, etc.). Therefore, achievement of projects is never assured. There are many instances of project failure due to time, cost and quality non-achievement. Projects are complex to implement with respect to lack of experience in relation to certain design conditions being exceeded (water depth, ground condition, pipeline size, etc.), the influence of external factors that are beyond human control, external causes which limit resource availability (of techniques and technology), various environment impacts, government laws and regulations, and changes in the economic and political environment. Cost and time overruns and the unsatisfactory quality of a project are the general sources of disappointment to the management of organizations. In such circumstances, a conventional approach to project management is not sufficient, as it does not enable the project management team to establish an adequate relationship among all phases of project, to forecast project achievement for building confidence of project team, to make decisions objectively with the help of available database, to provide adequate information for effective project management and to establish close co-operation among project team members.

Projects in India suffer from accurate prediction of demand that calls for augmentation of facilities soon after completion of a project, design optimization with the consideration all technical, economical as well as environmental factors throughout project life, poor performance of contractors, suppliers, lack of managing ability of client and consultants. The foreign investment projects in India are more complex as, along with the project variables as stated above, cultural difference plays major role. These projects also suffer from issues related to supply chain integration, relationship management, project planning, dealing with economical and political challenges, environmental regulation and social needs. Therefore, an effective project management method is needed to implement and operate foreign investment project in India. The main objective of this chapter is to analyse the project management maturity of an organization in the Indian oil industry and suggest improvement measures so as to depict issues and challenges of managing projects in India and means for achieving success. The second section elaborates the methodology. The third demonstrates causes of project failure as reported in the literature. The fourth section illustrates a few examples of issues and challenges of project management of the organization under study and provides root-cause analysis of non-achievement. The fifth section derives project management maturity of the organization under study. The sixth suggests improvement measures, the seventh discusses the dos and don'ts of managing projects in India and concludes the study.

Methodology

This analysis is based on critical review the literature on causes of project failure in general along with the risk factors for achieving project success in the Indian oil industry in order to provide empirical based support to the analysis. An organization in the Indian oil industry has been identified to highlight project management maturity. Further, a few examples have been captured from the organization under study on project failure using informal discussions with relevant people followed by root-cause analysis. Subsequently, a questionnaire survey quantitatively captures the perceptions of the project executives of the organization under study. Moreover a review of project documents and informal interviews with the project executives validates the findings from this exercise. Lastly, a benchmarking exercise determines the relative project management performance of the participating organizations, which identifies the improvement measures and their priorities for the organization under study. The following paragraph introduces the organization.

Born from the vision of achieving self-reliance in oil refining and marketing for the nation, the organization under study has gathered a luminous legacy of more than 100 years of accumulated experiences in all areas of petroleum refining from 1901. At present, it controls ten of India's twenty refineries, with total refining capacity of 60.2 million metric tonnes per annum (mmtpa) or 1.2 million barrels per day – the largest share among refining companies in India. It accounts for 33.8 per cent share of national refining capacity. It operates more than 10,000 km of pipeline network (69.60 mmtpa) across the country. It has one of the largest petroleum marketing and distribution networks in Asia, with over 34,000 marketing touch points. Its world-class R&D centre, established in 1972, has state-of-the art facilities and has delivered pioneering results in lubricants technology, refining process, pipeline transport, bio-fuels and fuel-efficient appliances.

Causes of project failure

Both academics and industry practitioners extensively research causes of project failure. They have derived many risk events that might cause negative impact on projects (Songer *et al.*, 1997; Tammala *et al.*, 1999; Dey and Ogunlana, 2001; Belout and Gauvreau, 2004; Dey *et al.*, 2009, Dey and Kinch, 2008). There are instances of project failure due to operational risks, such as technical complexities, contractors' and suppliers' incapability, government red tape, etc., which remain unidentified till they occur. Dey *et al.* (1994) and Dey (2001) reported cost and time overrun respectively due to implementation issues of cross-country oil pipelines in India. Ogunlana *et al.* (1996) reported cost overrun in high-rise building projects in Thailand due to contractors' failure. Social and environmental issues caused prolonged postponement of Chad–Cameroon oil pipelines (Ndumbe, 2002). Several projects in the Vietnam oil industry were delayed due to government approval (Thuyet *et al.*, 2007). A thorough review of such researches reveals a few generic risk events. These are valid for the Indian context as well as foreign companies investing in India. Table 9.1 shows risk events across phases (planning, implementation and evaluation) and risk categories (project management processes, organizational transformation and technology management).

Occurrence of any one of the above events may cause failure of projects to achieve time, cost and quality targets. The following examples show causes of project failure in the Indian oil industry.

Examples of issues and challenges of project management in an organization in the Indian oil industry

The following incidents demonstrate the project management problems experienced by the oil pipeline operators of the organization under study while managing oil refinery and related construction projects.

In 1995 a 60 km long pipeline (diameter 12 in.) was planned for replacing the transportation mode of crude oil and petroleum products via vessels in the eastern part of India. The project duration was eighteen months. The project consisted of laying pipe across the River Ganges (river width 2 km at the point of crossing) along with other work packages (laying main-line pipes, station construction, cathodic protection, and telecommunication). The river crossing work package was planned to be executed by a turnkey contractor to be selected

Table 9.1 Risk events in project management

Project phases	Risk categories		
	Project management processes	Organizational transformation	Technology management
Planning	Inaccurate business case	Lack of management/executive commitments and leadership	Inappropriate technology selection
	Unclear objectives	Lack of synergy between technology strategy and organizational competitive strategy	Sub-optimal design
	Weak implementation team	Unclear change strategy	Lack of communication with end users
	Inappropriate supplier, contractor and consultant selection		Inadequate training plan for users
Implementation	Inappropriate management of scope	Inappropriate change management	Business process re-engineering incompetence for use of new technology
	Lack of communication between implementation team, designers, supplier, contractor and consultant	Inappropriate management of culture and structure	Inappropriate system integration
	Poor contract management		Inaccurate performance data
	Not meeting statutory requirements (e.g. environment and safety, etc.)		Inappropriate user training
Hand-over, evaluation and operations	Inappropriate contract close-out	Inadequate organizational readiness	Inappropriate system testing and commissioning
	Inappropriate disbanding of team	Resistance to change	Lack of clarity on inspection and maintenance
	Lack of knowledge management	Lack of user training	Inaccurate performance measurement and management framework

through the global tendering method. As the owner had previous experience of laying pipe across river/canal (width maximum 1 km) using horizontal direction drilling through turnkey contractors, no study was made either during feasibility analysis nor during planning phase to check whether laying pipe across a river of 2 km is technically feasible or not through some experienced turnkey contractors. From previous experience, the bid document was prepared for engaging a turnkey contractor for laying pipe across the river and floated for receiving offers globally. However, no offer was received within the due dates and subsequent checking up with the prospective contractors revealed that they didn't have experience in laying pipe across a river of width 2 km. The case was referred to Bechtel, Houston (global consultant), for identifying a suitable contractor for the project. They reported that there were only two contractors having experience of laying pipe across a river of 1.8 km width. They recommended selecting one of them and checking up with them the applicability of using their technology for laying pipe across 2 km-wide river. However, they cautioned that the owner had to take the risk of failure. Alternatively, they suggested constructing a bridge across the river and laying pipe along the piers of the bridge. This option was not suitable to the owner, as constructing the bridge across the river does not come under scope of their business, which will cause huge extra expenditure. The owner decided to abandon the project in its current form and decided to look into the alternative techno-economic feasible solutions. The project had been commissioned in 1999 with laying branch pipeline from an existing pipeline by suitably augmenting the capacity of the existing pipeline through river crossing at the upstream where the river width is within the limit of available experienced contractors for laying pipe across river.

This clearly shows pitfalls of project management practices of the organization understudy. The technical feasibility analysis was poor as implementation methodology selection and procurement plans were not developed through a thorough analysis. They were mainly experience-based. Project management practices are more reactive than proactive as a crisis management approach was adopted in order to resolve the issues.

Another pipeline in north-west part of India had been commissioned in 1996 with huge cost escalation (more than 125 per cent) from the original estimate due to devaluation of Indian currency during the project duration, changing contract type (unit contract to turnkey contract), distance management with main international turnkey contractor, and many design alterations mid-way. Although the project was completed on schedule, the dispute between owner and the main contractor in connection with extra claims reached such an extent that they went for arbitration. The hearings are reported to be still continuing. This shows the incapability of managing scope of this project along with managing relationship with the contractors.

An oil refinery project in central of India was commissioned in 2002 with substantial time overrun because of delayed delivery of a few vertical turbine pumps by a supplier in the Indian public sector. The bid for supplying the pumping units was awarded to them on competitive basis with the consideration of past performance including delivery schedule. Although the financial performance of the company had been deteriorating over the past few years, this was ignored while evaluating their offer. During the manufacturing of the referred order the management of the supplier decided to reduce the production capacity so as to minimize the loss. This caused disruption of delivery schedule of all of their orders, including the vertical turbine pumps under consideration. However, the project owner could not anticipate the delayed delivery until the due date reached, as they didn't establish many follow-ups with the supplier. Later they improved the follow-up with the supplier and got the delivery of the pumping units after five months of scheduled delivery. These caused overall delay in completing the project by more than a year.

This shows that procurement management is one of the important issues of managing projects in India. The organization under study lacks procurement planning for all project materials and implementation activities. A strong synergy between design and detailed engineering and procurement planning needs to be adopted in order to strengthen project management practices.

In 2007 an oil refinery (7.5 mmtpa) at the eastern part of India was commissioned with offshore crude oil-receiving facility in the Bay of Bengal using single buoy mooring (SBM). The project was delayed by two and a half years mainly because of not being able to complete the implementation of SBM on time. This had a cascading effect on other work packages such as laying of offshore pipeline and related hydro-testing. The work package of implementing SBM was initially entrusted to an Iranian turnkey contractor on the basis of competitive bidding. The Iranian contractor couldn't complete this work package within the stipulated time period, and additionally there were many quality issues. Their contract was terminated before completion by the client after many negotiation meetings failed. Subsequently the SBM was commissioned by another turnkey contractor with substantial cost overrun. Moreover, the offshore pipeline observed many failures during its operations, which affected refinery operations substantially. This demonstrates lack project planning ability, which includes technical feasibility analysis and risk analysis. More proactive approach is needed in order to management project effectively in Indian industry. All the above examples show clear evidence of the lack of appropriate project management practices of the organization under study.

The root causes of project non-achievement

The root causes for project failure at the organization was analysed with the involvement of a few relevant project executives through informal discussions. Discussions with them revealed that project non-achievement in the Indian oil industry is due to mainly two reasons – sub-optimal design and poor project management. Inappropriate site selection, technology selection and implementation methodology selection are attributed for sub-optimal design. Improper project planning (scoping, scheduling, budgeting and specification), inefficient project organization, and ineffective supply chain management are the causes of poor project management. The root causes of project failure have been depicted in Figure 9.1.

Project management maturity of the organization

Project management maturity of the organization under study was carried out using the protocol shown in Figure 9.2. The project management maturity self-assessment questionnaire (Grant and Pennypacker, 2006) utilized in stage one. The questionnaire is based on the Project Management Institute's nine project management knowledge areas (PMI, 2004). The purpose of this study is to analyse the project management maturity of the organization under study and to provide recommendations in order to achieve 'world-class capital project delivery'. The paragraphs below depict the following:

- Feedback on the project management maturity questionnaire from stage 1.
- Feedback on the follow-up interviews and documentary analysis conducted in stage 2.
- New practices and knowledge transfer opportunities identified by stage 3.

Stage 1: quantitative analysis

The self-assessment questionnaire contains nine subject areas and an 'overview', with each subject area containing multiple questions. Each question is rated from level 1 (lowest rating) through to level 5 (highest rating). The nine subject areas consisted of project integration management, project scope management, project time management, project cost management, project quality management, project human resource management, project communications management, project risk management and project procurement management. Six senior staff were invited to participate in the self-assessment questionnaire from all functions of the business involved in capital project

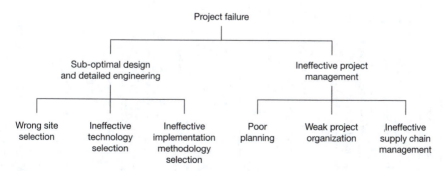

Figure 9.1 Root cause analysis of project failure in the Indian oil industry.

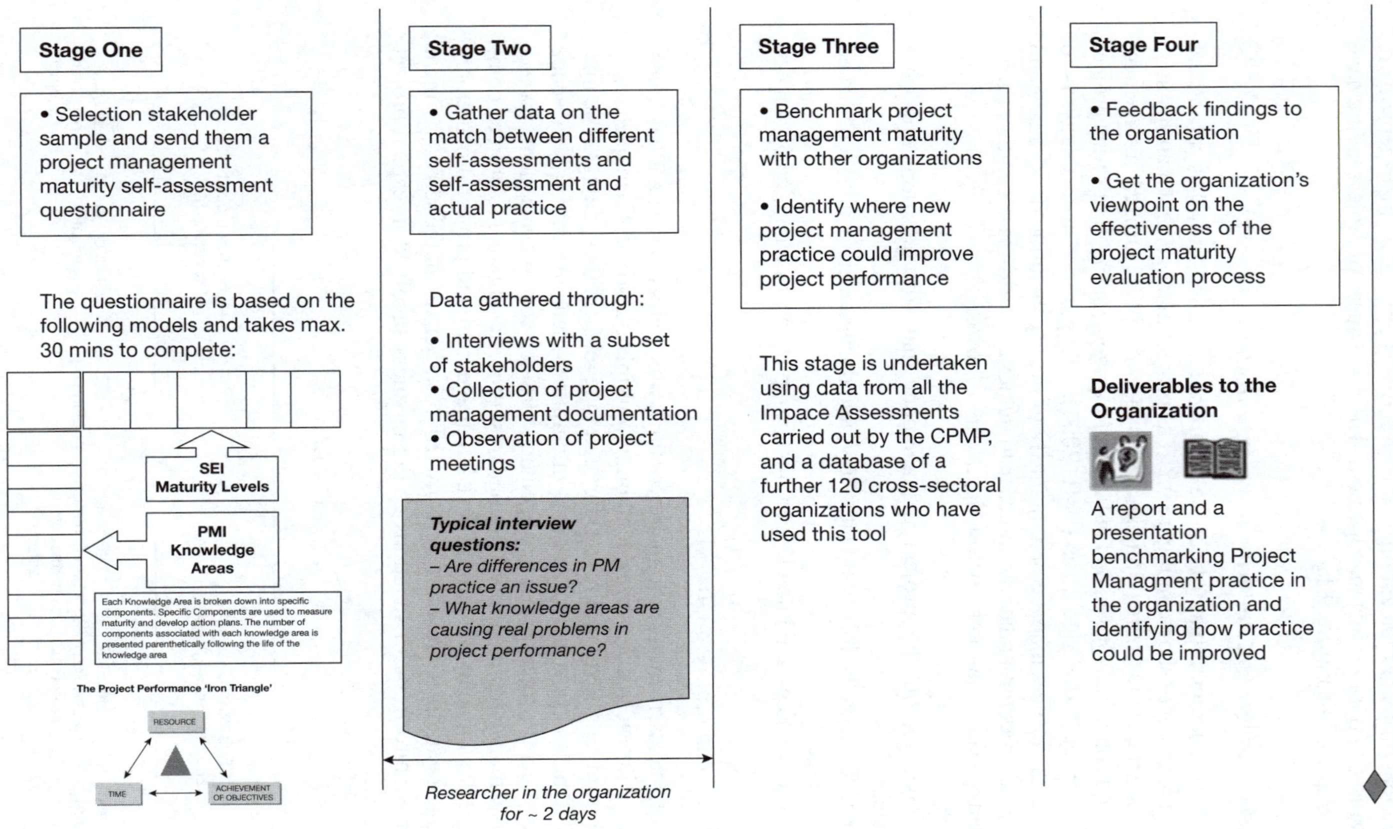

Stage One

- Selection stakeholder sample and send them a project management maturity self-assessment questionnaire

The questionnaire is based on the following models and takes max. 30 mins to complete:

SEI Maturity Levels

PMI Knowledge Areas

Each Knowledge Area is broken down into specific components. Specific Components are used to measure maturity and develop action plans. The number of components associated with each knowledge area is presented parenthetically following the life of the knowledge area

The Project Performance 'Iron Triangle'

RESOURCE

ACHIEVEMENT OF OBJECTIVES

TIME

Stage Two

- Gather data on the match between different self-assessments and self-assessment and actual practice

Data gathered through:

- Interviews with a subset of stakeholders
- Collection of project management documentation
- Observation of project meetings

Typical interview questions:
– Are differences in PM practice an issue?
– What knowledge areas are causing real problems in project performance?

Researcher in the organization for ~ 2 days

Stage Three

- Benchmark project management maturity with other organizations
- Identify where new project management practice could improve project performance

This stage is undertaken using data from all the Impace Assessments carried out by the CPMP, and a database of a further 120 cross-sectoral organizations who have used this tool

Stage Four

- Feedback findings to the organisation
- Get the organization's viewpoint on the effectiveness of the project maturity evaluation process

Deliverables to the Organization

A report and a presentation benchmarking Project Managment practice in the organization and identifying how practice could be improved

Figure 9.2 Project management maturity assessment protocol for the organization under study.

Source: Grant and Pennypacker (2006)

delivery. This was a sufficiently representative cross-section of the organization's business. The average maturity levels against each knowledge area are shown in Table 9.2. The table reveals that the organization under study has gross average maturity very close to 2. Project quality management and project procurement are relatively strong areas, whereas project cost management and project risk management are the weakest areas. Overall the organization lacks in managing project risks, controlling scope, time and cost, and organization planning and team development.

Stage 2: interview outcomes

Two project executives were interviewed (semi-structured) together to understand project management maturity of the organization. The discussion was limited within the nine knowledge areas of project management body of knowledge. Along with the discussion, various project management documents were reviewed. There was no major disagreement on organization's project management practices/maturity as revealed in the questionnaire survey. Both of them agreed on the following points with respect to each knowledge area.

- *Integration management.* Although the organization under study has ISO 9000 certification, project management practices are experience based. There are project plans (business case, activity network, budget, specification, design and drawings, etc.), but there are no customized documented

Table 9.2 Project-management maturity level of the organization under study

Project management knowledge areas	Average maturity level	Prioritized problem areas
Integration	2.13	Absence of customized project management processes, change control
Scope	2.06	Change control
Time	1.97	Schedule control
Cost	1.53	Cost control
Quality	2.50	Suppliers' and contractors' quality improvement
Human resources	2.00	Organization planning and team development
Communications	1.88	Performance reporting and issues tracking and management
Risk	1.63	All sub-areas need attention
Procurement	2.29	Stakeholders selection on the basis of quality

project management processes for each strategic project. Project planning and implementation are managed through individual project management skill using meetings and other communication methods. Project changes are not formally documented if these do not have time and cost implications. Project changes that have time and cost implications are hierarchically approved through the organization's governance. There is project management office (PMO), which is manned by experienced persons with functional (mechanical, electrical, civil, telecommunication, human resource management, finance and information) expertise. Each project forms a matrix organization to manage projects. Formal contract closings are done for all the projects. However, there is no formal project evaluation report covering lessons learned. *Key message.* Develop a project management office and establish a standardized project management practices across various phases of project. Customize the standard project management practices as per requirement.

- *Scope management.* Project scope is developed from the business case with the involvement of the concerned stakeholders. There is no protocol for project scope change control. Project review meetings address the issues of scope management. Anything beyond the control of the project manager goes to organizational hierarchy to address. There is no formal procedure. *Key message.* There should be a scope management plan in place, which will enable the project management team to make decision on scope change quickly.

- *Time management.* Project activities are evolved from project scope (work breakdown structure). Activity duration estimation is deterministic and mainly based on planners' past experience. Suppliers and contractors are also involved in many cases for providing valued information on activity durations. Therefore, development of accurate project schedule is an issue. Activity network is developed using MS Project. However, the major challenge in time management is schedule control. *Key message.* A realistic schedule development for every project activity is the key. Schedule implication of any scope change decision should be appropriately evaluated.

- *Cost management.* The business case for a specific project indicates the resource requirements, and forms the basis for cost estimate. There is no cost database. Both past data and supplier budgetary quotations help develop project cost estimate. The cost estimates are not linked with activity network in MS Project. Project budget is controlled by the finance department and produce report on a regular basis. There is no earned value management practice in the organization. Cost control is one of the major issues in the organization's project management. Both time and cost management are directly related to scope management. An integrated approach to change management is absent in the current project management practice. *Key message.* Appropriate contingency planning is vital for the project. Cost and schedule control along with scope management helps achieve success.

- *Quality management.* Specification for every project is incorporated in the business case. Depending on the type of project, detailed specifications are developed by the concerned stakeholders (e.g. suppliers, designers, contractors, etc.) and approved by the project manager or appropriate competent authority in the organizational hierarchy. Inspections are carried out as planned either on-site or supplier premises. However, there is no standardized process for managing project quality. Involving quality suppliers and contractors is the major issue as contemporary approach to supplier and contractor selection is governed by least-cost criteria. *Key message.* Developing quality plan for each project activity and material, selection of quality suppliers and contractors, and monitoring of quality/specifications of every project activity help achieve desired project quality and ultimate customer satisfaction.

- *Human resource management.* There is no formal process for project organizational planning, forming responsibility matrix and team development activities. However, project specific organization breakdown structure is developed. There is no formal project personnel selection and work package authorization process in place. Although the project personnel are technically/functionally qualified, they may not have project management experience. In many projects, basic project management skill gaps are quite visible. *Key message.* Identifying appropriate project manager and right personnel and fostering project management culture across the project supply chain would be critical for the organizational leadership in order to achieve success.

- *Communication management.* Although there are a few report formats mainly to monitor and control project progress, the communication across project stakeholders is mostly informal. Although information technology-based communication systems (MS Project, MS Office, e-mail, etc.) exist, there is no formal protocol for inter- and intra-organization communication. The minutes of project review meeting work as authentic documents for project control. *Key message.* Identifying appropriate project stakeholders, understanding their requirements from the project and making the right information available in right time will not only help making right decision on time, but also keep the project affected people aware on progress.

- *Risk management.* Risk management culture exists within the organization. In fact many projects are initiated to mitigate business and technical risks. However, there is no formal risk management practice (e.g. logging risks using a risk register, planning, monitoring and controlling risks) in managing projects. However, informal risk identification and analysis are carried out and suitable mitigating measures are suggested mainly using past experience. A project management approach is more reactive than proactive. *Key message.* As a foreign investment project is always risky, the overall project plan must consider risks that are involved in the project. Identifying them at the early stage of the project, analysing their impact and developing responses to mitigate are the key to success of many foreign projects.

- *Procurement management.* Project procurement planning is undertaken in the early stage of the project along with activity planning. Normal tendering processes are adopted to engage suppliers and contractors. Major suppliers and contractors are selected on the basis of their technical attributes along with price offer. There is no long-term relationship among the project stakeholders (suppliers and contractors). *Key message.* Long-term partnership, relationship development, selecting suppliers/contractors on the basis of total cost ownership, will certainly be an added advantage in managing projects in India.

It has been observed from the stakeholder interviews that the overall project management maturity of the organization under study is medium to low. Although projects are planned/scheduled using leading project management software, monitored and controlled through number of project review meetings throughout the project phase, they lack effective project management approaches. The interviewees agreed that standardized project management processes with project specific customization will help practice better project management throughout the organization.

Stage 3: benchmarking

Project management practices of the organization understudy was benchmarked against six other organizations in various industries (e.g. manufacturing, services, retail, etc.) across the world and the results of the project maturity self-assessments of all the participating organizations are summarized in Figure 9.3. Figure 9.3 shows the level of maturity of project management practices of the organization under study in the nine project management knowledge areas as compared with other participating organizations. This demonstrates that the concerned organization has a low level of maturity in all nine areas compared with the participating organization. There is room for improvement across the project management knowledge areas.

Improvement measures

On the basis of the PMM analysis (self-assessment questionnaire survey, focused interview and benchmarking) the following recommendations are made. Table 9.3 shows the suggested improvement measures along with the relevant project management references for the best practices.

Discussion and key issues

This study contributes a method to analyse project management maturity of any organization using triangulation approach – case studies to capture real-

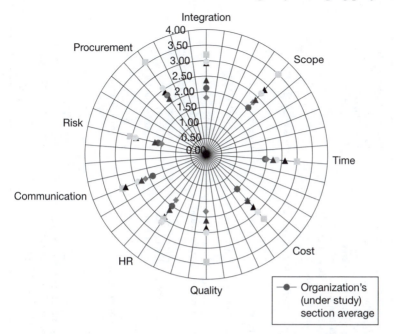

Figure 9.3 Comparative project management maturity levels in India

life project experiences, questionnaire survey to statistically observe project management maturity, and personal interview and project document reviews to validate the maturity. The proposed method has five steps. They are as follows:

- Developing examples of issues and challenges of project management practices of the organization and analysing their root causes.
- Pursuing questionnaire survey among the key executives of the organization under study, which is followed by statistical computation of their responses.
- Interviewing a few selected senior project executives informally in order to capture their perceptions on project management maturity and to validate the outcomes of the earlier step.
- Benchmarking project management maturity of the organization with other organizations.
- Suggesting improvement measures.

The proposed method helps measure absolute project management perform-ance of any organization and as well as benchmark performance with other organizations. The study further reveals that the organization under study suffers from low project management maturity. The project management practices

Table 9.3 Recommendations for improving project management practice

Knowledge areas theories	Problem areas	Recommendations	Relevant best practices
Project integration management	Absence of customized project management processes, Change control	Fostering project management culture across the organization, developing project governance structure for each project, continuous improvement of standard project management processes, customizing project management processes for each strategic project, organizing relevant project management training, managing project portfolio across the organization	Dai and Wells (2004) Dey (1999) Dey (2006) Ibbs *et al.* (2001)
Project scope management	Change control	Practising customized project management through appropriate training	Ibbs *et al.* (2001)
Project time management	Schedule control	Practicing customized project management through appropriate training	Ibbs *et al.* (2001)
Project cost management	Cost control	Practising customized project management through appropriate training	Ibbs *et al.* (2001)
Project quality management	Standardized processes for project quality management is absent	Developing a robust quality management plan for each project by linking material specifications and activity specifications	Arditi and Gunaydin, (1997) Winch *et al.* (1998)
Project human resource management	Organization planning and team development	Developing project governance structure for each project with clear roles and responsibility of each stakeholder, objective selection of project people and assigning responsibilities	Belout and Gauvreau (2004) Bubshail and Farooq (1999) Loo, R. (2000)
Project communications management	Performance reporting and issues tracking and management	Developing an integrated planning, monitoring and controlling framework with clear links with the concerned stakeholders	Charoemgam *et al.* (2004)
Project risk management	All sub-areas need attention	Developing an integrated project risk management framework, training the project personnel to practise it	Dey (2002) Raz and Michael (2001) Vrijhoef and Koskela (2000)
Project procurement management	Supplier and contractor relationship management	Developing procurement portfolio for each project, establishing desired relationship with all the stakeholders	Dey *et al.* (2008)

suffer from both design optimization and effective project management. The study argues that the organization under study needs improvement in project site selection, technology selection, implementation methodology selection, project planning, organizing and managing project supply chain.

The study recommends that the organization under study could improve project management by fostering project management culture across the organization, developing project governance structure for each project, continuous improvement of standard project management processes, customizing project management processes for each strategic project, organizing relevant project management training, and managing project portfolio across the organization. Additionally, practising customized project management through appropriate training, developing a robust quality management plan for each project by linking material specifications and activity specifications, developing project governance structure for each project with clear roles and responsibility of each stakeholder, objective selection of project people and assigning responsibilities, developing an integrated planning, monitoring and controlling framework with clear links with the concerned stakeholders, developing an integrated project risk management framework, training the project personnel to practise it and developing procurement portfolio for each project, and establishing desired relationship with all the stakeholders.

Through the case study this research demonstrates issues and challenges of managing projects in India. The author suggests that organizations planning major projects in India must analyse their project management maturity using the proposed project management maturity model and improve their performance. Additionally, they must emphasize the following in order to have success in implementing and operating major projects in India.

- Detailed project feasibility analysis covering market, technical, financial, environmental and social needs to be carried out before investment decision. Moreover, the best project alternatives in terms of technology, market, etc., is to be analysed using multiple criteria such as complexity, flexibility, adaptability, return on investment, cost, environment friendliness and employability.
- Risk analysis should be carried out by identifying risk factors, analysing their effect (probability and impact) and developing risk responses in order to justify the investment.
- Detailed project planning covering scope, schedule, budget, quality, human resources, procurement, communication, and risk should be done before implementation. Project organizing and procurement must be emphasized in overall planning. Appropriate leadership, project governance and communication across the project stakeholders need proper attention.
- Relationship management across the supply chain (upstream suppliers and downstream customers) could be the key to success not only during the implementation stage of the project but also in operations.

- Keeping the project plan flexible would be an added advantage to adopt the necessary changes in projects as they proceed. There should be a scope management plan in place.
- Integrating the decisions in strategic, tactical and operational levels in both project implementation and operation stages could help achieve desired goals of projects.
- Dynamic evaluation of projects is the absolute necessity to track the project progress and make quicker decisions in order to remain on time and within budget.

References

Akintoye, A. S. and MacLeod, M. J. (1997) Risk Analysis and Management in Construction, *International Journal of Project Management*, 15 (1): 31 – 38.

Arditi, D. and Gunaydin, H. M. (1997) Total Quality Management in the Construction Process, *International Journal of Project Management*, 15 (4): 235–43.

Ashley, D. B. and Bonner, J. J. (1987) Political Risks in International Construction, *Journal of Construction Engineering and Management*, 113 (3): 447–67.

Belout, A. and Gauvreau, C. (2004) Factors Influencing Project Success: The Impact of Human Resource Management, *International Journal of Project Management*, 22 (1): 1–11.

Bubshail, A. A. and Farooq, G. (1999) Team Building and Project Success, *Cost Engineering*, 41 (7): 34–8.

Charoenngam, C., Ogunlana, S.O., Ning-Fu, K. and Dey, P. K. (2004) Reengineering Construction Communication in Distance Management Framework, *Business Process Management Journal*, 10 (6): 645–672.

Dai, C. X. and Wells, W. G. (2004) An Exploration of Project Management Office Features and their Relationship to Project Performance, *International Journal of Project Management*, 22 (7): 523–32.

Dey, P. K. (1999) Process Re-engineering for Effective Implementation of Projects, *International Journal of Project Management*, 17 (3): 147–59.

—— (2001) Decision Support System for Risk Management: A Case Study, *Management Decision*, 39 (8): 634–48.

—— (2002) Project Risk Management: A Combined Analytic Hierarchy Process and Decision Tree Analysis Approach, *Cost Engineering*, 44 (3): 13–26.

—— (2006) Integrated Approach to Project Selection using Multiple Attribute Decision-making Technique, *International Journal of Production Economics*, 103: 90–103.

Dey, P. K. and Kinch, J. (2008) Managing Risk in Information Technology Projects, *International Journal of Risk Assessment and Management*, 9 (3): 311–29.

Dey, P. K. and Ogunlana, S. O. (2001) Project Time Risk Analysis through Simulation, *Cost Engineering*, 43 (7): 24–32.

Dey, P. K., Tabucanon, M. T. and Ogunlana, S. O. (1994) Planning for Project Control through Risk Analysis; Case of Petroleum Pipeline-laying Project, *International Journal of Project Management*, 12 (1): 23–33.

Dey, P. K., Charoenngam, C., Ogunlana, S. O. and Kajornkiat, D. (2009) Multi-party Risk Management helps manage Cement Plant Construction, *International Journal of Service Technology Management*, 11 (4): 411–35.

Dey, P. K., Ho, W., Charoenngam, C. and Deewong, W. (2008) Relationship Characteristics within the Supply Chain of Small and Medium-sized Construction Enterprises in Thailand. *International Journal of Manufacturing Technology and Management*, 15 (1): 102–18.

Grant, R. R. and Pennypacker, J. S. (2006) Project Management Maturity: an Assessment of Project Management Capabilities across and between Selected Industries, *IEEE Transactions on Engineering Management*, 53 (1): 59–68.

Ibbs, C. W., Wong, C. K. and Kwak, Y. H. (2001) Project Change Management System, *Journal of Management in Engineering*, 17 (3): 159–65.

Loo, R. (2000) Journaling: a Learning Tool for Project Management Training and Team Building, *Project Management Journal*, 33 (4): 61–6.

Ndumbe, J. A. (2002) The Chad–Cameroon Oil Pipeline: Hope for Poverty Reduction. *Mediterranean Quarterly*, 13 (4): 74–87.

Ogunlana, S. O., Promkuntong, H. and Jearkjirn, V. (1996) Construction Delays in a Fast- growing Economy: Comparing Thailand with other Economies, *International Journal of Project Management*, 14 (1): 37–45.

PMI (2004) *A Guide to Project Management Body of Knowledge*, 2nd edn. Upper Darby PA: Project Management Institute.

Raz, T. and Michael, E. (2001) Use and Benefits of Tools for Project Risk Management, *International Journal of Project Management*, 19 (1): 9–17.

Songer, A. D., Diekmann, J. E. and Pecsok, R. (1997) Risk Analysis for Revenue-dependent Infrastructure Project, *Construction Management and Economics*, 31: 377–82.

Thuyet, N. V., Ogunlana, S. O. and Dey, P. K. (2007) Risk Management in Oil and Gas Construction Projects in Vietnam, *International Journal of Energy Sector Management*, 1 (2): 175–94.

Tammala, V., Rao, M. and Leung, Y. H. (1999) Applying a Risk Management Process (RMP) to manage Cost Risk for an EHV Transmission Line Project, *International Journal of Project Management*, 17 (4): 223–35.

Vrijhoef, R. and Koskela, L. (2000) The Four Roles of Supply Chain Management in Construction, *European Journal of Purchasing and Supply Management*, 6 (3–4): 169–78.

Winch G., Usmani, A. and Edkins, A. (1998) Towards Total Project Quality: a Gap Analysis Approach, *Construction Management and Economics*, 16 (2): 193–207.

10 Management of human resources

Pawan S. Budhwar and Arup Varma

The aims of this chapter are fourfold: first, to report on the evolution of the human resource (HR) function in the Indian context; second, to highlight the key factors determining HRM policies and practices in firms operating in India; third, to highlight the nature of HRM systems prevalent in foreign firms operating in India; and lastly, to provide a list of key issues, based on our analysis, which should prove helpful for policy makers.

Developments in Indian HRM

The Indian HR function has a long history. A number of key developments over the past century or so have been responsible for its growth and development. Indeed, the origins of the personnel function in India can be traced back to the 1920s when several groups expressed concern for the welfare of factory labour. The Trade Union Act of 1926 gave formal recognition to workers' unions. The Royal Commission of Labour 1931 recommended the appointment of labour welfare officers and the Factories Act of 1948 laid down the duties and qualifications of labour welfare officers. Further, the Indian judiciary played an important role in expounding the correct scope of the protection envisaged to the working class by the legislation that was enacted in several spheres of industrial relations (IR) as per the spirit of the Constitution. Consequent to the passage of a number of labour and industrial relations laws, personnel managers began performing industrial relations as a significant role. The IR role of personnel managers formed such an important part of their work that they came to be known as children of the Industrial Disputes Act 1947 (IDA). All these developments formed the foundation of the personnel function in India (Balasubramanian, 1994, 1995; Saini and Budhwar, 2007; Budhwar, 2009). These seem to parallel the initial development of the British personnel function. For example, as early as the 1920s the Indian business house, the Tata group, made provision for their workers that were similar to those provided by Cadbury in Britain (see Budhwar, 2009).

A few years after India's independence, two professional bodies emerged – the Indian Institute of Personnel Management (IIPM), a counterpart of the Institute of Personnel Management in the United Kingdom, was formed at

Calcutta, and the National Institute of Labour Management (NILM) at Bombay. In the 1960s the personnel function began to expand beyond the welfare aspect, with three areas, Labour Welfare, Industrial Relations and Personnel Administration, developing as the constituent roles for the emerging profession (Venkata Ratnam and Srivastava, 1991). In the 1970s the thrust of the personnel function shifted towards greater organisational 'efficiency', and by 1980s it began to use and focus on terms and issues such as HRM and human resource development (HRD). The two professional bodies (i.e. IIPM and NILM) merged in 1980 to form the National Institute of Personnel Management (NIPM), based in Bombay. As we can see, the personnel function in India has continued to evolve over the years (Sparrow and Budhwar, 1997; Saini and Budhwar, 2007). Table 10.1 provides a summary of the evolution of the personnel function in India.

In the mid to late 1990s the liberalisation of economic policy led to increased competition for Indian firms – from foreign firms. As a result, Indian firms came under great pressure to change from indigenous, costly and probably less effective technology to a high, more effective and costly technology (Sparrow and Budhwar, 1997; Venkata Ratnam, 1995). This also led to the need to upgrade the infrastructure, address bureaucracy at operating level and revisit organisational culture. The policies of the time implied (to some extent they still do) a switch from labour-intensive to more capital-intensive methods of production, and therefore required organisations to remove surplus labour and generate new sustainable employment. The challenge arose regarding how to increase productivity, as well as how to reduce costs and overmanning whilst generating employment, improve quality, and reduce voluntary and involuntary absenteeism (see Budhwar, 2009). Such challenges demanded changes in the Indian personnel function.

As a result, from early 1990s onwards, HRD in India became the most dominant topic in the broad area of personnel function (see Rao *et al.*, 1994; Saini and Budhwar, 2007). The origins of the Indian approach to HRD can be traced back to the 1970s when it was articulated by Pareek and Rao (see Silveria, 1988), however, the pressure created by the economic reforms of the early 1990s on the Indian personnel function to modernise and become efficient, brought the field into prominence. Accordingly, both public and private-sector organisations began to create, as well as adopt, HRD and organisational development (OD) programmes. The formation of the HRD Network, which today has one of the largest memberships of academics and HRM and other managers, acknowledging the importance of employee development and the need to sharpen the abilities of HR professionals. During this period, the HR profession developed in leaps and bounds in both a positive and negative sense. Indeed, several organisations resorted to indiscriminate appointment of HRD managers. This period also saw an elevation in the status of personnel managers to the board level; though only in a few professionally managed organisations. There was also a massive upsurge in relabelling the title of personnel mangers to HRD managers and personnel departments as HRD

Table 10.1 The evolution of the Indian HR function

Period	Development status	Outlook	Emphasis	Status
1920s–30s	Emerging	Pragmatism of capitalists	Statutory, welfare, paternalism	Clerical
1940s–60s	Establishing	Technical legalistic	Introduction of techniques	Administrative
1970s–80s	Impressing with sophistication	Professional, legalistic, impersonal	Regulatory conformance, imposition of standards on other functions	Managerial
1990s	Promising	Philosophical	Human development, productivity through people	Executive
2000–	Rationalisation and formalisation	Strategic and change agent	Organisational performance	Strategic and change partner

Source: Venkata Ratnam and Srivastava (1991); Budhwar (2009).

department. Interestingly, however, some employers also perceived disillusionment with their decision as they felt that the investment in HRD did not deliver any tangible results. Thus they started downsizing or even abolishing their HRD departments. It also gave rise to the need for the measurement of HR performance – and thus the concept of 'HR audit' came into practice. As a result of this, several employers like Aditya Birla asked all their companies to get their HR systems audited by consultants. Indeed, the concept of the HRD scorecard is being used as a device to measure effectiveness of people-development activities (see Saini and Budhwar, 2007).

HRD then became the more often used term to denote personnel function than HRM in India in the late 1990s. It has been seen as a continuous process to ensure the planned development of employee competencies and capabilities, the motivation and exploitation of inner capabilities for organisational development purposes, and the pursuit of dynamism and effectiveness (see Rao *et al.*, 1994). It also emphasised the provision of tools and techniques to the line managers who encourage its philosophy. Some scholars (see Sparrow and Budhwar, 1997) have criticised it as being too prescriptive, unpragmatic and far removed from the reality of people management in Indian organisations.

The changes in response to the pressure created by economic reforms on the traditional Indian personnel/management system are now clearly noticeable in the way organisations are managed in India, especially in the modern sectors and the ones that are professionally managed. Nevertheless, the proportion of such organisations is in a minority. Since the traditional Indian HR system was developed over a very long time, understandably it will take some time to change. However, the change symptoms are quite prominent as HRM is playing a noticeable role in bringing about changes in Indian organisations and an increasing number of Indian organisations are creating a separate HRM/HRD department. There has also been a significant increase in the level of training and development of employees (Budhwar and Sparrow, 1997; Saini and Budhwar, 2007). Further, there are also indications of a movement towards performance related pay and promotions. Indeed, such developments have already matured in modern industrial sectors such as business process outsourcing (see Budhwar *et al.*, 2006). Similarly, in comparison to the public sector, the internal work cultures of private enterprises now place greater emphasis on internal locus of control, future orientation in planning, participation in decision making, effective motivation techniques and obligation towards others in the work context (Budhwar and Boyne, 2004). Overall, it would be appropriate to say that the HR function in India is in a phase of rapid transition. A collective effort is now required from both practitioners and researchers to support each other and share the on-going developments in the field with different audiences.

To summarise, it seems that HRM in India is defined as a holistic concept, which is more focused and proactive than personnel management (PM); it integrates and incorporates both PM and HRD, and deals with satisfying and developing employees. HRD on the other hand implies a long-term perspective for developing the potential and capabilities of HR for future organisational needs. PM is seen as more of a policing type of department as it is now a secondary function, also called transactional HRM. This aspect of HRM is concerned with the day-to-day activities of control, attendance, compliance with legislation, discipline aspects and IR. The majority of Indian managers believe that the future of the HRM function is good and its status is improving. Some managers, however, feel that the existing legislation can be restrictive in this regard. Perhaps rightly, they lament the functioning of the 'Exit' policy (a policy for voluntary retirements) as problematic due to the rigidities created by the IR laws (for more details see Saini and Budhwar, 2007).

On the HR research front, an analysis of the existing literature highlights that scholars have been pursuing research on a variety HR related topics in the Indian context. These include the evolution of the personnel function in India; role of unions and industrial relations in the new economic environment, factors determining HRM, HRM and firms' performance, HRM in multi-nationals, strategic HRM and organisational learning capability, employee relations, comparative HR in public and private sector organisations, emerging patterns of HRM in the business outsourcing sector, applicability of Western HR models in India, HRD and training and comparative HR between India and other countries. Also, a number of researchers have examined various aspects of organisational behaviour and organisational dynamics and influence of national culture of Indian HRM (for details see Budhwar, 2009). For policy makers it is important to have a good understanding regarding the main factors and variables that influence HRM in the Indian set-up. The next section highlights the same.

Determinants of HRM in India

Several scholars have highlighted the importance of studying HRM in a given context, as it is more meaningful and useful for both practitioners and researchers (see, e.g. Schuler *et al.*, 2002). An ideal way to better understand the context-specific nature of HRM systems is by examining and highlighting the impact of key factors and variables on HRM policies and practices at a given period of time and set-up (Budhwar and Sparrow, 2002a; Schuler *et al.*, 2002). In this section we present the main determinants of HRM in the Indian context. An understanding of the same should prove very useful for policy makers.

An analysis of the existing literature reveals the existence of both 'culture-bound' (such as national culture and national institutions) and 'culture-free' (such as age, size and nature of the firm) determinants of HRM (Budhwar and Debrah 2001; Budhwar and Sparrow 1998; 2002a). For the convenience of both researchers and practitioners these can be classified into three levels – the national factors (i.e. national culture, national institutions, business sectors and dynamic business environment), the contingent variables (such as age, size, nature, ownership, life cycle stage of organisation, presence of trade unions and HR strategies and interests of different stakeholders) and organisational strategies (such as the ones proposed by Miles and Snow, and Porter) and policies (related to primary HR functions, internal labour markets, levels of strategic integration and devolvement of HRM, and the nature of work). Policy makers need to have a good understanding of the various aspects and measures of such factors and variables in order to better understand how these impact their HRM functions. Budhwar and associates (e.g. Budhwar and Singh, 2009) have identified and developed a detailed list of such factors and variables along with empirical evidence regarding their applicability and suitability in better understanding the context-specific nature of Indian HRM – presented below is an overview of their typology.

National factors

The prominent processes or aspects of *national culture* include: the socialisation process through which managers are 'made'; the basic assumptions which shape managers' behaviour; their common values, norms of behaviour and customs; the influence of pressure groups unique to a country; and the unique ways of doing things and the management logic in a particular country which are reflective of a broader national business system. Given the regional/national focus of HRM, five *institutions* are worth considering regarding their influence on HRM in a given national context: national labour laws; trade unions; educational and vocational training set-up; role of professional bodies; and international business institutions. The aspects of a *dynamic business environment* identified as influencing HRM policies and practices in a cross-national context are: an increase in competition and pressures on productivity, quality or social costs of employment at both national and international level; the resulting growth of new business alliances or forms of corporate governance; automation of information systems and their impact on international business structures and co-ordination systems; change in composition of the work force; downsizing of organisations and transfer of work across a new international division of labour; and transfer of convergent best practice or creation of like-minded international cadre of managers. Finally, different aspects of *sector* which are known to influence HRM can include: common strategies, business logic and goals; sector-specific regulations and standards; specific requirement/ needs of supply chain management; need for sector-specific knowledge; informal or formal bench marking; cross-sector co-operative arrangements; common developments in business operations; and a sector-specific labour market or skill requirements (for details see Budhwar and Sparrow, 2002a, b). It is important to acknowledge that the above is by no means an exhaustive list, but is intended to serve as a starting point for such an analysis, and the resultant discussions.

Contingent variables

The existing research also highlights the influence of a number of contingent variables on HRM policies and practices in India. They are the artefacts through which the above-mentioned four national factors may easily be measured and operationalised. The main *contingent variables* shown to influence HRM policies and practices are size, age, nature, type of ownership, and life-cycle stage of the organisation; level of technology adopted; presence of a formal HRM department; existence of training units in the HR department; type of organisational strategy; union status; interests of influential stakeholders; structure of organisation and HR strategy.

Given the changing nature of the Indian HRM function, it seems clear that a combination of the above-mentioned factors and variables (and more) are significantly determining Indian HRM policies and practices. However, given the variations in the developments in Indian HRM (e.g. based on the ownership of firms – Indian versus foreign), the impact of different combinations of such factors and variables on HRM will continue to change (e.g. impact of unions in different sectors). It will be useful for policy makers to consider possible factors and variables (depending on their suitability) and then accordingly develop their HRM policies and practices. There is now reliable research evidence which highlights the practical implications of various national factors and organisational level variables on HRM (e.g. Budhwar and Sparrow, 1998; Budhwar, 2003). It is beyond the scope of this chapter to provide empirical evidence regarding how different factors and variable impact HRM systems in a given context. Given that national level factors tend to vary significantly for foreign investors and also they are known to play a significant role in determining relevant HRM practices for specific set-up. Below we illustrate how different national factors influence HRM in the India. This is based on empirical investigations conducted by Budhwar (2003) and Budhwar and Sparrow (2002b) conducted by help of a survey of 137 firms and 22 in-depth interviews with top HR managers in as many firms.

National culture and HRM

On average, Indian HR managers give high priority to the importance of cultural assumptions that shape the way employees perceive and think about the organisation, as well as common Indian values, norms of behaviour and customs and the way in which managers are socialised in India. Indian managers believe that social relations play an important role in managing human resources. Indeed, managers' actions are often dictated by these values and norms of behaviour. Indian managers also feel that pressure groups (such as unions) act as saviours of employees, dictate the terms and conditions of certain agreements, yet are often perceived as creating trouble for management.

To further put the above findings in the Indian cultural context, we now utilise Hofstede's (1991) five standardised dimensions (power distance, uncertainty avoidance, individualism–collectivism, masculinity–femininity and long-term–short-term orientation) as an illustration of how they impact Indian HRM. Similarly, other contributions on national culture can be utilised to reveal how it influences national HRM systems.

India scores high on the power distance dimension and accordingly Indian HR managers tend to rely on the use of power in superior–subordinate relationships, and thus, are not actively inclined towards consultative or participative styles. Indeed, such barriers are slowly being overcome in the new sectors like IT and BPOs (see Budhwar *et al.*, 2009) – though managers are often observed misusing their power, due to different pressures (such as political, caste, group and bureaucratic). They operate within a logic of 'power myopia' which has created a culture of psychophancy, inequality, apathy, triggered by a feudalistic outlook of employers and a strong backing of political parties by unions. A possible explanation for such behaviour can be traced to the long imperialist history of India (Thomas and Philip, 1994) and the traditional hierarchical social structure of India that has always emphasised respect for superiors – they can be elders, teachers or superiors at work, i.e. the nature of Hinduism evidenced by the caste and social systems (Sahay and Walsham, 1997).

The analysis of existing empirical evidence also reveal less importance given to the dimension of uncertainty avoidance indicating that, for Indians, uncertainty is inherent in life and they are well prepared to take each day as it comes. It is understandable to have such a behaviour in a country with a high rate of poverty, unemployment, corruption in government offices, political instability, casteism, low per capita income, prone to natural and man-made disasters and an increasing gap between rich and poor. Accordingly the personnel function places more emphasis on training and development and career development to reduce uncertainty at the work place. The element of uncertainty forces Indian managers to take calculated risks, which means that people value job security and stability. Clearly, this has implications for the recruitment function. It should be noted here that, in comparison with the private sector, the public sector in India offers more secure jobs.

On the third cultural element of individualism–collectivism, traditionally the Indian national culture shows a strong emphasis on collectivism (Hofstede, 1991; Shenoy, 1995), though our analysis reveals a mixed picture. There is an increased emphasis on individualism at the managerial level and collectivism at the shop-floor level. The emphasis on collectivism for the lower level of employees is mainly dictated by the strong trade unions. A strong interference of social relations, caste and religion dynamics at work place is still observable in Indian organisations (Sahay and Walsham, 1997; Sparrow and Budhwar, 1997).

As far as the dimension of masculinity–femininity is concerned, the results show that Indian male managers appear to exercise their superiority and assertiveness over their female employees by expressing their reluctance to recruit them irrespective of their performance during the recruitment process.

Such behaviour is based on the cultural roles of men and women in traditional Indian society, where women are expected to devote themselves to internal household affairs and men are required to work outside to provide the economic maintenance of their households (Sinha and Sinha, 1990). This social norm is now seriously challenged as more and more females are entering the workplace, especially in the new sectors of software, IT, R&D and BPOs (Budhwar *et al.*, 2005). Nevertheless, the masculine nature of the Indian society has clear implications for most HR functions such as job design, recruitment and promotions.

Traditionally, India has been a long term-oriented country (see Hofstede, 1991). However, in the ever increasing uncertain and competitive business environment, Indian HR managers feel that the question is that of immediate survival, hence it seems that there is now more emphasis on short-termism. Similar propositions are made by other researchers (see Sparrow and Budhwar, 1997). Accordingly, it is contributing to the development of performance-based systems and abolition of the lifelong employment and tenure-based compensation.

The above was an illustration of how national culture influences Indian HRM. It is worth acknowledging that, given the complexity of both the construct of national culture and Indian society, it is important to adopt a variety of dimensions of national culture while developing HRM policies and practices for the Indian context. For example, Budhwar and Sparrow (2002b) asked Indian HR managers to highlight which other dimensions of national culture they feel should be there for the Indian context to develop relevant HRM systems. Indian HR manager provided dimensions such as 'ascribed' versus 'achieved' status, 'pragmatism' versus 'fatalism' (taking a practical approach to doing things such as promotion based on performance versus leaving things to 'fate', such as saying 'If it is in my fate only then will I get promotion'), 'materialism' versus 'inner satisfaction' (doing things totally for monetary rewards versus doing things because they give internal satisfaction), 'honesty' versus 'corruption' (employees who are and believe in honest work versus employees involved in corrupt practices), and the impact of a nation's relatively short versus long history and identity. This shows the diversity of Indian national culture. Although it will not be sensible to classify all these constructs as dimensions of national culture, certainly they are worth considering while developing HRM policies practices.

National institutions and HRM

Regarding the influence of national institutions on HRM, Indian HR managers give a high priority to national labour laws, trade unions and educational and vocational training set-up, regarding their influence on HRM policies and practices. HR managers believe that Indian national labour law influences their HRM policies and practices the most because they limit the actions that can actually be implemented. Moreover, they are 'pro-labour' and compliance with them is important for maintaining good industrial relations and therefore the survival of organisations. Indian managers also feel that trade unions and educational vocational training set-up of India are important influences of their HRM policies and practices. The presence of the latter is helpful in increasing employees' efficiency, contributes to the process of updating their skills and facilitates better stress management.

The high priority attached to the influence of national labour laws on their HRM policies and practices is understandable as at present there are over 150 state and central laws in India which govern various aspects of HRM at the enterprise level. Unfortunately, while there is a proliferation of legislation, the implementation is weak (Venkata Ratnam, 1995; Saini and Budhwar, 2007). Unions still significantly influence HRM policies in India. At many places, they still have an antagonist nature, which is mainly due to the strong political support they have and the existence of pro-labour laws. A number of institutes such as Indian Society for Training and Development, management associations (both at local and national level) and HRD academy are now well established. These and many similar bodies emphasise on vocational training in India, especially to combat the pressures thrown up by foreign competition, who at the moment are working hard towards the regular upgrading of skills. Nevertheless, the rapid developments in the new sectors (like IT, software and BPO) are too fast and the Indian educational–vocational training set-up is struggling to meet their demands.

Dynamic business environment and HRM

An analysis of the existing empirical evidence highlights that on average Indian managers give a relatively high priority to customer satisfaction and increased competition/globalisation of business structure regarding their influence on HRM policies and practices. Managers also believe that their personnel function is under severe pressure to improve productivity by developing an efficient and responsible work force. The emphasis is on the need for teamwork, enhanced training programmes, HRD, skills improvement and retraining of employees by providing technical skills. HR managers feel that the personnel should contribute more actively in the restructuring of the business, i.e. facilitating delayering, downsizing, decentralisation and cost reduction. Managers also feel that competitive pressures have resulted in enhanced levels of manpower planning to assure that the right man is at the right place at the right time, and a need to attract and retain scarce skilled labour and improve the efficiency and quality of their work.

Nevertheless, as indicated earlier in this chapter, economic liberalisation in India has resulted in stiff competition for national firms from overseas operators. As a result of the liberalisation of the economy, the number of business alliances has also increased in India. Understandably, then, HR managers feel a significant influence of both these aspects of dynamic business environment on Indian HRM. They suggest that the rapid developments in information technology have implications for functions such as recruitment, training and development and performance appraisals. In summary, in the liberalised economic environment Indian managers perceive the key roles of the HRM function as being those of increasing productivity, reducing costs, rationalizing and controlling over-staffing whilst generating employment, improvement in quality and reduction in voluntary and involuntary absenteeism. The new paradigm has brought a shift towards more professional management and new opportunities for technology upgrading, human resource mobilisation from previously untapped sources, expansion, diversification, business turnaround and internationalisation. To a great extent, the multi-national companies (MNCs) operating in India are leading on this front. Next we provide empirical evidence from a study of MNCs operating in India about the kind of HRM systems they are operating in India and the kind of HR challenges they are experiencing. This information should be useful for policy makers to further develop their HRM policies and practices.

Patterns of HRM in foreign firms operating in India

The information in this section is based on in-depth interviews in 103 MNCs operating in India. The interviews were conducted during late 2002 and early 2003 with one top HR specialist in as many foreign firms (see Budhwar *et al.*, 2009). Discussions were carried out along the core HR functions (such as what and how of recruitment and selection, training, appraisals, compensation, retention), and themes such as the nature of organisational structure, relationship between India units and headquarters and different learning experiences related to key HR functions were examined in the research. On average, each interview lasted for ninety minutes. The interviews were tape-recorded, transcribed and later content analysed. The views presented here are those of a minimum of 40 per cent of the interviewees.

HR department

Most of the top HR managers recruited to head the India operations are from within India (recruited from the Indian partner in the joint venture, from an Indian company, or from another Indian unit of the MNC). The commonly used job designations of senior HR personnel are HR Manager, General Manager and HR Director. HR managers are helping to establish the HR function both as a 'business partner' and a 'change agent' in their Indian operations. Recruiting an Indian as the HR manager in India has a number of advantages such as: they have a better understanding of the local social, cultural, political and legal environment; can be recruited for a relatively small compensation package in comparison with an expatriate; knows the ways of working around the local system; can easily become part of relevant networks (not only related to HRM but also related to customers, suppliers and distributors); and can easily be moved between different units of the MNC (not only between joint ventures but also to wholly owned subsidiaries). Similarly, all other HR people in the operations units are local.

Working in a MNC is a new experience for a majority of Indian employees. Considering the unique ways of doing things in MNCs (mainly related to their global standardised HRM practices), the HR departments in India based MNCs have to work very hard to change the established mind set of new employees (who have not previously worked in a MNC) as per their own liking. Hence a strong emphasis is placed on training, orientation and related programmes.

Most MNCs in India have established HR departments and HR is represented at the board level and there are specialists heads within the HR department such as for HRM, industrial relations (IR), administration and HRD. In the majority of firms the HR department is actively involved in the strategic planning processes and it is viewed as a partner in the management of business and agent of change by people outside the HR function. Further, most firms make an explicit effort to align business and HR strategies. Generally, someone at the position of vice president or director heads the HR department. S/he is followed by senior manager, manager, senior executives, executives and staff. Perhaps an important challenge to HR in foreign firms operating in India is to eliminate some hierarchies from their HR departments as these have been found to be affecting their efficiency. Moreover, there is also a need to further devolve routine HR activities to line, something which is not usual in the Indian context (see Budhwar and Sparrow, 1997).

HR functions

Many of the sample firms have been successful in adopting the MNCs' global HR policies related to recruitment, employee development, performance appraisals and compensation of local employees, to a great extent with some local adjustments. For example, most MNCs are able to use global recruitment and selection policies with minor local adjustments. All the MNCs adopt a formal, structured and systematic approach to recruit new employees. Interestingly, this is not so in the case of many Indian national companies (especially in the private sector) which adopt an informal and unstructured approach to recruitment function (for details see Sparrow and Budhwar, 1997). A number of methods are adopted by MNCs to find new recruits such as consultants, employee referrals, the internet, campus interviews, and through advertisements. When it comes to adopting different criteria and methods to select new candidates, the global HR polices of the MNC are seriously considered. For example, at Motorola, 'skills as per Motorola specification, integrity, honesty and ethics' are looked for in all candidates. To achieve such requirements, MNCs adopt different criteria during the selection process. It generally starts with job specification, by defining the profile of person(s) required, the kind of competencies one should have and finally matching the needs of the person with the company. A strong emphasis is given to the attitude of the person, along with different skills, educational qualifications and the institute from which the candidate has graduated. Many MNCs conduct different general tests to evaluate the general ability, technical competency, behavioural competence and aptitude. Due to the existence of many educational institutions and the drastic variation in the nature and quality of education standards of the same, most MNCs strongly look for graduates from the premier institutions to fill various positions.

The majority of HR managers have had some bad experiences with their recruitment programmes, for example, with advertising of jobs in the newspapers or magazines. These often lead to large numbers of applications from unqualified and/or unsuitable candidates. Another problem faced by HR managers is acquiring a new employee after a formal job offer is made. At times, after getting the appointment letter, the candidates do not take up the job and use it to get a job in their preferred organisation. Further, at times, the same candidate's profile comes to an organisation from two or three consultants. In such cases, it becomes a difficulty for the HR manager to figure out if there are different candidates or there is a single candidate. Similarly, many MNCs (that are not well known) are unable to get an early date for campus interviews. As a result, they end up with below-average students. In the Indian context, where social relations are important, most MNCs are using this to their advantage to attract good candidates via techniques like 'word of mouth' and 'employee referral' and with the help of structured and formal approaches bring in objectivity in the recruitment process.

All employee development is also clearly structured, formal in nature and most of the time linked to the performance system of the MNC (this is another strong deviation from local firms). The training programmes used in India are to a great extent a reflection of the global training set-up of the MNCs. For example, companies like Max New York Life Insurance, Honda, Motorola, GE, Siemens, Hyundai and Hughes Software Systems have established their own 'management training centres' in India, where the courses offered are similar to those offered in other parts of the world in their affiliates or headquarters. Apart from in-house training facilities, the help of external training consultants is also taken. A variety of area-specific training programmes are provided by MNCs in their Indian operations. These include both soft (such as behavioural, supervisory, management, leadership, communication, ethics, culture, team building) and hard skills (such as operational, technical, quality). The majority of the MNCs do not have any serious problem in adopting such training programmes in the Indian context, but they do make amendments to them to suit the local context.

Despite the systematic and formal approach to employee development, the HR managers report some problems with the training programmes. First, trainers, especially internal, find it difficult to train a higher status employee due to high power distance. Second, during the induction and orientation programmes, due to less inter departmental co-operation (i.e. when new recruits are sent to different departments for orientation they are not given the required attention), some MNCs find it hard to achieve the required training results. Third, at times, some companies have a limited training budget. Fourth, HR managers also report the scarcity of training experts in some specific areas (such as quality control and new management interventions). Lastly, a more serious problem is regarding the older employees, who do not have a proper university education and often hesitate to adopt new technologies and modern approaches to management. Some MNCs make an attempt to train such staff by sending them to special institutes.

A formal and structured approach to the performance appraisal system is common in most MNCs operating in India. To a great extent, the majority of firms have introduced a periodic appraisal or assessment system, generally developed in their headquarters, which form part of their global policies concerning performance appraisal in India. The majority of firms have an annual appraisal system. Some firms have it on a six-monthly basis and some even on a quarterly basis tied to the yearly cycle. All the firms have a structured format and a clear set of parameters for appraisals. In many cases the appraisal starts with a self appraisal, in which the individual writes about oneself and then s/he is appraised by the immediate supervisor. However, the general trend is that the immediate supervisor appraises the employee and gives their report to the person. They then read it and have to counter sign before it is submitted to the section head. A number of issues related to future movement, cross-functional movement, training needs identification, key performance areas and possible targets are analysed. The above discussed appraisal system, which is quite comprehensive, has some drawbacks. For example, in the present system there is relatively low participation of individual employees regarding their goal setting (though some companies claim to be doing this). This reflects the hierarchical nature of Indian society. Perhaps, a more participative approach could be beneficial (as experienced by some Japanese firms operating in India).

It seems that by far the most different amongst the global HR policies is the compensation of local employees in the Indian units. The main reasons in this regard are the low labour costs and the availability of large number of skilled human resources in India. Still in comparison with Indian national companies the compensation packages of MNCs are far more attractive (see Venkata Ratnam, 1998). Many MNCs adopt a grading system to compensate their employees. Others, on top of it also practise performance-related compensation – a mixture of company and individual based performance. Almost all the firms pay a bonus to their employees. A significant number of MNCs do not have a formal career planning system for their Indian operations. Possibly, some are still working on it (as claimed by the HR managers) and others do not feel the need of one due to the existence of a good labour market. However, well educated Indian employees expect a clear career progression and with the increasing level of competition both from national and international firms, it soon is expected to become an important tool to retain the best employees. Until recently, Indians have been used to lifetime permanent employment with some sort of clear career progression.

Globalisation versus localisation

Despite the clear differences in national, regional and organisational differences, most MNCs are able to adopt many global HR practices in Indian units with minor adjustments. Perhaps the key reason for this is the awareness of Indian employees about the ways of doing things in different parts of the world (due to their management education system). Still, the importance given to social networks can be a big hindrance in further reducing the gap. Many MNCs send their senior managers for training at headquarters. Also working with expatriates in India is helping to minimise such gaps significantly. However, many global HR policies are being modified to fit Indian conditions. For example, the policy of many MNCs to 'fire' people without any explanation is totally against the Indian culture and legislation. It is now slowly modified and an explanation is now provided while removing someone from a job. Similarly, the compensation policies and practices are modified as per the local standards. Many MNCs also localise recruitment practices as per the qualifications and the graduating institution.

Nevertheless, it is important to keep in mind that India is a large country with massive regional differences – cultural, economic and political. Accordingly, the employment conditions (such as for the availability of labour, cost of living, state taxes, etc.) vary significantly. For example, it is costly to set up a plant in one of the metropolitan cities in comparison with less populated and less costly areas. Hence, it is not sensible for MNCs to establish strict nationwide policies such as for compensation and various benefits (such as housing and travel). There are then many opportunities for MNCs to learn from and teach to local partners in India. A number of established HR-related networks exist in India. Almost all the HR managers of India are in one way or other affiliated to these. These networks form the part of many forums (such as Delhi, Bombay chapters of HRD network), professional bodies, national and regional HRD network, local and national management association (such as All India Management Association), Confederation of Indian Industries (CII), Indian Society for Training and Development. Such bodies organise a number of conferences, seminars and workshops. Information related to different HR trends such as compensation, recruitment practices, retrenchment, work environment, new developments in the area, staff welfare, competition, etc are shared during such meetings on a regular basis.

Conclusions and key issues

As more and more MNCs are lining up to enter India, and as national firms are modifying their HRM systems in order to compete with them, the management of human resources has become crucial in the Indian context.

This chapter discussed the evolution of the HRM function in India, the main factors influencing HRM in the Indian context and the emerging patterns of HRM in foreign firms operating in India. By doing so, we have presented an overview regarding the HRM scenario in India, and also has provided useful information to policy makers which should assist them to further develop relevant HRM systems for their Indian operations. Below are the main takeaways from the above analysis.

- The developments in Indian HRM have been significant, however, they vary from public, private, local/national owned to foreign owned firms and from traditional manufacturing to modern service based sectors. Thus, it is possible to develop and successfully practice formal, rationalised and structured HRM systems in India.
- A combination of both national and organisational level factors and variables significantly influence HRM in India. HR managers need to have a good understanding of such determinants of HRM in order to develop relevant HRM policies and practices for the Indian context.
- The socio, political, legal and economic context of India needs to be clearly understood in order to be successful there. For example, trade unions, labour legislations and social networks play a significant role in the development and successful implementation of HRM policies and practices. If their dynamics are not carefully understood and accordingly handled properly, then they can have a detrimental affect.
- India has a long list of labour legislations, whose provisions in many cases are dated, and they lack easy implementation. Nevertheless, foreign firms are expected to fully adhere to such provisions. Understanding of such provisions is crucial – in this regard, local experts can prove to be very handy.
- A number of HR-related professional bodies and networks exist in India. Memberships of such bodies are very helpful for learning, networking and sharing of best HR practices.
- Talent acquisition, management and retention are a major issue in the Indian dynamic business environment. A combination of both indigenous and global standardised approaches to HRM will work well in the Indian markets.
- It seems that with minor modifications, foreign firms are able to adopt their global HRM systems in India. The adoption of the 'polycentric approach' to HRM might seem to be the most appropriate for the Indian environment.
- Given the drastic variations in the skills inculcated in new graduates by different institutions; training needs to stay a priority in order to raise the level of Indian employees to the required standards and also to inculcate the philosophy of a given MNC.
- In order to handle things like 'job hopping' and high levels of attrition in the Indian context (as is evident in the BPO sector), HR managers need to be continuously innovating new HR practices.

- A clear career system, based on objective criteria can be useful for retention of talent.
- Indian graduates are full of enthusiasm, energy and exciting ideas – the right kind of support and encouragement can help lead to desired results.

References

Agarwala, T. (2003) Innovative Human Resource Practices and Organizational Commitment: An Empirical Investigation. *International Journal of Human Resource Management*, 14: 175–98.

Balasubramanian, A. G. (1994) Evolution of Personnel Function in India: A Re-examination, Part I. *Management and Labour Studies*, 19 (4): 196–210.

—— (1995) Evolution of Personnel Function in India: A Re-examination, Part II. *Management and Labour Studies*, 20 (1): 5–14.

Baruch, Y., Budhwar, P. and Khatri, P. (2007) Brain Drain: The Inclination of International Students to Stay Abroad after their Studies. *Journal of World Business*, 42: 99–112.

Bjorkman, I. and Budhwar, P. (2007) When in Rome . . .? Human Resource Management and the Performance of Foreign Firms Operating in India. *Employee Relations*, 29 (6): 595–610.

Bjorkman, I., Budhwar, P., Smale, A. and Sumelius, J. (2008) Human Resource Management in Foreign-owned Subsidiaries: China versus India. *International Journal of Human Resource Management*, 19 (5): 966-80.

Bordia, P. and Blau, G. (1998) Pay Referent Comparison and Pay Level Satisfaction in Private versus Public Sector Organisations in India. *International Journal of Human Resource Management*, 9 (1): 155–67.

Budhwar, L., Reeves, D. and Farrell, P. (2000) Life Goals as a Function of Social Class and Child-rearing Practices in India. *International Journal of Intercultural Relations*, 24: 227–45.

Budhwar, P. (1998a) Comparative Human Resource Management in India and Britain. PhD thesis, Manchester Business School, UK.

—— (1998b) National Factors determining Indian and British HRM Practices: An Empirical Study. *Management International Review*, special issue, 38 (2): 105–21

—— (2000) Factors Influencing HRM Policies and Practices in India: An Empirical Study. *Global Business Review*, 1 (2): 229–47.

—— (2001) Doing Business in India. *Thunderbird International Business Review*, 43 (4): 549–68.

—— (2002a) An Integrative Framework for Determining Cross-national Human Resource Management Practices. *Human Resource Management Review*. 12 (3): 377–403.

—— (2002b) Strategic HRM through the Cultural Looking Glass: Mapping Cognitions of British and Indian HRM Managers. *Organization Studies*, 23 (4): 599–638.

—— (2003) Employment Relations in India. *Employee Relations*, 25 (2): 132–48.

—— (2004) Introduction. HRM in the Asia-Pacific Context. In P. Budhwar (ed.) *Managing Human Resources in Asia-Pacific*. London: Routledge, 1–15.

—— (2009) Managing Human Resources in India. In J. Storey, P. Wright and D. Ulrich (eds) *The Routledge Companion to Strategic HRM*. Routledge: London, 435–446.

Budhwar, P. and Boyne, G. (2004) Human Resource Management in the Indian Public and Private Sectors: An Empirical Comparison. *International Journal of Human Resource Management*, 15: 346–70.

Budhwar, P. and Debrah, Y. (2001) Rethinking Comparative and Cross-national Human Resource Management Research. *International Journal of Human Resource Management*, 12 (3): 497–515.

Budhwar, P. and Debrah, Y. (2004) (eds) *HRM in Developing Countries*. London: Routledge.

Budhwar, P. and Khatri, P. (2001) HRM in Context: The Applicability of HRM Models in India. *International Journal of Cross-cultural Management*, 1 (3): 333–56.

Budhwar, P. and Singh, V. (2007) Introduction. People Management in the Indian Sub-continent. *Employee Relations*, 29 (6): 1–14.

—— (2009) Factors Influencing Indian HRM Policies and Practices. In P. Budhwar and J. Bhatnagar (eds) *The Changing Face of People Management in India*. London: Routledge, 95–112.

Budhwar, P. and Sparrow, P. (1997) Evaluating Levels of Strategic Integration and Devolvement of Human Resource Management in India. *International Journal of Human Resource Management*, 8 (4): 476–94.

—— (1998) Factors Determining Cross-national Human Resource Management Practices: A Study of India and Britain. *Management International Review*, special issue, 38 (2): 105–21.

—— (2002a) An Integrative Framework for Determining Cross-national Human Resource Management Practices. *Human Resource Management Review*, 12 (3): 377–403.

—— (2002b) Strategic HRM through the Cultural Looking Glass: Mapping Cognitions of British and Indian HRM Managers. *Organization Studies*, 23 (4): 599–638.

Budhwar, P., Luthar, H. and Bhatnagar, J. (2006) Dynamics of HRM Systems in BPOs operating in India. *Journal of Labor Research*, 27 (3): 339–60.

Budhwar, P., Saini, D. and Bhatnagar, J. (2005) Women in Management in the New Economic Environment: The Case of India. *Asia Pacific Business Review*, 11 (2): 179–93.

Budhwar, P., Varma, A., Malhotra, N. and Mukherjee, A. (2009) Insights into the Indian Call Centre Industry: Can Internal Marketing help tackle high Employee Turnover? *Journal of Services Marketing*, 23 (5): 351–62.

Budhwar, P., Varma, A., Singh, V. and Dhar, R. (2006) HRM Systems of Indian Call Centres: An Exploratory Study. *The International Journal of Human Resource Management*, 17 (5): 881–97.

Devi, R. D. (1991) Women in Modern Sector Employment in India. *Economic Bulletin for Asia and the Pacific*, June–December: 53–65.

Hofstede, G. (1991) *Culture's Consequences: Software of the Mind*. London: McGraw-Hill.

Jain, H., Lawler, J. J. and Morishima, M. (1998) Multinational Corporations, Human Resource Management and Host-country Nationals. *International Journal of Human Resource Management*, 9: 553–66.

Kakar, S. (1971) Authority Pattern and Subordinate Behaviours in Indian Organization. *Administrative Science Quarterly*, 16: 298–307.

Kanungo, R. and Mendonca, M. (1994) Culture and Performance Improvement. *Productivity*, 35 (4): 447–53.

Krishna, A. and Monappa, A. (1994) Economic Restructuring and Human Resource Management. *Indian Journal of Industrial Relations*, 29 (4): 490–501.

Kuruvilla, S. (1996) Linkages between Industrialization Strategies and Industrial Relations/Human Resource Policies: Singapore, Malaysia, the Philippines and India. *Industrial and Labor Relations Review*, 49: 634–57.

Rao, T. V., Silveria, D. M., Shrivastava, C. M. and Vidyasagar, R. (1994) (eds.) *HRD in the New Economic Environment*. New Delhi: Tata McGraw-Hill.

Sahay, S. and Walsham, G. (1997) Social Structure and Managerial Agency in India. *Organisation Studies*, 18: 415–44.

Saini, D. and Budhwar, P. (2007) Human Resource Management in India. In R. Schuler and S. Jackson (eds) *Strategic Human Resource Management*. Oxford: Blackwell, 287–312.

Schuler, R. S., Budhwar, P. and Florkowski, G. W. (2002) International Human Resource Management: Review and Critique. *International Journal of Management Reviews*, 4 (1): 41–70.

Sharma, I. J. (1984) The Culture Context of Indian Managers. *Management and Labour Studies*, 9 (2): 72–80.

Shenoy, S. (1995) Organisation Structure and Context: A Replication of the Aston Study in India. In D. J. Hickson and C. J. Macmillan (eds), *Organisation and Nation: The Aston Programme IV*, London: Gower Publishing, chapter 5.

Silveria, D. M. (1988) *Human Resource Development: The Indian Experience*. New Delhi: New India Publications.

Sinha, J. B. P. (1990) *Work Culture in Indian Context*. New Delhi: Sage.

Sinha, J. B. P. and Kanungo, R. (1997) Context Sensitivity and Balancing in Indian Organization Behavior. *International Journal of Psychology*, 32: 93–105.

Sinha, J. B. P. and Sinha, D. (1990) Role of Social Values in Indian Organisations. *International Journal of Psychology*, 25: 705–14.

—— (1990) Role of Social Values in Indian Organisations. *International Journal of Psychology*, 25: 705–14.

Sparrow, P. R. and Budhwar, P. (1997) Competition and Change: Mapping the Indian HRM Recipe against Worldwide Patterns. *Journal of World Business*, 32 (3): 224–42.

Tayeb, M. (1987) Contingency Theory and Culture: a Study of matched English and the Indian Manufacturing Firms. *Organisation Studies*, 8: 241–61.

—— (1994) Organisations and National Culture: Methodology Considered. *Organisation Studies*, 15 (3): 429–46.

Thomas, A. S. and Philip, A. (1994) India: Management in an Ancient and Modern Civilisation. *International Studies of Management and Organisation*, 24: 91–115.

Tripathi, R. C. (1990) Interplay of Values in the Functioning of Indian Organizations. *International Journal of Psychology*, 25: 715–34.

Venkata Ratnam, C. S. (1995) Economic Liberalization and the Transformation of Industrial Relations Policies in India. In A. Verma, T. A. Kochan and R. D. Lansbury (eds) *Employment Relations in the Growing Asian Economies*. London: Routledge.

—— (1996) *Industrial Relations in Indian States*. New Delhi: Global Business Press.

—— (1998) Multinational Companies in India. *International Journal of Human Resource Management*, 9: 567–89.

Venkata Ratnam, C. S. and Srivastava, B. K. (1991) *Personnel Management and Human Resources*. New Delhi: Tata McGraw-Hill.

Yadapadithaya, P. S. (2000) International Briefing 5. Training and Development in India. *International Journal of Training and Development*, 4 (1): 79–89.

11 Conflict management and negotiation

Jacob D. Vakkayil and Rajiv Kumar

Anyone exploring India or its neighboring countries in South Asia would be amazed at the scale and variety of conflicts this region lives with. The noted historian Ramchandra Guha observed that the range of conflicts in this region is unmatched even when compared with those seen in the Balkans (2007). This variety is also reflected in the ways in which people express and address conflicts, such as *gherao* (surrounding a person or building and preventing them from moving away until demands are met), hunger strikes, non-cooperation, and acts of extreme violence and destruction.

In this chapter, we examine how conflict handling and negotiation in the Indian context can be understood from a behavioral perspective. We initially highlight examples of conflict in the context of Indian businesses at the macro and micro levels. Then we examine some evidence on the conflict management styles adopted by Indian managers. The possible relationships between cultural values and conflict handling behaviors are explored next. Finally, we provide a few guidelines for negotiation that could be of practical use to non-Indian managers operating in India.

Macro-level issues

According to the Ministry of Labour and Employment (2008), cases of strikes and lockouts in the country have steadily decreased over the last two decades. In 1992, the number recorded was 1,714, in 1998 it had come down to 1,097, and there were only 440 reported cases in 2006. However, this decreasing trend is not reflected in the number of workers involved or person-days lost. On an average, the country has lost approximately 24 million person-days annually due to strikes and lockouts in the period mentioned above. This data indicates that comparatively larger organizations are increasingly involved in disputes. Even a single day's strike in a large organization would lead to the loss of a sizeable number of person-days.

In India, unions are active in manufacturing industries, and a number of instances of conflict involving workers have been reported in the past few years. One example is the violent police action on striking workers, at the plant of Honda Motorcycle & Scooter India, in Gurgaon near the capital Delhi in 2005.

The workers were protesting the dismissal of four of their colleagues and the suspension of twenty-five others by the management, in an alleged attempt to prevent them from forming unions. The Chief Minister of Haryana, the state where the plant is located, eventually brokered a peace agreement and the management had to take back all the employees it had previously sacked.

Unlike manufacturing, emerging and rapidly growing sectors such as information technology (Budhwar, 2001) and biotechnology have so far been unaffected by strikes and lockouts as unions have failed to emerge in such sectors. The companies in these emerging sectors offer better working conditions and compensation, and are more proactive in adopting advanced human resource management practices. Hence even politically affiliated unions find it difficult to gain a foothold in these sectors.

The Industrial Disputes Act of 1947 forms the base for dispute resolution in Indian industry. It provides for a variety of resolution mechanisms, including provisions for bipartite agreements, conciliation, voluntary arbitration and adjudication. Many Acts and legal provisions have since been introduced, such as the establishment of joint works councils with equal participation from management and workers in 1958, the Scheme of Workers Participation in Industry in 1975, and the Participation of Workers in Management Bill in 1990. Many companies, especially those in the public sector, have adopted the Code of Discipline for industry announced in 1958. Prominent organizations such as the Railways and Department of Post and Telegraph have established permanent negotiating machineries to quickly address disputes.

However, there are a number of impediments to the effective implementation of these provisions (Saini and Budhwar, 2008). Political undercurrents and their resultant influence on decision making are all too obvious in the Indian business arena. In a study of a large integrated steel plant in India, Varman and Bhatnagar (1999) found that the impartiality of "due procedures" specified for employee grievance handling was often subverted through devices such as the declaration of "special cases." Conflict management requiring mediation or arbitration can thus be long drawn or may not meet the stated objectives fully. These and other characteristics of the Indian political and legal environment are elaborated in Chapter 3 and elsewhere in this volume.

Apart from conflicts involving labor, many family-run firms are characterized by ownership disputes. A highly visible case involved Reliance – one of the largest conglomerates in India. A major dispute between Mukesh and Anil, heirs to the business empire built by their father, Dhirubhai Ambani, was settled with the demerger of the company through the intervention of their mother. However, disagreements have persisted. In 2008, the younger brother filed a Rs 10,000 crore defamation suit against the elder brother for some remarks made about him by the latter during an interview to the *New York Times*. Another instance of a long-standing feud involving the Bajaj family was also settled in 2008. Major conflicts have also been reported in the past from many other prominent business families such as the Chhabrias, Srirams, Mafatlals, and Goenkas.

Bist (2008) opines that after liberalization, the increased pace of economic growth and the incorporation of professional management practices have contributed to a spurt in the number of conflicts. The barriers between family and business interests have also been not very clear in the Indian context. This leads to decision making processes that can be contested. Non-vigilant boards, filled with cronies of the family acting as independent directors, might also lead to high levels of questionable decisions and resultant conflicts. More recently, a few family run firms are waking up to the reality of conflicts and taking proactive steps to prevent them. A major example is the GMR group, a key builder of airports in India. The group has hired the London-based advisor Peter Leach to help in specifying a constitution and code of conduct for the family and to plan a succession blueprint involving the two sons of the founder (Singh, 2007).

Land acquisition for industrial activities is another prominent source of conflicts which some major corporations have faced in the post-liberalization era. Quite predictably, poor planning and implementation by the government machinery dealing with land acquisition and compensation to affected people have been held responsible for such conflicts. For example, the Tatas faced opposition at their steel plant in Kalinga Nagar in Orissa and their proposed small car factory at Singur in West Bengal. In Kalinga Nagar, in January 2006, thirteen people from the local tribal community who were protesting against the acquisition of their land for the Tata steel plant were shot dead by the police. This triggered further protests and road blockades for months. The company has since taken active steps to diffuse the tension. They have built a rehabilitation colony and settled many local people there, besides training young people in industrially relevant skills. Partially due to these efforts, the company has managed to continue its operations. However, they have not been so successful in Singur in the neighboring state of West Bengal. After repeated attempts for a settlement that did not bear fruit, the small car project had to be relocated to the state of Gujarat. A second case of conflict was reported from Nandigram in West Bengal, where the state government was trying to acquire land so that Indonesia-based Salim group could build a special economic zone and a chemical hub. After months of conflicts involving major political parties active in the area, violent police action left fourteen people dead and at least seventy injured in 2007. Protests have also been encountered by the South Korean steel giant Posco in Orissa and by Indian companies such as Dabur in Himachal Pradesh. While some of these have been at least partially settled, these instances of conflicts have led to uncertainties and loss of time as well as revenue for the companies involved.

Companies that are entering the Indian market through mergers, acquisitions or joint ventures need to take into account the above-mentioned factors. For these ventures, the willingness to engage with the gap between legal provisions and their implementation, and understanding the implications of the introduction of professional management to family firms can be especially beneficial. They also need to take note of the apparent mistrust of foreign investors, which is probably a result of India's long experience with colonialism (Kumar and Worm, 2005). Although the people from urban middle class have reaped the benefits of economic liberalization, vast tracts of rural India are still untouched by these developments, and their initial contacts with the industry may not be smooth. Companies need to invest resources, time and effort in creating goodwill and educating people on the implications of their activities. Democratic political processes in India can make this engagement especially challenging, as various political parties and pressure groups can use these issues for their own political ends.

Micro-level issues

There is evidence (e.g., Budhwar and Sparrow, 2002; Sparrow and Budhwar, 1997) to believe that the Indian organizations differ from their Western counterparts in conceptualizing and enacting HR practices. These and other differences often lead to some unique forms of conflicts at the micro-level. Drawing from our training and consulting experience with various companies in India, we highlight a few prominent factors leading to micro-level conflicts in Indian organizations.

We have come across many instances where apparent *breach of contract* led to conflicts. In one instance, a British national, working for an Indian family-owned firm, found that some previously agreed perquisites were not given to him. While the company had promised him fully furnished accommodation at the time of hiring, he found that his residence was only semi-furnished when he shifted there. He was also promised that some portion of his tax liability while working in India would be cushioned by the company. This too was subsequently not done. When he raised these issues before the HR director, he was asked to wait for a decision on these matters by some higher authority. A second case concerns a senior executive of US nationality working at a high-technology firm. A few years after joining the company, he was asked to shift from his allocated residential apartment in a centrally located area to another one which was at some distance from his office in the suburbs. Though he protested, he was told that the decision was driven by the unanticipated increase in the rental for the property which was allocated to him. While the British national in the first case eventually left his company, citing breach of contract as one of the reasons for doing so, the US national continued with obvious dissatisfaction. While narrating his experience, he remarked that contracts were never final in India. His views were based on what he observed his Indian employers doing, not only to his own employment contract, but also to negotiated contracts with several suppliers as well. This disregard for the sanctity of contractual agreements has also been highlighted by many authors. For example, Misra and Kanungo (1997, p. 1270) state that the Indian "work relationships are personalized rather than contractual. They work for their superiors, friends and relatives rather than for accomplishing a task of organizational goals under contractual obligations."

This emphasis on *personalized nature of relationships* in organizations, as pointed out by Misra and Kanungo (1997), can often lead to conflicts of varied kinds. Expatriate managers in Indian companies may find the uneasy fusion of the personal and the professional realms in Indian companies somewhat puzzling. In an illustrative case, a German national, working for a family-owned engineering firm in India, was not given enough autonomy to make decisions that were required for his role. When he pointed this out to the authorities, he was told that he needed to develop an understanding of the culture and decision making processes of the company before he could be completely trusted with important decisions. This wait was inordinately long and difficult for him especially since he had a highly successful track record in his previous organization. He found it disturbing that though his professional competence was not in doubt, his autonomy was curtailed because of lack of personal relationships with the promoter and the top management at the headquarters in India. This was the main reason behind his subsequent resignation from the organization.

High levels of hierarchy and power distance can also be troubling for managers unfamiliar with the Indian context. Professional managers who join family-run Indian firms often find that loyalty and deference to authority find diverse expressions in these companies. An instance was narrated to us by a professional executive with proven track record, who was hired to steer a family-run manufacturing firm in India during a period of expansion. He often had experiences of organizational norms which ran counter to the professionalism he expected in such a large company. For example, he was once asked to stay well beyond his normal office hours as the promoter wanted to meet him. Despite his waiting for more than an hour, the promoter did not call him for the meeting. Upon inquiring with the promoter's secretary, he came to know that the promoter had already left his office some time ago. This, he suspected, was a normal experience which would not warrant any protest from a person who had been with the company for a longer period of time.

Many instances of interpersonal conflicts can be attributed to the *complexities of socio-cultural affiliations of individuals* in the Indian society. In a large software company, a person hailing from the state of Orissa in eastern India and another from the state of Tamil Nadu in southern India were jointly responsible for managing a team. Both these people reported to a person who happened to be from Tamil Nadu who in turn reported to another person, again from Tamil Nadu. For some reason the manager from Orissa formed an impression that his Tamil colleague got more favors from his superiors because of their common regional affiliations. This led to repeated instances of conflict between the two. When one of them would recommend a candidate for hiring, the other would opine against hiring the person; if one would ask a subordinate to do something, the other would ask the same subordinate not to follow the previous instruction. Ultimately they had to be put in two separate teams to avoid the escalation of conflict to unmanageable levels. India is characterized by a large number of social divisions and many Indians have strong caste or religious affiliations. These have often caused tensions in the social realm, and sometimes these conflicts spill over to business organizations too.

Based on these evidences, we believe that foreign executives should be mentally prepared to encounter a diverse set of people who may get into conflicts because of their demographic diversity. To compound matters further, higher acceptance of hierarchy may come as a surprise for foreigners. They may also find it difficult to establish the trust and personal relationships during their initial contacts with Indian executives. And as we highlighted, contracts in India are likely to have a less strict meaning than in some more developed societies. Considering the time-consuming and expensive legal processes in India, foreign executives should pay special attention to this aspect.

Managerial strategies

Conflict handling behavior has often been explored utilizing a framework that classifies behavior on the two dimensions of "concern for self" and "concern for the other" (e.g., Thomas and Kilmann, 1974; Rahim, 1983). A combination of these results in five distinctive styles of approaching conflict, namely, avoiding, obliging, dominating, compromising, and integrating. *Avoiding* denotes low concern for self and the other party and is associated with withdrawal from the conflict. *Obliging* denotes low concern for self and high concern for the other party and is associated with yielding to the other, thus smoothing the differences. *Dominating* denotes high concern for self and low concern for the other party and is associated with forcing one's interests through. *Compromising* denotes moderate concern for self and the other party and is associated with finding middle-of-the-road solutions that are partially acceptable to the parties concerned. Lastly, *integrating* denotes high concern for self and the other party, and is associated with finding an integrative solution that fully satisfies the interests of the parties concerned. There have been a few attempts to understand conflict handling behaviors of Indian managers using this schema.

For example, Das (1987) examined the conflict management styles of ninety-eight "efficient" bank managers in India. *Avoiding* and *obliging* were found to be used in relation to superiors, *compromising* was used more in relation to subordinates, and *integrating* was used equally with respect to both subordinates and superiors. The *dominating* style was used the least. Pandey (1992) studied various dimensions of superior–subordinate conflicts in Indian organizations, especially with regard to leadership styles and power bases. The data were drawn from a questionnaire administered to 252 executives from seven manufacturing firms. Overall, *integrating* emerged as the most frequently used strategy, while *compromising* was the least used strategy in handling conflicts with subordinates. Three styles of leadership behavior (participative, nurturant-task, and authoritarian) were examined in relation to the use of these strategies. Participative leaders tended to use *collaborating, obliging, compromising* and *avoiding* for conflict resolution. Nurturant-task leadership was closely associated with *integrating* and *compromising* while authoritarian leadership was characterized by *competing, avoiding* and *obliging* strategies. It was found that five bases of power (reward, personal, coercion, information and connection) were also associated with these strategies. While reward power was associated with all except *avoiding* and *obliging*, personal power predicted *collaborating, avoiding* and *obliging* strategies. Predictably, coercive power was associated with *dominating* strategy and information power interestingly was related to *obliging* strategy and connection power was associated with the use of *competing, obliging* and *compromising* strategies. In an earlier study Sayeed and Mathur (1980) had examined the relationship between leadership behavior of managers and strategies adopted for conflict resolution. Apart from the conflict resolution strategies indicated above, they found that these managers utilized three more strategies. These were *following rules* (often used in order to gain time and to be fair), *consulting others* (taking other parties' opinions) and *toning down differences* (which involved an emphasis on common interests). Leadership behavior was examined utilizing the four concepts of support behavior, interaction facilitation, goal emphasis and work facilitation. The first two constituted the relationship dimension and the last two constituted the task dimension. The hypothesis was that a relationship-oriented manager would opt for compromising and toning down differences while a task-oriented manager would opt for forcing and consulting others to resolve conflicts. The study did not find support for these hypotheses, indicating that dimensions of leadership behavior alone were not sufficient to predict effective conflict handling strategies. Morris *et al.* (1998) examined conflict handling behaviors in four countries (United States, China, Philippines and India). According to them, Indian managers tend to use *avoiding* and *competing* styles more as compared to the managers from the other three countries examined.

With only a few studies that examine conflict handling behaviors of managers in the Indian context, it is indeed difficult to draw conclusions regarding the propensity of managers to use certain styles or strategies more than others. From the studies reported above, it seems that the Indian managers may prefer integrating style the most. In order to attain a little more clarity, we conducted two exploratory investigations that assessed managerial behaviors in Indian companies utilizing the above schema. In the first study we administered the inventory reported by Rahim (1983) to fifty-one top management executives from two large public-sector undertakings in India and found that the most preferred conflict management style was indeed integrating.

We explored this further by assessing what mangers may actually do as opposed to what they report. For this, we made use of a group exercise during training on conflict management for branch managers of a public-sector bank in India. Individual branch managers ranked five different alternatives of managing four different conflict scenarios. Then these managers were divided into groups of four or five and they discussed the same five alternatives of managing each of the four different scenarios of conflict. For over twenty to twenty-five minutes, these managers discussed the alternatives in their group in order to arrive at a group ranking of the alternatives. We found that *avoiding* was the least preferred style and *integrating* was the most preferred style, if enough information was available for decision making. If the information was not enough, the groups of managers preferred *dominating* style.

Across most of the above investigations, *integrating* emerges as a prominent style that Indian managers tend to adopt. This has practical implications for conflict management and negotiation. For example, the search for integrating solution might result in time-consuming efforts for a solution that satisfies all. This would lead to unwillingness to compromise on any aspect in arriving at a solution. When fast decisions need to be made, this tendency might some-times be counterproductive. Secondly, providing more information regarding the reasons behind the other party's actions may be useful in scenarios of conflict. Indians' propensity for analytic decision making involving accumu-lation of more and more information has also been indicated by Kumar and Worm (2005). In their efforts to mange conflicts, executives need to balance the requirement for more and more information with a need for efficiency in the process and the constraints imposed on them by the situation.

Conflict management and Indian values

Researchers often try to understand conflict handling behaviors by examining the underlying values in a society. For example, Morris *et al.* (1998) compared managers in Asia and the United States in terms of their conflict-handling behaviors and found that Chinese managers tend to show a preference for avoiding style while mangers in the United States preferred the dominating style. They argued that these differences reflect underlying differences in value orientations between these societies. They suggest that the value of "societal conservatism" (Schwartz, 1992, 1994) adequately explains the differences in the preferences of both the societies. In this light it is probably worth while to examine how underlying cultural values might affect conflict handling in managerial situations in India.

Many researchers (e.g., Kakar, 1971; Sinha and Sinha, 1994; Gopalan and Rivera, 1997; Budhwar and Bhatnagar, 2009) assert that Indians structure all relationships in a hierarchical manner. According to a number of authors, this stems from societal devices such as the caste system and the joint family in India. There is great respect and deference for people in power and those powerful people on the top are expected to protect and provide patronage to people below them. Due to this, Indian organizations often reward deference to authority and loyalty even at the cost of professional competence. Such notions clash with the increasing professionalism after liberalization. In a study that examined influence tactics of bank managers on superiors and sub-ordinates, Bhatnagar (1993) pointed out how they were severely restricted in the number of tactics for upward influence. Reason alone emerged as appropriate and effective in influencing superiors whereas for downward influence on their subordinates, they used a number of tactics such as friendliness, coalition and reason. She suggested that a broader range of options indicated a greater maneuverability in handling differences with subordinates than in the case of superiors.

The image of the family and associated hierarchy are highly visible in the workplace in India. Jet Airways, one of the leading airlines in India, laid off 800 employees out of its total work force of approximately 13,000 during the festival season in 2008. Compelled by rising costs and hike in fuel prices, the company announced that it would lay off another 1,100 soon. Employees who lost their jobs protested, and they were supported by various political parties. A few days later, the chairman of the company, Naresh Goyal, announced that all the employees who lost their jobs would be reinstated. "I apologize for all the agony you went through," he said. "The management will have to understand sometimes in a family there are disagreements but the father of the family decides" (Chandran, 2008). The predominance of the family image is also evident in other aspects of managerial decision making. As illustrated above, managers often resort to personalized rather than purely contractual or role-related relationships in organizations. The intermingling of the professional and the personal in India is quite evident in India. Due to this, the differentiation of task and relationship conflict (e.g., Jehn, 1997) often tends to be hazy in India.

Responses to conflicts should also be understood in the context of the collectivistic orientation that is often attributed to Indians and other cultures of the East. However, dubbing Indian managers as either collectivistic or individualistic is likely to be simplistic and erroneous as collectivism in India is also coupled with a strong streak of individualism. Sinha *et al.*, (2002) found that the intentions and behaviors of Indians will be more collectivistic in matters concerning extended family. Therefore, we anticipate that though family-owned firms might be having conflicts among themselves, they might come together when one of them is threatened by an external entity. In situations other than those involving family, Indians may exhibit more (but not completely) individualistic attitudes and behaviors (Sinha and Kanungo, 1997). We have seen above that organizations in India are also arenas where religious, caste-related, regional and linguistic forces become active leading to peculiar situations of conflict. For example, Kumar (2007) found that informal interactions at the workplace are also influenced caste and kinship considerations in Indian companies. An effective approach to conflict management would arguably be one that recognizes these complex social dynamics.

The presence of such apparent contradictions makes Indian managers' behavior hard to predict. For example, the following two cultural characteristics of Indians could result in varied stances in a situation of conflict. Over centuries, India has developed renowned philosophical and spiritual traditions.

This has resulted in a heightened awareness of the various systems of thought and the sensitivity to possibilities. This might be the reason for predominance of managers who seek the integrative solutions as they are able to delineate faults easily and are eager for the best possible solution. This would often result in lengthy negotiations that do not conclude unless an integrative solution is reached. On the other hand, there is another characteristic of Indians that would seem to predispose them to avoiding rather than to integrating. Traditionally Indians tend to view their events and situations as the result of past deeds and thus unchangeable to a degree. This has led to a sense of fatalism and a resultant unwillingness to engage in creating change (Gopalan and Rivera, 1997), often leading to a tendency to avoid conflicts in the hope that things will sort themselves out in due course. However, this linkage between the value of fatalism and avoiding style of conflict management may indeed be weakening with the new economic scenario after liberalization.

Thus, the identification of uniformly applicable values in a highly complex country such as India might be challenging. Such complexity is often attributed to geographical vastness and the fabled diversity of India. It is a country with a large number of languages, races, geographical features, religious traditions, and social practices. Scholars have argued that this diversity has been nurtured because of the tendency to "enfold" (Sinha and Sinha, 1994) and thus preserving the differences, rather than to absorb these into a coherent whole. As a consequence, India is the site of a variety of practices and values that often seem contradictory to one another.

Such encompassing and enfolding is also visible in the organizational sphere. Many large-public sector companies in India have colonial roots and are being managed by incorporating many elements of such a work organization. However, Tripathi (1994) opines that although the colonial legacy has resulted in the incorporation of Western values at work in organizations, traditional values have a very strong influence on the Indian mind set. While designing organizational systems in India, one needs to consider both this colonial influence and the more deep-rooted set of traditional values. With the liberalization of the Indian economy, another era of Western and global influences has opened up. This makes an analysis of managerial choices in India somewhat complex (Chatterjee and Pearson, 2000). Managers who take up assignments in India would need to consider this complexity and invest time and effort in understanding the nuances of managerial action in this context.

Guidelines for negotiation

Negotiation is a decision-making process occurring among interdependent parties who do not share identical preferences (Neale and Bazerman, 1992). Previously negotiation skills were considered essential for only those managers who dealt with collective bargaining, but increasingly more and more managers are expected to possess good negotiation skills. Hence for non-Indian managers intending to do business in India or with Indian managers overseas, it will help to note which unique factors may drive different preferences of their Indian counterparts during negotiations.

Research on negotiation with respect to India is sparse (Kumar, 2005). At the same time, Indian economy and socio-political contexts have been experiencing rapid changes after the onset of economic liberalization in 1991. Yet, as Kumar (2005) points out, socio-cultural changes in India are likely to be slower than the pace of economic changes. Hence we have considered the available evidence regarding socio-cultural context of India, and built upon this somewhat thin base to offer some working propositions to practicing managers.

Nakamura (1964) argued that Indians search for a grandiose solution to problems which may not be in harmony with the pressing empirical reality. Sinha and Kanungo (1997) believed that Indian managers are likely to approach problem solving from moral dimensions. As mentioned earlier, Indians tend to have a philosophical orientation that drives them to look for an ideal solution to problems, and at times such quest for the best could jeopardize even the betterment of the current state. Probably this pursuit of the ideal or perfect solution leads to delays in negotiations and Indian managers appear to tolerate long-drawn-negotiations. As some researchers (e.g., Kumar, 2005; Salacuse, 2004) have pointed out, Indians are unlikely to find long-drawn-out negotiation a waste of time; they seem not to be in a hurry to finish a negotiation. In fact, the perception of haste on the part of the other party may work against a successful negotiation. As Salacuse (2004) argued, perceived haste by the former energy multinational Enron during their negotiations with Indian government officials was a major reason behind the ultimate ouster of Enron from India.

There is another facet of the relationship between time and negotiation that should be considered by foreign negotiators. Tinsley (2001) found that polychronic use of time predicted more integrating style as the polychronic negotiators could think of multiple points of view while negotiating. As Indian managers are likely to be more polychronic in their time utilization, they are more likely to understand the multiple viewpoints of foreign negotiators. However, as highlighted earlier, such sensitivity of Indian negotiators is subject to an overall tolerance for a long-drawn-out negotiation process.

Salacuse (2004) found that only 33 percent of Indian negotiators examined in the study viewed a "signed deal" as the goal behind their negotiations. Majority of them viewed the negotiation process as a means to weave long-term relationships. This finding is consistent with the previously mentioned characteristic of tolerance for prolonged negotiations. As the negotiation process unfolds, Indian managers seem to be willing to invest in building the long-term relationship rather than finishing the task at hand. This also relates to how personal and professional concerns often get intertwined for Indians, as pointed out earlier. Foreigners negotiating with Indians should incorporate this attribute in their negotiation plans.

As illustrated above through the experience of two Western managers working for Indian companies in India, contracts in India do not have the same sanctity as one expects to find in the West. This has dual implications for foreigners negotiating with Indian companies. Firstly, the pursuit of finer details in the contract before the deal is signed may not yield proportionate benefits. Secondly, they should also be prepared for possible violations or renegotiations as the contract is being implemented.

Mutual expectations during negotiation and subsequent reactions to the negotiated settlement are shaped by the sense of fairness as perceived by the parties involved. Here it is noteworthy that Indians are likely to view fairness of outcomes as based not only on the ratio of input and output for parties involved, but also on the perceived capacity of the parties to pay (Murphy-Berman *et al.*, 1984). Hence the wealthier party is expected to provide more concessions, irrespective of what the less wealthy party is exchanging in the deal.

Foreign executives intending to work in India need to negotiate with Indian regulators, apart from their counterparts in Indian businesses. Hence it will be germane to describe the key characteristics of this category of Indian negotiators. As Narlikar (2006) points out, an Indian bureaucrat negotiating in multilateral as well as bilateral arenas has traditionally been viewed as a "naysayer." The preference for an ideal solution is frequently reflected in international trade negotiations also. Representatives of the Indian state exhibited similar idealistic posturing during international negotiations on nuclear non-proliferation and disarmament. The unwillingness of Indian negotiators to yield to external demands has frequently led to India's isolation in international negotiations. The unique expectation of equity mentioned previously that considers the paying capacity of the other party apart from the actual constituents of exchange has also been repeatedly exhibited in international negotiations. Such rigid stances adopted by Indian regulators are driven not only by idealistic considerations, but also by a lingering suspicion of foreigners due to the colonial experience of the past (Kumar and Worm, 2005). Such considerations frequently drive the policy-making in India – for example, foreign direct investment (FDI) policies – and it has obvious implications for foreigners intending to do business in India.

Kumar and Worm (2005) also point out that due to the peculiarities of the socio-political and legal context in India, negotiators need to give special emphasis on post-negotiation phase where decisions are implemented. A number of contingencies can arise in this phase and these can often be frustrating for the manager who is uninitiated to India.

Summary and key issues

The following is a list of key issues that readers may derive from this chapter. We are presenting them here in a highly condensed form for readers' convenience.

- Manifestations of conflict that foreign managers are likely to face in India might be driven by both macro- and micro-factors. The macro-variables such as political scenario, historical imbalances, and socio-cultural dynamics might often lead to conflicts. Executives, therefore, need to develop an awareness of the macro drivers for potential conflicts in their spheres of operation.

- India has a complex system of legal provision aimed at the reduction of industrial conflicts. However, its implementation in spirit is often hampered by many factors outlined earlier. Foreign executives can often be baffled by this. Thus they need to develop an appreciation of the gap between what is ideal or desirable and what is practical in the Indian context.

- An understanding of Indian cultural values can be extremely useful for a foreign executive in India. For example, the propensity to seek ideal solutions may prompt many Indians to wait and hope for perfect answers, even though this may be impractical. This can be puzzling for those who are not familiar with India, and they should be prepared to deal with such perfectionist tendencies.

- Respect for elders or hierarchy and an assertion of the primacy of family in all spheres of human action are highly conspicuous in India. These would create or add to the complexity of conflicts experienced in corporate houses across the country. Often foreign managers might not find neat divisions between personal, familial, or professional spheres that they are used to elsewhere.

- Newcomers to India are often not prepared for the diversity that they would face in this country. This includes diversity of languages, geographies and cultural norms. The cultural values pointed out earlier might thus be manifested in varied ways and standard responses might often be insufficient. Managers need to be versatile in adapting their behaviors in line with this diversity in different parts of India.

- Due to the long history of colonialism and the subsequent protectionist economic policies in India until liberalization, many Indians, in particular the regulators, may be skeptical about the motives of foreign companies and their representatives. Thus executives arriving in India would need to work hard to establish trust and convey their intentions for non-exploitative and mutually beneficial relationships.

- While negotiating with Indian companies, we suggest that foreign managers should be prepared for a long-drawn-out process with an emphasis on building relationships. They should also consider the Indian approach to fairness and idealism displayed during negotiations.

- We find that many companies in India are in the throes of a contradictory pattern wherein they want to professionalize their operations in line with Western multinationals, while holding on to older attitudes, beliefs, values and systems. Foreign managers need to be ready for reconciling these opposing trends in creative ways to achieve their objectives.

In this chapter we have highlighted some aspects related to conflict management and negotiation in the Indian context. We initially outlined a few macro- and micro-level issues that lead to conflicts while doing business in India. We then tried to identify preferred styles of conflict handling that are likely to be adopted by Indian managers by examining the scant research available in the area and through our own inquiry. The results showed a preference for the integrating style. Next, we tried to examine the linkages between cultural values that are prominent in India and how they could affect conflict management behavior. We highlighted a few guidelines for managers engaging in negotiation with Indian companies, institutions or government bodies. Finally the gist of key issues from the chapter is outlined for readers' convenience.

References

Bhatnagar, D. (1993) Evaluation of Managerial Influence Tactics: A Study of Indian Bank Managers. *Journal of Managerial Psychology*, 8 (1): 3–9.

Bist, R. (2008) Family feud, India style. Retrieved January 27, 2009 from http://www.asiasentinel.com/index.php?option=com_content&task=view&id=986&Itemid=32.

Budhwar, P. (2001) Doing Business in India. *Thunderbird International Business Review*, 43 (4): 549–68.

Budhwar, P. and Bhatnagar, J. (2009) (eds) *Changing Face of People Management in India*. London: Routledge.

Budhwar, P. and Sparrow, P. (2002) Strategic HRM through the Cultural Looking Glass: Mapping Cognitions of British and Indian HRM Managers. *Organization Studies*, 23 (4): 599–638.

Chandran, R. (2008) Update 1: India's Jet Airways Reinstates Sacked Employees. Retrieved October 25 from http://www.reuters.com/article/rbssIndustryMaterials UtilitiesNews/idUSDEL38865020081016.

Chatterjee, S. R. and Pearson, C. A. L. (2000) Work Goals and Societal Value Orientations of Senior Indian Mangers: An Empirical Analysis. *Journal of Management Development*, 19 (7): 643–53.

Das, G. S. (1987) Conflict Management Styles of Efficient Branch Managers as perceived by others. *ASCI Journal of Management*, 17 (1), 31–8.

Gopalan, S. and Rivera, J. B. (1997) Gaining a Perspective on Indian Value Orientations: Implications for Expatriate Managers. *International Journal of Organizational Analysis*, 5 (2): 156–79.

Guha, R. (2007–08) The Beauty of Compromise. *World Policy Journal*, 24 (4): 77–89.

Jehn, K. A. (1997) A Qualitative Analysis of Conflict Types and Dimensions in Organizational Groups. *Administrative Science Quarterly*, 42 (3): 530–57.

Kakar, S. (1971) Authority Patterns and Subordinate Behavior in Indian Organizations. *Administrative Science Quarterly*, 16 (3): 298–307.

Kumar, R. (2005) Negotiating with the Complex, Imaginative Indian. *Ivey Business Journal*, 69 (4): 1–6.

—— (2007) Tacit Knowledge and Organizational Citizenship Performance. Unpublished doctoral dissertation, Indian Institute of Management, Ahmedabad.

Kumar, R. and Worm, V. (2005) Institutional Dynamics and the Negotiation Process: Comparing India and China. *International Journal of Conflict Management*, 15 (3): 304–34.

Ministry of Labour and Employment (2008) Year-wise Man Days lost due to Strikes and Lockouts: Year 1985–2004. http://labourbureau.nic.in/id2K4%20Graph1. htm.

Misra, S. and Kanungo, R. N. (1997) Bases of Work Motivation in Developing Societies: A Framework for Performance Management. In M. Warner (ed.) *Comparative Management: Critical Perspectives on Business and Management*. London: Routledge.

Morris, M. W., Williams, K. Y., Leung, K., Larrick, R., Mendoza, M. T., Bhatnagar, D., Li, J., Kondo, M., Luo, J. and Hu, J. (1998) Conflict Management Style: Accounting for Cross-national Differences. *Journal of International Business Studies*, 29 (4): 729–47.

Murphy-Berman, V., Berman, J. J., Singh, P., Pachauri, A. and Kumar, P. (1984) Factors affecting Allocation to Needy and Meritorious Recipients: A Cross-cultural Comparison. *Journal of Personality and Social Psychology*, 46 (6): 1267–72.

Nakamura, H. (1964) *Ways of Thinking of Eastern Peoples: India, China, Tibet and Japan*. Honolulu HI: East–West Center Press.

Narlikar, A. (2006) Peculiar Chauvinism or Strategic Calculation? Explaining the Negotiating Strategy of a Rising India. *International Affairs*, 82 (1): 59–76.

Neale, M. A. and Bazerman, M. H. (1992) Negotiating Rationally: the Power and Impact of the Negotiator's Frame. *Academy of Management Executive*, 6 (3), 42–51.

Pandey, M. (1992) Managing the Superior–Subordinate Conflict: Strategies and some Correlates. Unpublished doctoral dissertation. Department of Humanities and Social Sciences, Indian Institute of Technology, Kanpur. Retrieved December 10, 2008 from http://www.new.dli.ernet.in/scripts/FullindexDefault.htm?path1 = /rawdataup load/upload/0120/626&first = 1&last = 203&barcode = 5990010120624.

Rahim, M. A. (1983) A Measure of Styles of Handling Interpersonal Conflict. *Academy of Management Journal*, 26 (2): 368–76.

Saini, D. and Budhwar, P. (2008) Managing the Human Resource in Indian SMEs: The Role of Indigenous Realities in Organizational Working. *Journal of World Business*, 43: 417–34.

Salacuse, J. W. (2004) Negotiating: The Top Ten Ways that Culture can Affect your Negotiation. *Ivey Business Journal*, September–October: 1–6.

Sayeed, O. B. and Mathur, H. B. (1980) Leadership Behaviour and Conflict Management Strategies. *Vikalpa*, 5 (4): 275–82.

Schwartz, S.H. (1992) Universals in the Content and Structure of Values: Theoretical Advances and Empirical Tests in Twenty Countries. In M. Zanna (ed.) *Advances in Experimental Social Psychology*, San Diego CA: Academic Press.

—— (1994) Beyond Individualism/Collectivism: New Dimensions of Values. In U. Kim, H. C. Triandis, C. Kagitcibasi, S. C. Choi and G. Yoon (eds) *Individualism and Collectivism: Theory Application and Methods*. Newbury Park CA: Sage.

Singh, P. (2007) Beyond the Family Feud. *Business World*, December 7, 2007. Retrieved January 27, 2009 from http://www.businessworld.in/index.php/Corporate/ Beyond-The-Family-Feud.html.

Sinha, J. B. P. and Kanungo, R. N. (1997) Context Sensitivity and Balancing in Indian Organizational Behavior. *International Journal of Psychology*, 32 (2): 93–105.

Sinha, J. B. P. and Sinha, D. (1994) Role of Social Values in Indian Organizations. In H. S. R. Kao, D. Sinha and Sek-Hong N. (eds) *Effective Organizations and Social Values*. New Delhi: Sage, 164–73.

Sinha, J. B. P., Vohra, N., Singhal, S., Sinha, R. B. N. and Ushashree, S. (2002) Normative Predictions of Collectivist–Individualist Intentions and Behavior of Indians. *International Journal of Psychology*, 37 (5): 309–19.

Sparrow, P. and Budhwar, P. (1997) Competition and Change: Mapping the Indian HRM Recipe against Worldwide Patterns. *Journal of World Business*, 32 (3): 224–42.

Thomas, K. W. and Kilmann, R. H. (1974) Thomas–Kilmann Conflict MODE Instrument. Tuxedo NY: Xicom.

Tinsley, C. H. (2001) How Negotiators get to Yes: Predicting the Constellation of Strategies used across Cultures to Negotiate Conflict. *Journal of Applied Psychology*, 86 (4): 583–93.

Tripathi, R. C. (1994) Interplay of Values in the Functioning of Indian Organizations. In H. S. R. Kao, D. Sinha and Sek-Hong N. (eds) *Effective Organizations and Social Values*. New Delhi: Sage, 174–92.

Varman, R. and Bhatnagar, D. (1999) Power and Politics in Grievance Resolution: Managing Meaning of Due Process in an Organization, *Human Relations*, 52 (3): 349–82.

Part III

India and the world

12 Outsourcing and offshoring to India

Charmi Patel and Pawan S. Budhwar

With an average growth of GDP of 6.2 per cent (in the last decade), an international exchange seven times larger than in 1991 and a value of investments more than thirty times greater, India is the second best economy in the world (after China) for its growth rate (Nassimbeni and Sartor, 2008). In fact India's GDP at 9.4 per cent was the second fastest-growing GDP after China in 2007–08. As per Reserve Bank of India (RBI), India's actual outbound foreign direct investment (FDI) in 2007–08 was an estimated US$ 17,436 million, an increase of 29.6 per cent over US$ 13,454 million in the previous fiscal year (NASSCOM[1] Newsline, 2008). India is the fifth largest economy on basis of GDP calculated on purchasing power parity (PPP) basis (CIA, 2009). One of the key industries that have propelled this rise and growth is that of information technology (IT). It includes a vast range of activities, from IT-enabled services (ITes) to development and maintenance of software. What was, at first, the externalization of singlular activities has now become a phenomenon involving entire processes: business process outsourcing (BPO).

India has taken this advantage, emerging as a preferred destination for several kinds of processes. The Indian IT–BPO industry is estimated to achieve revenues of US$ 71.7 billion in FY 2009, with indirect employment levels estimated to be around 8 million. Export revenues are estimated to gross US$ 47.3 billion in financial year (FY) 2009, accounting for 66 per cent of the total IT-BPO industry revenues. As a proportion of national GDP, the sector revenues have grown from 1.2 per cent in FY 1998 to an estimated 5.8 per cent in FY 2009. Net value added by this sector to the economy is estimated at 3.5–4.1 per cent for FY 2009. The sector's share of total Indian exports (merchandise plus services) has increased from less than 4 per cent in 1998 to almost 16 per cent in 2008 (NASSCOM Strategic Review, 2009). At the same time, despite these major strides, the IT–BPO sector is facing significant challenges that could impact its future growth if corrective actions are not taken (Budhwar *et al.*, 2006a; 2006b).

This chapter is organized as follows. The first section begins with a clarification of relevant terms such as outsourcing, offshoring, ITO, BPO and KPO. The next talks briefly about the background and evolution of outsourcing/offshoring industry in India. It further focuses on destination India and why it is the favoured land for offshore outsourcing, its trends and challenges. The third section focuses on how to start an offshore outsourcing project in India. In this section we propose a theoretical model; some methodological indications useful in choice-making and planning activities for creating sourcing channel in India and the difficulties met by firms in this market. Moreover, by proposing a scheme that describes the strategic path for developing a sourcing channel in India, we will combine the experiences of some selected firms and suggestions from the past and present literature. In the fourth section we shall briefly discuss some common myths that vendors and clients cling to about offshore outsourcing and lastly, crafting the vision ahead, i.e. the idea to articulate long-term growth perspective that can be achieved by the industry. Finally, we conclude the chapter with some key messages for policymakers.

Outsourcing and offshoring: some clarifications of the terms

'Outsourcing' and 'offshoring' are terms that are often used interchangeably by both practitioners and research scholars despite some important technical differences. Outsourcing can be defined as the shifting or delegating a company's day to day operations or business process to an external service provider, done in anticipation of a better quality, lower rates and in a sense getting an edge over one's competitors. Whereas offshoring is the transfer of an organizational function/operation to another country, regardless of whether the work is outsourced or stays within the same corporation/company (Kroll, 2005; Monczka *et al.*, 2005; Rutherford and Mobley, 2005). Thus the term outsourcing refers to the ownership of productive assets, while offshoring refers to a geographic connotation (Huws *et al.*, 2004).

With increasing globalization of outsourcing companies the distinction between outsourcing and offshoring has become less clear over time. This is evident as increasingly companies are outsourcing their operations or business processes to firms in foreign countries, often to take advantage of cheap skilled labour, resulting in offshore outsourcing.[2] For example, in the electronics industry, several of the large contract manufacturers, like Flextronics, are US-based multinationals. When IBM outsources to Flextronics, it is outsourcing its business to another US firm. By contrast, if IBM outsources to an Indian contract manufacturer, we call this offshore outsourcing.

Some studies mention still another term: nearshoring (Gupta *et al.*, 2003; Ganesh, 2004;). It refers to offshoring activities in countries close to that of origin. For example, some US companies resorting to services provided in Canada, as well as the delocation (transfer) of processes from European industrialized countries tow other European recently developed countries (such as Romania and the Czech Republic) are sometimes defined as nearshoring (Baldwin, 2003; Nassimbeni and Sartor, 2008).

Nassimbeni and Sartor (2008) using the geographic dimension (offshoring) and the assets ownership dimension (outsourcing) have identified a useful typology of similar terms like 'domestic insourcing' where services are generated and supplied within the company or branches located in the domestic territory (other terms used in literature are 'onshore' and 'domestic in-house production') and 'offshore insourcing' where services are provided by foreign branches of the company. Synonymous with the term are 'captive outsourcing', 'captive offshoring' or 'offshore in-house production' (Nassimbeni and Sartor, 2008).

A further literature classification deals with the typology of outsourced services. The prevalent distinction is between three types of outsourcing services: (1) information technology outsourcing (ITO), (2) business process outsourcing (BPO) and (3) knowledge process outsourcing (KPO) (see Figure 12.1 for more details). While it is more difficult to rigorously delineate the three corresponding types of sourcing, nevertheless it is quite easy to distinguish the literature associated with these two forms. According to Willcocks *et al.* (1999), on the same lines as Sen and Shiel (2006), Scholl (2003) and Dharmawat (2003), ITO refers to the outsourcing of activities linked to the management of technological infrastructures and software, with its main objective being to reduce the cost of IT systems or site/data centres while BPO refers to the outsourcing of supply (moving, storing, making and buying of goods and services) and demand (customer selection, acquisition, retention and extension) management, and certain enterprise services (human resources, finance and regulatory, IT and facilities management). ITO is typically service-based. It is a vendor-driven market with its main objective being to reduce the cost of IT systems or site/data centres whereas BPO goes beyond that, it has to do with improving the performance, efficiency and productivity of a business. BPO is more focused on changing and improving a firm's competitiveness in the market place, such that it will generate more revenues, more margin, etc. With ITO, firms are trying to make cost reductions in the 3 per cent of the operating expenses that make

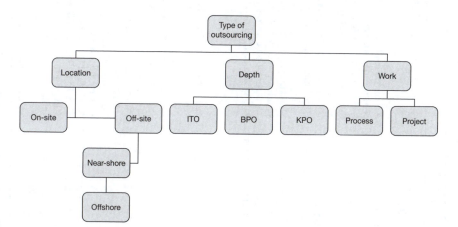

Figure 12.1 Types of outsourcing to India.

Table 12.1 Key differences between KPO and BPO operations

Parameter	KPO	BPO
Primary value proposition	Generating revenues (bolstering top line)	Cost arbitrage process improvements and process efficiency via learning curve and economies of scale across one or more clients
Staff skill sets	Advanced studies and industry recognised certifications such as Chartered Financial Analyst (CFA), Chartered Accountant (CA), Actuarial Studies, Master in Statistics, Engineering and MBA	Undergraduates in commerce and finance
Billing rates	US$ 10 to US$ 45 per hour	US$ 4 to US$ 15 per hour
Process complexity	High-complexity, judgement-based work	Basic processes involving standard procedures and templates
Process quality management and techniques	Standard project management applications supplemented by in-house modelling and documentation controls	Robust six sigma-driven quality techniques with focus on accuracy of output
Staff retention policies	Equity and equity-linked incentives Technical excellence and globally accredited certifications such as CFA and Fellow of Institute of Actuaries Lateral movement across various industry groups Professional growth into client relationship management path	Focus is on monetary incentives such as annual bonuses and increments. However, some BPO's have started focusing on advanced education via MBA programmes to retain staff
Regulatory issues	Strict conflict-of-interest management particularly with respect to insider trading Focus on intellectual property (IP) ownership and management issues	Focus is on Data Protection and Privacy law issues relating to customer data Compliance requirements such as SAS 70
Scalability driver	Staff capabilities and expertise	Staff numbers, volume and accuracy of output
Typical resource cost	US$ 15,000 to US$40,000 (in India) per FTE	US$ 4,000 to US$ 10,000 (in India) per FTE
Control over IP	Key controls required over IP protection	IP is generally not an issue
Common destinations	India	India, China, Vietnam, Philippines and Eastern Europe
Sample activities	Equity research initiation of uncovered stocks and valuation modelling	Finance and accounting outsourcing – accounts receivables and payables, HR

Source: Adapted from KMPG study, 2008.

up their IT budget. With BPO, firms are looking to increase the overall productivity, efficiency and competitiveness of their processes, which can result in huge gains.

On the other hand KPO is a form of outsourcing, in which knowledge-related and information-related work is carried out by workers in a different company or by a subsidiary of the same organization, which may be in the same country or in an offshore location to save cost. Unlike the outsourcing of manufacturing, this typically involves high-value work carried out by highly skilled staff (e.g. valuation research, investment research, patent filing, legal and insurance claims processing, medical diagnostics, clinical trials, etc.). KPO firms, in addition to providing expertise in the processes themselves, often make many low-level business decisions – typically those that are easily undone if they conflict with higher-level business plans. Thus, BPO has a process which is much simpler than KPO. While BPO places an emphasis on low level processes, KPO places an emphasis on high-level processes such as patent filing, investment research, and legal issues. (Table 12.1 represents key differences between KPO and BPO operations, adapted from KPMG's study, 2008.)

Background and evolution of outsourcing/offshoring industry in India

The historical evolution of the ITO, BPO/KPO has been traced by many contributors (Kern *et al.*, 2002; Bajpai *et al.*, 2004). With respect to India, the origin of the ITO/BPO industry goes back to mid-1980s. (See Figure 12.2 for a graphical representation of the stages of evolution.) The first stage deals with transfer to low-cost locations of some IT activities. For example, several European airlines in the 1980s started using New Delhi as base for their back-office operations, British Airways (BA) being one of them. In the second half of the 1980s, Amex consolidated its Japan–Asia Pacific (JAPAC) back-office operations in New Delhi. In 1990s GE set up its back-office operations in Gurgaon, New Delhi. Around the same time Citibank also started its back-office operations and call centre in Chennai. At the same time an organization called EXL started in Noida, Efunds started its operations in Mumbai and Gurgaon, Daksh started its operations in Mumbai and Gurgaon, and 24*7 Customer and Customer Asset started their operations in Bangalore. While Daksh was acquired by IBM and Customer Asset by First Source, EXL, Efunds, and 24*7 continued to be successful players. Having created capacity, companies were hoping that the dot-com boom would translate into larger customer service business through e-mail and chat. Unfortunately the dot-com business crashed in 2001. Start-ups had to do a quick course correction to ensure that the capacity they had built was utilized. The call centre business was a low-hanging fruit, and they capitalized on it. The second stage can be defined as 'growth' which involved some simple back-office services like call centres or invoicing processes as well as more complex IT activities. To simplify the matter, BPO industry can be broadly classified into voice and non-voice

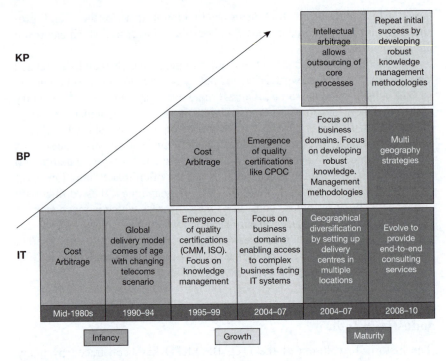

KP					Intellectual arbitrage allows outsourcing of core processes	Repeat initial success by developing robust knowledge management methodologies
BP		Cost Arbitrage	Emergence of quality certifications like CPOC	Focus on business domains. Focus on developing robust knowledge. Management methodologies	Multi geography strategies	
IT	Cost Arbitrage	Global delivery model comes of age with changing telecoms scenario	Emergence of quality certifications (CMM, ISO). Focus on knowledge management	Focus on business domains enabling access to complex business facing IT systems	Geographical diversification by setting up delivery centres in multiple locations	Evolve to provide end-to-end consulting services
	Mid-1980s	1990–94	1995–99	2004–07	2004–07	2008–10

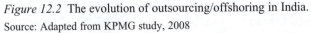

Infancy   Growth   Maturity

Figure 12.2 The evolution of outsourcing/offshoring in India.
Source: Adapted from KPMG study, 2008

processes. The non-voice component is also called transaction processing (TP), and has a closer relationship with IT business. There are huge technical differences between the two sets of businesses processes (Table 12.2 provides key differences between voice and non-voice components of BPO industry).

In the successive stage, that of 'consolidation', services associated to human resources management, administration, finance became candidates for offshoring. The big daddies of the business are keenly looking at this top tier of the business. This is an area where the global players like IBM, Accenture and Capgemini have consolidated their place. Their consulting background has helped them win large contracts spread over extended durations. The jargon used for such deals is 'total outsourcing' and every year we see a multi-billion dollar total outsourcing deals being awarded. For example, International Business Machines Corporation, Hewlett-Packard and India's Infosys Technologies won deals worth US$ 1.2 billion over five years from Australia's Telstra Corporation for application development and maintenance services (NASSCOM, 2009).

Finally, in the current phase, processes destined to offshoring seem more complex and numerous and involve still other functional areas from legal consultancy to R&D. KPO has emerged as an acronym in the early 2000s as a marketing term to highlight the unique aspects of niche BPOs. The requisite

Table 12.2 Comparison between voice and non-voice processes in India

Voice	Non-voice
Real-time	Real-time and batch
It is difficult to provide multi-country support because of language challenges	Easier to provide multi-country support
Customer identifies you with the brand. For example, a Dell computer user calling a call centre thinks he is talking to a representative from Dell	Since it is not interactive, there is no direct correlation with a brand
The focus of training is first on communication, accent, etc., before moving on to processes	The focus is on processes
Need for specialization in domain is limited	Requires specialization and can evolve into a professional career track
Errors, if any, have limited liability	Errors/delays, if any, can have high liability. For example, change in interest rate can wipe away huge amounts of money if the work is not completed as scheduled
Requires large investment in technology, links, etc.	Requires smaller investment

Source: Adapted from Anandkumar and Biswas (2008).

workers need to have deeper functional or domain expertise. Unlike voice BPO operations, non-voice operations are a complete paradigm shift and are closer in relationship to IT business. This is the business on which people are betting on future growth. A spate of new companies like MarketRx, Sigma, etc., has been set up in recent years that focus on very niche areas. Many of these companies have been acquired by larger BPO companies at astronomical valuations (Anandkumar and Biswas, 2008).

As indicated above, the Indian ITO–BPO industry has had an incredible run over the last two decades, gaining a poster-boy image and placing the country on the global map. What was a US$ 4 billion industry in 1998 has grown into a US$ 52 billion sector in 2008, employing over 2 million people. The industry's vertical market exposure is well diversified across several mature and emerging sectors. Banking, financial services and insurance (BFSI) remained the largest vertical market for Indian IT–BPO exports, followed by hi-tech/telecom, which together accounted for 61 per cent of Indian IT–BPO exports in FY 2008. Direct employment in Indian IT–BPO crossed the 2.2 million mark, an increase of about 226,000 professionals over FY 2008. According to the Global Services Location Index compiled by A. T. Kearney (2007), India is still the most attractive country to which to move back-office operations. The index evaluated fifty countries according to three main categories: financial attractiveness, availability of skilled workers, and the business environment. India stays ahead of China, ranked second, still offers an unbeatable mix of low costs, deep technical and language skills, mature vendors and supportive government policies. In both India and China, double-digit growth rates have fuelled wage inflation, with average compensation costs for sample functions rising by around 30 per cent in China and 20 per cent in India. But these cost escalations have been matched by corresponding increases in skill supply and quality indicators. India maintains a strong lead in terms of language skills and vendor maturity. For example, Citigroup announced it would move as many as 8,000 positions to India, particularly in equity research, investment banking and back-office transaction-related activities. This is in addition to its 12,000 employees in the BPO division there. In-country shifts of resources away from expensive and overburdened tier-one cities to tier-two and tier-three cities, with their higher quality of life and lower costs, can also be credited in part for the country's continued competitiveness (A. T. Kearney, 2007).

The neoIT study (2005), which analyses separately ITO and BPO projects, also confirms that India is still a privileged destination of service offshoring. The attractiveness of India is particularly clear for IT and BPO services, justified by the experience gained year after year by local providers, the technical competences, the quality of the adopted processes, the dimension and rate of growth, the adequacy of the legislation on intellectual property protection, the skills of the employees and their cost.

The emergence of India as a key IT–BPO destination is a relatively recent phenomenon. However, its roots go back to the then evolving ITSS (Indian information technology and software sector) industry in India. Two major factors responsible for the growth of ITSS sector within India were the high-quality academic institutions in India which produced high-quality graduates every year and the liberalization of Indian economy in 1991 (Budhwar, 2001). This is probably the main strength of this market. The Indian educational system provides a number of engineers, physicians, chemists, biologists, mathematicians and IT experts that is highest in the world. Every year 2.3 million graduates enter the working world. The integration of foreign units with Western headquarters, and in general the commercial relationships between India and Western companies, are favoured by the perfect knowledge of the English language. It's an advantage often underlined in the literature and particularly evident when comparing India with other locations as China (Kobayashi, 2004; Rutherford and Mobley, 2005; Nassimbeni and Sartor, 2008). Secondly, in India cost goes hand in hand with a quality of services. Since the 1990s the Indian IT sector has looked for international recognition for quality of processes. Many companies have obtained ISO 9000 and/or SEI-CMM level 5 certification. Three out every four SEI-CMM[3] level 5 companies worldwide are located in India (NASSCOM, 2005a).

Not only these, but several other advantages offered by India have led to the emergence and success of the IT–BPO sector. Among these (1) the availability of good talent, (2) a strong base of blue-chip companies, (3) significant government support to the sector, (4) a number of tax incentives, i.e. export services largely being tax free, (5) the existence of ITSS and call centre industry, (6) competition among state governments to attract BPO investments, (7) powerful venture capital interest in investing in growth opportunity, (8) developing track record of proven delivery and systems/process, (9) improved international bandwidth situation, (10) the time difference between India and main clients (based in the UK and US), along with comparative national cost advantages. etc., have contributed significantly to the rapid growth of the IT–BPO industry in India (Prahalad, 2005; Punch 2004; NASSCOM 2005a, b; Pritchard, 2003; Chengappa and Goyal, 2002; Read, 2001). However, going back to comparative studies, many of them underline some challenges of the Indian market: the lack or the inadequacy of transport infrastructure (Gartner, 2003; UNCTAD, 2005; neoIT, 2005), the bureaucracy (neoIT, 2005), the geopolitical instability (Gartner, 2003; UNCTAD, 2005) and high employee attrition rates, not to forget the changing global economic uncertainties (NASSCOM, 2008).

An analysis of the existing literature highlights that the Indian outsourcing industry has a number of barriers for its growth. These include (1) relatively poor infrastructure and electricity, (2) the lack of a customer service culture, (3) cultural differences between employees and clients, (4) under-trained representatives speaking English with a heavy accent (in the case of voice-based captive call centres), (5) scarcity of language skills other than English, (6) employees with relatively little work experience in the outsourcing sector, (7) increasing automation of customer interaction technologies, (8) regional political instability, (9) lengthy periods required to acquire government clearance to allow foreign firms to start operations, (10) increasing competition from other low-cost providers in the Philippines, China, Eastern Europe, South Africa, and (11) increasing costs. (For details see Budhwar *et al.*, 2006a; b; Budhwar *et al.*, 2009.) The impact of such constraints is clearly demonstrated by the fact that a number of outsourcing operators have gone bust in the past. There have also been several emerging reports that highlight a number of issues related to the management of human resources (HR) in the outsourcing sector, such as high attrition rates, motivation, efficiency, and the well-being of employees (Budhwar *et al.*, 2006a).

If not addressed, these could adversely affect the growth of Indian BPO and also impact all the overseas businesses that are outsourcing work to India. For example, many BPO employees (call centres in particular) are asked to assume multiple identities by expecting them to change their names, acquire foreign accent(s), and develop new interests and hobbies to better converse with and satisfy the clients. This often causes psychological problems such as 'multiple personality disorder' while at present a lot of outsourcing firms do not seem to be concerned about the long-term effects of such issues. Things are further complicated by the use of 'graveyard shifts' to match working hours in the Western countries. These erratic long working hours make normal socialization difficult, leading to alienation, withdrawal and increased irritability. Psychologists note that many young individuals employed in Indian call centres are susceptible to burn-out stress syndrome (BOSS), symptoms of which include chronic fatigue, insomnia and alteration of the body's twenty-four-hour biological rhythm. In addition to this, disturbed sleep and prolonged working hours may lead to gastric ulcers, high blood pressure, diabetes or clinical depression. Other aliments ranging from hypertension and asthma to spondylitis are also reported as an outcome of working in outsourcing centres. Other factors contributing to stress, especially in international outsourcing centres is the problem of working at odd hours, especially night shifts, which often leads to family and social problems, including problems with traditional 'arranged' marriages.

To summarize, the problems faced by employees within the Indian BPO industry range from stressful work environments, adverse working conditions and a lack of control to the absence of career development opportunities, physical confinement, over-regimentation, unsociable working hours and abusive clients. However, it is important to note that the very nature of the outsourcing industry (e.g. its emphasis on speed and quality) is such that some of these problems are inevitable and might still continue. But it also raises the serious issue regarding the extent to which organizations are pursuing different initiatives to tackle these emerging problems. If they are not handled properly then they may be disastrous for the sector.

In light of the above highlighted HR related problems in the outsourcing sector, a number of initiatives are being pursued by some BPO companies in India and others will find them helpful to minimize HR related problems. These will include provision of flexible work arrangements (including flexible working day, week, shift, and job sharing), better working conditions, creating a career path for lower level employees (their attrition rate is the highest and the absence of a clear career is acting as a major factor for high attrition), adoption of improved motivation and retention mechanisms, and further professionalism of managerial systems. At a macro level, organizations can work with respective governments and bodies to create a more robust infrastructure to support the outsourcing sector, develop rigorous norms for job-hoppers, institutions are working on the creation of appropriate skills for this sector and a combined effort is needed from all the stakeholders of this sector to improve the image of working in it. (At present it is socially not considered good to work in the BPO sector.) Despite the above-mentioned problems, the future of outsourcing sector is very promising, but regular improvement will be needed for it to flourish. In the last section of this chapter we further map out the way forward in this regard.

Starting an offshore outsourcing project in India

As per Monczka *et al.* (2005) and Nassimbeni and Sartor (2008) the strategic path for IT/BP offshoring experiences that we have gathered can be theorised into three successive phases: strategic analysis and planning, selection of suppliers and definition of contracts and implementation (see Figure 12.3 for more details). Starting with this scheme, each phase is explained in detail below.

Phase 1: strategic analysis and planning

The first step of this phase consists of preventive analysis. Before choosing an international sourcing type, it is vital to have in-depth knowledge of the activities that could be developed abroad. The identification of input variables, output performance expectations, constitutive stages, work procedures, lead times, organizational interdependences and the concomitant creation of the documents stating these aspects are prerequisites for a well informed choice of outsourcing, especially when offshore (Ganesh, 2004; Nassimbeni and Sartor, 2008). At GSK[4] the company's analysis of its internal know-how and documentation is the starting point for every sourcing project. Further strategic evaluation follows, aimed at defining the relative importance of each activity with respect to the core business. The distinction between 'core' and 'non-core' activities is one of the key aspects of global sourcing projects. In GSK every choice of service offshoring is assessed in order to quantify the value added by each activity.

Evaluation of the level of outsourcing and offshoring propensity is the next step, which involves the study of two decisive variables in order to choose the localization and ownership of the productive assets: the outsourcing and offshoring propensity of the activities/processes considered. The two variables are linked to some factors such as level of tacit knowledge, level of separability between activities, comparison of internal work performances and those offered by external, i.e. local/foreign supply sources, risk of negative repercussions such as loosing process know-how and control, need of proximity between buyer and supplier, need for linguistic competences, contractual

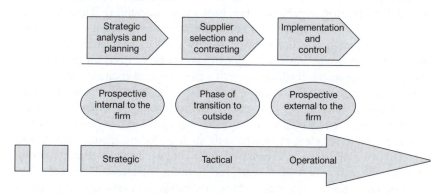

Figure 12.3 The macro-phases of outsourcing.

Source: Monczka *et al.* (2005); Nassimbeni and Sartor (2008)

legal restraints, digitalization level, need to know the context where client works, level of buyer–supplier interaction required to carry out the activity and level of standardization of activity (Willcocks *et al.*, 2004, 1995; UNCTAD, 2005; Ganesh, 2004; Gupta and Nidhin, 2003).

GSK, for example, resorts to offshoring for some repetitive back-office services such as the management of pay sheets and internal call centre. In this company, standardization precedes aggregation, i.e. the identification of the activities that are related to each other and can be potentially grouped into one. Through the composition of critical volume of purchases and co-ordinated management of the activities outsourced by its various units, GSK greatly improved the results of its sourcing process.

Having determined the activities' level of outsourcing and offshoring propensity, it is possible to start the decision-making process that will define the most suitable form for sourcing. For core activities, which can not be outsourced for obvious strategic reasons, the choice only concerns the place of production (in-house or captive foreign unit). Non-core activities on the other hand can have different destinations: outsourcing on the domestic market, international outsourcing, onshore or offshore insourcing. An example of offshore insourcing is that of the research and development activities carried out by GSK. Since these are characterized by a significant technological content, the absence interaction with the final client and a high level of separability, GSK established a subsidiary in India. Some of the main offshore insourcing forms available in India are: wholly owned subsidiaries (WOS), companies where 100 per cent of the capital is foreign (e.g. Citigroup[5] and Comau India;[6] joint ventures (JVs), joint-stock companies in which two or more partners collaborate to develop common entrepreneurial project (e.g. Sitel India[7] and Sella Bank[8]); build–operate–transfer (BOT) solutions where a provider starts an offshore service centre whose ownership passes to the buyer after a period of time which is defined by contract (Nassimbeni and Sartor, 2008).

In the presence of high degrees of externalization ability and global-level allocability, the most suitable solution is offshore outsourcing. There are three corresponding forms. Firstly, 'pure offshore outsourcing' consists in employing an independent supplier in order to buy services characterized by high standardization levels, limited complexity and reduced need for control (e.g. pay sheet management, feeding data into a database, call centres, and so forth). This type of sourcing does not require significant integration with the provider and shares common features with 'traditional direct sourcing' of material goods. Secondly, when greater control of processes is required or more complex activities must be developed, it is advisable in logic of balancing control and flexibility to establish a 'dedicated offshore centre'. The provider creates an operational centre where staff work full time for the client. However when this expertise is lacking the most suitable solution is an intermediary, i.e. 'third-party transplant'. This third party mediates the relationships between supplier (Indian) and customer (Western), and can provide the latter the competences in international sourcing, as well as consultancy services for redefining the company's processes and the management of transition (Nassimbeni and Sartor, 2008).

Dos

- Carry out strategic evaluation which aims at defining the relative importance of each activity with respect to the core business. The distinction between 'core' and 'non-core' activities is one of the key aspects for global sourcing projects.
- Focus on the expected goals: a sourcing project aimed at cutting costs will follow a different path from that of a project oriented towards qualitative improvement or the acquisition of external competencies.
- Ensure that the external supplier receives responsibilities over processes that are not critical for the creation and preservation of the competitive advantage.
- Reason in perspective, and try to understand and foresee how changes in technology or in the market can redesign the future map of core activities.

Don'ts

- Do not get carried away only with the perceived cost savings of outsourcing on a total cost/employee basis, as the productivity, delivery of the SLAs, quality of services and cost in managing the engagement are equally important.
- Do not rely on the services provider for business innovation. No one knows your business and your clients better than you do.
- Do not outsource the core applications or processes which have a direct impact in servicing your key clients. Fundamentally, the existence of the organization is dependent on their clients.
- Do not undervalue the importance of linguistic knowledge. This requirement can drastically reduce the number of locations or impose heavy effort for translation.

Phase 2: selection of suppliers and definition of contracts

The first step in this phase is to identify the criteria used to select a supplier. From Nassimbeni and Sartor (2008) study costs: the quality and competencies supplied, flexibility of the supplier, certification and quality of processes supplied, international presence of the supplier and experience in the management of offshore relationships are crucial in selecting the source basin (Ganesh, 2004; A. T. Kearney, 2004; Gupta, 2003). A further element is choice of location within India. India is really heterogeneous: the states forming it differ in terms of incentives and fiscal aid given to foreign operators, industry specialization and infrastructures. Thus the choice of location is as crucial as when opting for insourcing. Request for information (RFI) follows next, i.e. a questionnaire is sent to the selected suppliers in order to characterize their profile. RFI gathers general information on the size of the company, competences, production features, localization, certification and customers served. Finally, on final selection an RFP (request for proposal) is issued, requesting an offer regarding the activity in hand.

Dos

- Use your contractual terms as the basis for negotiations and include them in the RFP with a redline copy as a condition for response.
- Maintain a healthy competitive environment. Never sole source. You can have a primary partner (e.g. globally) and keep that partner honest with a mix of regional partners.
- Check out the supplier's expertise in the field of offshoring and its past and present customers. If possible talk to them about their experiences
- Clearly define the desired results and how they'll be measured.

Don'ts

- Do not treat the supplier as outsider. Once you outsource, your supplier is part of your company; treat it that way. Give them a sense of 'ownership' of their tasks.
- Do not fail to consider the long-term relationship dynamics.
- Do not impose, try to work with. Establish good lines of communication. There can be many things that can cause problems here such as; language barriers, time differences, cultural and economic environment differences. It is crucial that all parties can understand each other.

Phase 3: implementation

Having selected the supplier and defined the contract, the next phase is implementation. Offshore services, particularly those concerning activities that were previously carried out inside the company, can determine radical changes to organizational structure. It is therefore, necessary to carefully plan and manage this stage. During this stage it is useful to set up a pilot project so to clarify the dynamics and effect of change on the internal organization of the company. The next step is the gradual transfer of the activities involved in the project. During this step the supplier acquires, as well as a growing work load, greater responsibilities. The transition process is probably the most delicate stage of the implementation of a service offshoring strategy. The problems encountered during this phase by the companies analysed are numerous, from work interruptions to loss of data from spreading of uncertainty and loss of motivation by the firm's employees to complaints issued by trade unions.

These problems are frequently accompanied by the errors made when estimating transition costs. It is therefore useful to plan with the supplier, this transition period, taking care to define an accurate activity plan and control systems for the results brought about by the change. Once transition is complete the project enters the stage of 'ongoing management'. The need to control the outsourced processes, monitor the progress of the project and predict technological and organizational updates stresses the importance of relationship with the provider. The relationship with the provider has to be strengthened by sharing managerial and work policies, making an effort to understand the different organizational dynamics, mitigating cultural differences and adapting to the new leadership style. Whilst maintaining the relationship with the provider it is also important to monitor performance. The variables that are usually assessed are punctuality, costs, quality, problem-solving ability, safety and flexibility.

Relationship and negotiation dynamics concern all the stages mentioned previously. These dynamics are decisive for every sourcing process, but on an international scale they present country-specific criticalities linked to local laws and culture. The latter includes both implicit and explicit assumptions, perceptions and internal and external elements. It is difficult to fully understand these complex factors in a heterogeneous society like India. More details can be found in Chapter 11 of this book which reflects upon conflict management and negotiation dynamics in India.

Dos

- Seriously emphasize the governance model and mutually agreed pre-defined time bound escalations to stake holders. There are always identified and unforeseen risks in any engagement. For any identified risks, the critical path has to be monitored regularly on a proactive basis and the mitigation plan needs to be executed as planned.
- Get your act together internally. Ensure that you have the right cross-functional team formed to assess service options, including sourcing/procurement, financial and technical representation.
- Create and maintain an environment that fosters open, honest, transparent communications and mutual trust.
- Ensure periodic visits to development centres (especially for offshore services). Be explicit in governance meetings at all levels (eliminate use of colloquialisms).

Don'ts

- Do not undervalue performance control and monitoring of activities. The variables that are usually assessed are punctuality, costs, quality, problem-solving ability, safety and flexibility.

- Do not feel relieved of all responsibility and abdicate control to the supplier. In other words, sometimes companies think once they outsource they can wash their hands of it. Instead work with offshore managers on improvement plans and minimizing any risks.

Myths about outsourcing/offshoring

In recent years, there's been a seemingly endless boom in offshore outsourcing. But companies that think handing off an operation to an overseas partner is easy can get a rude awakening. The transition often proves out to be much more costly and complicated then expected. And companies often find that their high hopes about cost savings and greater efficiency don't pan out. To get a better understanding of the problems and solutions several surveys by various practitioners and research scholars have found some common myths that vendors and clients cling to about offshore outsourcing – false assumptions about how processes should work; these range from unrealistic expectations to poor ideas about how to structure contracts to mistaken views of risks. Its important to briefly reflect upon these myths, as they can prove detrimental to the success of outsourcing projects and even to an organization's overall sourcing strategy if not addressed timely (McKinsey Global Institute, 2006; Puranam and Srikanth, 2007; NASSCOM, 2005a).

- *We can have it all.* Puranam and Srikanth (2007) found in their survey that executives top criteria for judging the success of an outsourcing project are efficiency, or cost reductions; effectiveness, or improvement in service; and flexibility, or the ability to increase and decrease production rapidly. Each in itself is perfectly valid objective; however, the problem is that many clients expect and indeed many vendors promise all three in the same outsourcing project. The fact is, achieving one objective means making a trade-off in another area. Thus it is essential to define from the outset as to the real motive for outsourcing, as mixed motives are dangerous: if people inside the client company have different expectations about the outsourcing project, it's political trouble before it begins. It is important to prioritize outsourcing objectives and communicate them widely within the organization.
- *Outsourcing is like buying commodities.* Many companies think outsourcing is a 'frictionless market', with no transition costs or other restraints. In fact most managers feel that outsourcing back-office operations is like procuring stationery. On the contrary, outsourcing carries significant transaction costs, starting with finding a vendor and negotiating a contract to moving the operation from one location to another and subsequently keeping in sync with rest of the company (NASSCOM, 2005; Puranam and Srikanth, 2007).
- *We need an ironclad contract.* Outsourcing is not a one-time transaction, but an exchange that evolves over time as competitive conditions and

technology change. So, many executives try to write complex contracts that protect them in a host of possible circumstances. It is impossible to take all contingencies into account. Instead, companies should write a contract that ensures that all parties understand their role and responsibilities, and then put in place a process for negotiating changes.

- *Contracts don't matter.* On one hand companies might be too rigid with contracts; on the other sometimes companies try to rush into an outsourcing deal without a contract. They draft a memorandum of understanding or letter of intent – informal documents that set out grand visions of the client–vendor relationship rather than focus on nitty-gritty details, as a contract does. These documents are useful in setting out the joint vision of the relationship, but they are no substitute for contracts. Since they are usually vague on critical operational details, they may be hard to enforce in court, lead to different interpretations by different managers and ultimately undermine trust in the client–vendor relationship. Thus the process of negotiating a contract will enable the client and vendor to understand the risks, rewards and interests for both sides. That, in turn, will make it clear what should be on and off the table in the relationship (Puranam and Srikanth, 2007).

- *It's not our headache any more.* The biggest obstacle to a satisfactory partnership is that one party sees itself as relieved of all responsibility and abdicates control to the other. In other words, sometimes companies think once they outsource a process they can wash their hands of it. In fact the key to success for many companies has been the high level of engagement of their senior management. The senior managers should work with offshore managers on process-improvement plans. And the senior managers can ensure that the offshore managers are treated as part of their extended team, and conduct joint management development and training activities. Thus, outsourcing does not mean that the process is not your headache any more – though it is (one would hope) less of a headache! (Puranam and Srikanth, 2007; Anandkumar and Biswas, 2008.)

Creating the vision ahead

The Indian IT–BPO industry is at an interesting juncture of its history. After recording mind-boggling growth of nearly 37 per cent year after year since 2004, the sector is faced with a dynamic and volatile global scenario which is throwing up significant challenges. As the markets, where the industry predominantly plays are changing, and as customer needs are altering, the IT–BPO industry needs to reinvent itself in order to sustain its global leadership. At the same time, the debilitating impact of the economic slowdown sweeping across the world cannot be ignored by the BPO industry, which predominantly relies on exports. Matters are made worse by the fact that the Indian BPO industry banks significantly on the US market (with 60 per cent of the sector's revenues being realized from this geography) as well as the banking, financial services and insurance (BFSI) vertical (which accounts for 50 per cent of BPO exports), as both these areas have been massively hit by the economic slowdown. The crisis has also led to a complete change in the way global customers are now approaching outsourcing. It is becoming apparent today that a sliver-centric approach is becoming key for the BPO sector, with companies building a strong and unmatched value proposition for themselves in specific, focused niche segments. The move by Indian BPOs to sub/micro-verticals is a sign that super-specialization is being actively explored by these companies. Since the BPO industry is expanding in width (with completely new industry segments opting for outsourcing), it is imperative that Indian companies strengthen their capabilities in some of these emerging areas. Whether it is procurement BPO, legal BPO or domestic market BPO, the industry view is that these nascent segments with high offshore ability could hold the key to future growth. With innovation and niche orientation emerging as big differentiators, especially for emerging companies and start-ups, a number of companies within the BPO space have begun taking uncharted paths to make an impact. For example, SAVI Infoservices (India), a wholly owned captive centre for SAVI Group (see www.billingsavi.com for more details), a US-based outfit, is focused on delivering profitability to physician practices through a trained certified team and technology innovation. SAVI is the back-office prescription for healthcare providers. The company's clients are improving profitability through SAVI's proven best-practice processes, which eliminate no-shows and increase daily patient visits; maximize co-pay and deductible payments at time of visit, ensure insurance card collection and eliminate eligibility questions, capture all charges, identify missing information, and shorten follow-ups, improve first time payment percentage through coding and claim scrubbing, handle claims auditing, denial responses, and soft collections and provide an offsite secure technical platform at no cost to the physician. By combining technology and extensive experience SAVI has created practice management solutions which result in higher efficiency, greater productivity, and increased collections for customers (NASSCOM, 2009).

Keeping in view the prevailing economic conditions, BPO players will need to evolve new and innovative business models, based on gain sharing and outcome-based pricing. Going forward, it is suggested that BPO service providers consider multiple step-out business models to capture opportunities. The NASSCOM–McKinsey study (2009) states that these could be centred on several areas, including multi-client services/products; domain expertise, customer intimacy and delivery excellence. As a part of their domain approach for instance, BPOs can build specific solutions (accelerators, frameworks, next-generation process design) in a few chosen domains (verticals and horizontals). This could imply a process re-engineering play (e.g. designing next-generation F&A process) or vertical specialist play (e.g. clinical research). If they embrace a solution approach, companies can drive non-linear revenues by leveraging market leading intellectual property. This could include development of industry-standard utilities (e.g. carbon dioxide monitoring and optimization), software products (e.g. core banking platforms) and subsequent commercialization using a licence and maintenance fee model. These models will entail a distinct set of performance markers, capabilities and management philosophies, and should be managed separately from current traditional approaches, and as part of a portfolio. The players that emerge at the top in 2020 will have moved well beyond the traditional delivery approach to nimbly implement and outperform on other approaches as well. At the end of the day, it is becoming apparent that the Indian BPO industry has the intrinsic strengths to survive the downturn and thrive in the long term. The sector can achieve its medium to long-term goals by thinking beyond the mundane, exploring new and unbeaten paths and working in partnership with its peer sectors – the government and academia (*Economist*, 2008; NASSCOM, 2009; A. T. Kearney, 2007).

Key issues

- While India today has over a third of the world's BPO global sourcing market, other competing countries have scaled up their BPO supportive incentives and initiatives. However, India still remains one of the most favoured destinations for offshore outsourcing despite the economic slowdown. In order for India to remain in the global sourcing arena, all the stakeholders including government and industry need to collectively address challenges such as lack of public services, cost of training and infrastructure issues.
- Sending functions or business processes to an offshore destination can be a complex, frustrating and time-consuming venture. More care is needed for India due to differences in political environment, culture, infrastructure and business environment.
- While most companies go into offshore locales for the cost savings, there are longer-term implications that must factor into the decision such as quality of processes, workforce flexibility, external economic environment, relationship with supplier, country infrastructure, people and skills availability and so on.
- Selecting a right location with a long-term commitment to maintaining world-class levels of performance in a business process can help ensure satisfaction with the decision to offshore long after wage differentials have disappeared. The classic example is India and information technology, where companies now look to India as much for the quality of its IT professionals as for the price of its labour.
- Establish an accurate baseline that can help the offshore organization to set reasonable, achievable performance targets. Inflated opinions of existing service levels can be a barrier to consideration of offshoring, implementation and ultimate satisfaction.

- Don't offshore highly interconnected processes. The best candidates for offshoring are self-contained processes with minimal 'surface area'. The overhead associated with offshoring activities that cannot be easily and naturally decoupled from activities that will remain onshore generally exceeds projected savings from wage arbitrage. Adding an unnecessary handoff for purposes of offshoring also increases the chances of error or miscommunication.
- Don't leave process improvement entirely to the offshore organization. 'Lift and shift' has an intuitive appeal because it leaves offshore resources, often less expensive and more highly motivated, to make improvements that onshore resources have presumably failed to make for years. Despite lift-and-shift's intuitive appeal, experience suggests that the best time to make process improvements is in the transition from onshore to offshore, when the organization is in flux and methods of operating have yet to become entrenched. The price of the additional implementation time and effort will prove worth paying.
- Lastly, don't assume local culture can be finessed. Local culture impacts everything from how best to motivate people to methods of dealing with disagreement and conflict.

Notes

1   The National Association of Software and Services Companies (NASSCOM), the Indian chamber of commerce is a consortium that serves as an interface to the Indian software industry and Indian BPO industry.
2   There is not complete consensus on these definitions; however Bhagwati *et al.*, (2004) define outsourcing as the offshore trade in arm's-length services, while others such as Trefler (2005) adopt a broader perspective and refer outsourcing in either goods or services.
3   Capability Maturity Model (CMM) is a method developed (1984) for the development of software by Software Engineering Institute (SEI) at Carnegie Mellon University, Pittsburgh PA. It has five levels of 'maturity'; each of them represents an improvement in the processes and in the organization of software development.
4   GlaxoSmithKline, a multinational company in the pharmaceutical sector, localizes in India several of its back-office and support activities with the aim to reduce costs and increase operation flexibility.
5   Citigroup (branded Citi) is a major American financial services company based in New York. Citi India offers knowledge outsourcing services to Citi's investment bank and research teams across the globe.
6   Comau India (WOS of Comau since 1997) is a company that offers product engineering, production systems and maintenance services to automotive companies.
7   Sitel India is joint venture between the Tata group and Sitel Corporation, formed in 2000, with both parties holding 50 per cent of the equity. It is a global BPO leader.
8   Sella Bank have created a joint venture in India to develop some high-value-added activities for their software.

References

Anandkumar, V. and Biswas, S. (2008) *Business Process Outsourcing Oh! BPO-Structure and Chaos, Fun and Agony*. New Delhi: Sage.

A. T. Kearney (2007) Global Services Location Index (GSLI), www.atkearney.com http://www.atkearney.com/index.php/Publications/global-services-location-index.html (accessed 12 June 2009).

——— (2004) FDI confidence Index. *The Global Business Policy Council*, Vol. 7.

Bajpai, N., Sachs, J., Arora, R. and Khurana, H. (2004) *Global Service Sourcing: Issues of Cost and Quality*. CGSD Working Paper No. 16.

Baldwin, M. (2003) More than Offshoring: Smartsourcing. *Journal of Financial Transformation*, 8: 95–102.

Bhagwati, J., Panagariya, A. and Srinivasan, T. N. (2004) The Muddles over Outsourcing. *Journal of Economic Perspectives*, 18 (4): 93–114.

Budhwar, P. and Khatri, N. (2001) Comparative Human Resource Management in Britain and India: An Empirical Study. *International Journal of Human Resource Management*, 13 (5): 800–26.

Budhwar, P., Luthar, H. and Bhatnagar, J. (2006b) Dynamics of HRM Systems in BPOs operating in India. *Journal of Labor Research*, 27 (3): 339–60.

Budhwar, P., Varma, A., Singh, V. and Dhar, R. (2006a) HRM Systems of Indian Call Centres: An Exploratory Study, *International Journal of Human Resource Management*, 17 (5): 881–97.

Budhwar, P., Malhotra, N. and Singh, V. (2009) Work Processes and Emerging Problems in Indian Call Centres. In M. Thite and B. Russell (eds.) *The Next Available Operator: Managing Human Resources in Indian BPO Industry*. New Delhi: Response Books from Sage, 59–82.

CIA (2009) *World Factbook*, www.cia.gov https://www.cia.gov/library/publications/the-world-factbook/rankorder/2001rank.html (accessed 10 June 2009).

Chengappa, R. and Goyal, M. (2002) House Keepers to the World. *India Today*, November: 18–48.

Dharmawat, N. (2003) BPO: Destination India. *Patni*, http://www.patni.com/resource center/collateral/businessprocessoutsourcing/tp_bpodestination.pdf (accessed 20 June 2009).

Economic Times (2005a) Indian BPOs can save $30 billion for US, http://economic times.indiatimes.com/articleshow/msid-1171501,prtpage-1.cms (accessed 20 December 2006).

Economist (2004) India's Shining Hopes: A Survey of India. 21 February.

Economist (2005) Survey: Sweatshops and Technocoolies. 5 March.

Economist (2008) Management Idea: Outsourcing, http://www.economist.com/research/articlesBySubject/displaystory.cfm?subjectid=328221&story_id=E1_TNPNPNRS (accessed 20 June 2009).

Financial Express (2005) Call Centers turn Women Favourites. 8 March, http://www.financialexpress.com/fe_full_story.php?content_id=84677/headline=call (accessed 9 March).

Ganesh, D. (2004) Planning for Offshore Outsourcing. *National Computing Centre*, No. 286.

Gartner (2003) Choosing an Offshore Outsourcing Location. In Hillary M. Kobayashi (ed.) *Outsourcing to India*, Heidelberg: Springer.

Gupta S. and Nidhin V. (2003) 'Pete at night, Pradeep by day': The Offshore Contact Center Phenomenon. *Capco*.

Gupta, S., Singh, J., Regulapati, R., Nachum, L. and Mukherjee, M. (2003) *Managing Change in Offshoring*. Offshoring Survey Report. Baruch College/Paarus Group/ Capco.

Harrison, A. and McMillan, M. (2006) *Outsourcing Jobs? Multinationals and US Employment*. Washington DC: NBER.

Huws U., Dahlmann S. and Flecker J. (2004) *Outsourcing of ICT and related Services in the EU*. Dublin: European Foundation for the Improvement of Living and Working Conditions.

Kern, T., Kreijger, J. and Willcocks, L. (2002) Exploring ASP as Sourcing Strategy: Theoretical Perspectives, Propositions for Practice. *Journal of Strategic Information Systems*, 11 (2): 153–77.

Kobayashi, Hillary M. (ed.) (2004) *Outsourcing to India*. Heidelberg: Springer.

KPMG (2008) Knowledge Process Outsourcing: Unlocking Topline Growth by Outsourcing the core, www.in.kpmg.com. http://www.in.kpmg.com/TL_Files/ Pictures/KPO.pdf (accessed 12 June 2009).

Kroll, C. A. (2005) *State and Metropolitan Area Impacts of the Offshore Outsourcing of Business Services and IT*. Berkeley CA: Fisher Center for Real Estate and Urban Economics, No. 293.

McKinsey (2006) Benchmarking India's Business Process Outsourcers. http://www. mckinseyquarterly.com/Operations/Outsourcing/Benchmarking_Indias_business process_outsourcers_1788 (accessed 20 June 2009).

Monczka, R. M., Carter, J. R., Markham, W. J., Blascovich, J. and Slaight, T. (2005) *Outsourcing Strategically for Sustainable Competitive Advantage*. CAPS/A. T. Kearney.

NASSCOM (2008) Industry Trends, www.nasscom.in/Nasscom/templates/Normal Page.aspx?id=56966 (accessed 12 June 2009).

NASSCOM (2005a) BPO Job Potential Stays High: NASSCOM. Sify.com http:// sify.com/finance/fullstory.php?id=13866657?headline=BPO~job~potential~sta (accessed 20 December 2006).

NASSCOM (2005b) http://nasscom.org/artdisplay.asp?Art_id = 2781 (accessed 24 May 2007).

NASSCOM (2008) Newsline. Looking Ahead, http://blog.nasscom.in/nasscom newsline/2008/12/ (accessed 20 June 2009).

NASSCOM (2009) Strategic Review, www.nasscom.in, http://nasscom.in/Nasscom/ templates/NormalPage.aspx?id = 55816 (accessed 12 June 2009).

NASSCOM–McKinsey (2009) In focus: Newsline. www.nasscom.in. http://www. nasscom.in/Nasscom/templates/NormalPage.aspx?id = 11075 (accessed 12 June 2009).

Nassimbeni, G. and Sartor, M. (2008) *Sourcing in India*. Basingstoke: Palgrave Macmillan.

neoIT (2005) Offshore Insights. Market Report series, www.neoIT.com, http://cost killer.net/tribune/TribuPDF/OIv4i04_0506_ITO_and_BPO_Salary_Report_2006.pdf (accessed 12 June 2009).

Prahalad, C. K. (2005) The Art of Outsourcing. *Wall Street Journal*, Easter edition, 8 June, A14.

Pritchard, S. (2003) Heavy Costs of an Insecure World. *Financial Times*, 5.

Punch, L. (2004) The Global Back Office: Beyond the Hype. *Credit Card Management*, 16 (11): 26.

Puranam, P. and Srikanth, K. (2007) Seven Myths about Outsourcing. *Wall Street Journal*, http://sloanreview.mit.edu/business-insight/articles/2007/3/4935/seven-myths-about-outsourcing/ (accessed on 12 June 2009).

Read, B. B. (2001) Being There: Serving your US Customers from Afar. *Call Centre Magazine*, 14 (2), 85–92.

Rutherford, B. and Mobley, S. (2005) The Next Wave: Refining the Future of Offshoring. *Journal of Corporate Real Estate*, 7 (1): 87–95.

Scholl, R. (2003) Business Process Outsourcing at the Crossroads. White Paper. Stamford CT: Gartner Group.

Sen, F. and Shiel, M. (2006) From Business Process Outsourcing (BPO) to Knowledge Process Outsourcing (KPO): Some Issues. *Human Systems Management*, 25: 145–55.

Trefler, D. (2005) Policy Responses to the New Offshoring: Think Globally, Invest Locally. Mimeo, University of Toronto, April.

United Nations Conference on Trade and Development (2005) *Prospects for Foreign Direct Investment and the Strategies of Transactional Corporations, 2005–2008* (United Nations report). Geneva: UNCTAD.

Willcocks, L., Fitzgerald, G. and Feeny, D. (1995) Outsourcing IT: The Strategic Implications. *Long-range Planning*, 28 (5): 59–70.

Willcocks, L. P., Lacity, M. C. and Kern, T. (1999) Risk Mitigation in IT Outsourcing: Strategy Revisited: Longitudinal Case Research at LISA. *Journal of Strategic Information Systems*, 8 (3): 285–314.

Willcocks, L. P., J. Hindle, D. Feeny and M. Lacity (2004) IT and Business Process Outsourcing: The Knowledge Potential. *Information Systems Management Journal*, summer: 7–15.

13 Lessons from Indian success stories

Jyotsna Bhatnagar and Ashok Som

Given the ground reality of complex political, legal and socio-cultural nuances in the Indian diaspora, the need for an efficient, effective and innovative HR system becomes an imperative for all managers struggling to understand the upcoming Indian business context. This is an important contribution, to this volume, as the business challenges become more daunting when we find a mixed response within the Indian business context to the early 1990s initiated liberalization of the Indian economy. Managers struggle with HR systems, which are transforming from traditional ones to more efficient systems and practices. Yet most are lost in the cross-fire of change, especially when changing from the traditional HR systems. These traditional systems were based on personal status within the society, personal connections within an organization and one's social connections. Within this context when a manager in India would like to shift to innovative, cost-effective, efficient, and metric-driven HR system, he has to struggle with archaic rules within this business context and finds the navigation within the system still based on traditional ways of doing things and knowing the right people in the system.

The main aim of the chapter is to highlight two case studies which emphasize the post-liberalization challenges that the organizations were facing and were resultant in HR and OD interventions, which highlight efficient, effective, and innovative HR system. Further, the chapter builds on the unique lessons these companies provide which perhaps others may utilize. The first case study is of a large public-sector organization undergoing restructuring (Som, 2007b). Included in our examination are how the redesign had affected internal and external customers and also how the strategic HR service role by line managers is embedded in a transforming system. The second case study is of a private-sector company that made changes in its HRM practices, talent acquisition strategy and organizational culture which enhanced the firm's competitive advantage, leading to talent loyalty and high organizational commitment. Following the discussion of the two case studies the chapter focuses on implications for practicing managers and lessons and challenges in the Indian business context.

To understand the case studies we need to first navigate the changing Indian business context. We need to comprehend the ground reality pre- and post-liberalization. Before the liberalization of the Indian economy the Indian government had an extremely regulated and restrictive use of private, domestic and foreign investments, so that self-reliance on Indian socialistic systems might be attained. (Budhwar *et al.*, 2006; Amba-Rao *et al.*, 2000). The government-owned, public-sector firms dominated the organized or "modern" sector jobs, which employed two-thirds of the work force (Sodhi, 1994). Public-sector enterprises, constrained by government and union pressures, were compelled to accept this "entitlement" approach, which resulted in workforce inflexibility and lower productivity. The inefficiencies of central planning also created shortages of resources in all sectors and led to an abuse of power and questionable practices by various government officials (Mathias, 1994; Tayeb, 1988). This had led to a myopic vision within the Indian context (Bhatnagar, 2006). With the financial crisis that followed from depleting foreign reserves the Indian government felt compelled to move towards liberalization in the early 1990s. This led to both public and private-sector companies adopting restructuring and redesigning HR interventions (Som, 2008; Bhatnagar, 2007). Of special importance is the strengthening of the public sector, wherein functional autonomy was granted by withdrawing 696 guidelines, issued by the Department of Public enterprises. Granting freedom to eleven selected public-sector organizations (called *navratnas*[1]) to incur capital expenditure, raise finances and decide on joint ventures and strategic alliances (Bhatnagar, 2006: 416). There are now eighteen navratna public-sector organizations and fifty-eight mini- (small) navratna public-sector organizations, referred by the Indian government as central public enterprises (http://dpe.nic.in/newsite/navmini.htm).

Despite the government's impetus on public-sector navratna firms, and due to opening up of the Indian economy to foreign direct investment, soon the Indian market was dominated by global multinationals, business process outsourcing firms and private firms (Budhwar *et al.*, 2009). Given the signs of changing times, and with the increasing presence of global MNCs and private players in India, the new generation HR professionals in India have become key players in the design, development, restructuring, and realignment of a firm's business strategy to its HR strategy (Som, 2007a). The labor-intensive Indian market started becoming proactive to innovative, HR metric-driven, effective and efficient people management systems, which were adopted by the growing number of global MNCs, BPOs and other private firms. There was a change in the landscape of people management practices across all sectors of Indian industry with focus on upcoming themes of strategic innovative HR, talent management, six-sigma in HR function and commitment-based HR which best-place-to-work-in organizations implemented (Budhwar and Bhatnagar, 2009). Thus the HR systems in public-sector organizations, as well as in private-sector manufacturing companies, needed to undergo transformation, as these organizations had to compete with the innovative and proactive people management systems of global MNCs. Talent, which is one of the most important assets needed for an organization to run smoothly, witnessed a flow towards the MNCs, which offered not only better compensation packages but also a good-place-to-work-in culture. It became imperative for many Indian organizations to change, restructure and realign their systems, so as to tailor their systems to a changing business landscape.

However, the movement towards multinational service-intensive BPO sector is temporarily impacted by the advent of global meltdown, which may improve the Indian public sector's position. This may be due to the increased financial pressures on multinationals and private sector enterprises, from the global market (*Economic Times*, 2009).

Many research studies in India tested the business landscape and HR systems in public-sector and private/multinational firms but from empirical lens (Bhatnagar, 2006; Bhatnagar and Sharma, 2005; Budhwar and Boyne, 2004). Most of these studies provided valid information regarding the ground reality of the HRM systems that could enhance the innovativeness and competitiveness of firms. Most of the studies were data-driven and used hypothesis testing compared to relatively scarce, in-depth case study-based research studies to understand this emerging ground reality.

Given the above gap there is a need for in-depth case studies which clarify the issues organizations in India are dealing with and also introduce the managers to ground realities in the HR domain. The chapter is an important contribution to the current volume as it emphasizes important lessons for practitioners and academicians about post-liberalization restructuring. It also brings forth the role of strategic HR and talent management interventions, which become important with line functions, and hitherto known as embedded HR. The cases highlight how communication strategy is important to be synchronized with HR strategy. An important lesson is that the key driver to success is changing competences of Indian managers and the increasing complexities to deal with hypercompetitive environments using local and global workplace knowledge. Implications and lessons for managers interested in doing business with India and Indian managers are an important contribution of this chapter.

Case study – BPCL

Restructuring for success

BPCL is a Fortune 500 and Forbes 2000 list firm, as well as a leading navratna public-sector company with an all-India presence, engaged in the refining, marketing and distribution of petroleum products (http://www.bpclcareers. com/Overview.aspx). With liberalization, India's demand for petroleum products was expected to increase and was therefore attracting the attention of multinational oil companies, as well as private Indian firms, which were trying to complete construction of their refineries for future prospects. Competition would surely increase, and for the existing small order execution system (SOE) this meant a significant loss in market share. Deregulation would also impact prices and margins set by competitive pressures would become more volatile and uncertain. Dealers and distributors might shift their allegiance, possibly shutting retail sites of existing domestic firms which might react by offering minimal facilities in their highway segment to keep costs low and reduce lead times.

In addition, trained and experienced manpower could be lured away by the new entrants. Non-fuel offerings (convenience stores and automated teller machines) would become threshold activities, especially in metropolitan and urban markets. One manager summed up these thoughts: "The increasing demand for hydrocarbons in India is a tremendous opportunity. The major concern is the possible and inevitable loss of market share due to an increase in the number of players in the market place. The greatest challenge will be to retain our customers and to remain profitable." Deregulation of the industry forced top management to realize that BPCL had to be customer-focused, and its decision-making process had to be faster. These changes would be possible only by de-layering the hierarchical organization and by empowering staff. Two of the senior managers pointed out: "The aim of redesign was to be ready for change. This meant changing ourselves to be tuned to the external changes."

Organizational redesign started in 1998 with the help of consulting firm Arthur D. Little. The consultants formed a project group with more than thirty people drawn from different functions and regions and led by general manager. It was called Project CUSECS, which meant "customer satisfaction." The group's thrust areas were better customer service, profitability, the creation of strategic business units (SBUs), and dividing the organization into regions. BPCL's organizational structure would shift from a functional to a divisional enterprise, with six strategic business units – refinery, retail, industrial/ commercial, lubes, LPG, and aviation – spread over four geographic regions. The entities that supported the SBUs were Human Resource Services (HRS), Human Resource Development (HRD), Finance, Planning, Brands, Audit, Vigilance, Strategy, Information Services, Project Entrance, and Corporate Affairs (legal, PR, health, safety, and environment). HRM (both HRS and HRD) played a critical role in the redesign process.

BPCL's overall theme was "Business partner first, business partner last", and each SBU had its own theme. For example, the HRM department's theme was "It's a great place to be", for the lubes unit it was "Survive today, to be there in the future", and the retail SBU's theme was "People above oil. We care for you. We exist because of you".

The individuality of the themes worked to build teamwork and innovation. For example, one manager stated:

> The old commandant rule is gone and it is now more a team-based organization. There is lot more flexibility; it's like running your territory as your own business. It means I can do things differently, take risks, experiment and innovate. Now if my team performs well I can even think

of giving them a tour abroad. It's the attitude shift that has taken place, and all in a span of three years.

BPCL recruited generalists and trained some to become specialists; most of the senior managers at BPCL were generalists. One of the managers pointed out:

> The redesign is a good concept. It is an ideal one. The implementation also has taken place in a good way. The only problem I foresee is that the territory managers are not mature enough to handle their jobs properly. Due to historical recruitment structure the personnel are generalists while we need bright specialists like MBA. There would be a gap, if we cannot look into this matter, as 70 per cent of our recruits are not as good as our competitors, they are average. The profile, experience and expertise for the job are not there.

HRM at BPCL: "It's a great place to be"

As the redesign got under way, HRM was on the same level as other support services, like Finance and Information Systems. Support of HRM services was organized into three structures: Embedded Support Services, Shared Support Services, and Corporate Services. Embedded HRM refers to the HR role embedded within line managers' role. The embedded HRM had the following functions:

- Administering the performance management system.
- Workforce planning.
- Designing and delivering functional training.
- Anchoring organizational learning.
- Processing transfers within business units.
- Disciplining management.

The shared support services included tasks that had enterprise-wide and region-wide implications; they were not purely business-specific and were transactional in nature. These tasks were performed by shared teams across all business units and entities as pooling certain activities created economies of scale. An HRM services team was in each region and was led by the Head of Regional Services, who was supported by the HR Manager (Employee Relations) responsible for recruitment of non-management staff. The structure and role of the HRM department were explained this way:

> The HRM division between corporate HRM services and embedded HRM satisfies the role of HRM. The role of HRM is to help other areas and provide support to the main business. HRM should be ready to help and provide information and support in a proactive manner than what it is today.

HRM has changed a lot but HR still needed to be changed in terms of its functioning and proactive nature. Sometimes it is reactive. Last but not least, HRM should know the business we are in, and not only concentrate on HRM practices, but try to implement those practices in helping the business.

Hiring was done by matching the job profile with the applicant. A promotion could only be expected after three years; employees were expected to gain work experience in at least three departments, so a system of job rotation existed. The average age profile at BPCL was between thirty-five and forty years.

Retraining and redeployment became part of the organization's business strategy after the redesign process; excess manpower in certain areas was trained and redeployed. Retraining and redeployment were first discussed with the employee and then action was taken but this was a challenge because employees did not want to be redeployed.

Performance management systems

The extensive team-based structures proposed by the consultant, Arthur D. Little, were pilot-tested with six retail projects. Workshops were held to clarify shared visions, document the current situation and devise concrete plans for bridging the gap between vision and reality. For the redesign to be successful, the consultants understood, the new organization needed new competences and a new mind set that was team-based, collaborative, and cross-functional. It was a difficult task. Employees were invited to participate in learning experiences designed to teach them how to work in high-performing cross-functional teams.

For BPCL the biggest challenge would be to protect against competitors looking for bidding control in BPCL. Domestic firms, like, Reliance and Essar Oil, plus foreign operators including Shell, BP, Total Elf Fina, ExxonMobil, and Petronas of Malaysia are expected to bid for a controlling stake in BPCL. This private investment is expected to fuel expansion of the organization's marketing and retail infrastructure, which should lead to improved levels of service and lower prices. A surge in the organization's share price reflects investor confidence that the biggest hurdles have been navigated and should ensure that the government receives a good return on its investment.

Case study – Notel

Notel Group's journey began in 1973 with a vision to create a world-class organization. It was mainly into black-and-white television production. Pre-liberalization Notel was a small group with a transactional/administrative HR system which was rule-based and tilted towards a personnel, drawer maintenance function. Today, Notel Group, part of the private sector, is

India's largest manufacturer of displays for televisions, avionics, industrial, medical and professional applications, plus components for displays, machinery and engineering services. The group employs 6,000 employees in nine factories and has an annual turnover of Rs 12 billion (US$ 300 million). Notel Group boasts of innovative design and development skills and is considered a dependable player with strong technological capabilities and a long-term commitment to the display industry. Its products are known for their ruggedness and reliability and conform to the latest relevant quality standards. Notel has registered numerous patents for developments in display technology and also developed its own technology for automation. The organization's philosophy is "People come first, business follows. That is how we write our future . . . our destiny." It developed a vision: "To build a responsible mega-corporation – an institution with business excellence, which impacts nation building and cares for the environment and society. Our culture will be value-driven, self-searching and exploring to develop a mind of our own."

Changes in HR policy since liberalization of the Indian economy

The organization opted for a restructuring programme. There was a transition from pyramidal to a functional structure. There was no system of HR audit, though there was an internal audit system. A number of changes were made on how Notel structured its HR department. The organization's focus was to develop a competitive edge by tapping human energy and the unrealized potential of its employees. An environment to foster people to be driven from within was created. One of the top management officials commented in his interview: "If you take care of the people by developing the internal commitment, they will automatically take care of the organization." In other words, company officials knew that building on the competences of people would improve personal productivity. The company also attempted to build social capital by developing trust and building interdependences between the teams. For example, the top management tried to make Notel an organization where people were valued and they have sense of respect and significant value. The culture of individual learning and teamwork was institutionalized at Notel.

The role of HR

Earlier, in the Indian business context, the role of HR was that of record keeper, and at most it maintained industrial relations harmony. Employees were treated as part of the system that needed some amount of welfare activities. Post-liberalization saw many organizations in the Indian business context, give impetus to the strategic role of HR. In Notel, HR was known for maintaining healthy relations between employees and management. Employee voice is an important aspect of the system. Top management and HR leadership propelled this movement and change within Notel. HR is responsible for not being a bureaucratic department, which picks out unnecessary rules to harass employees. But, HR was responsible for letting go of control and building an organization based on employee voice, trust, learning and organizational commitment. HR facilitates employees to realize their full potential and within Notel, and move toward their career aspirations. Employee champion role of HR along with line manager support was present at Notel. This became a challenge when adversely conflicting views of management and employees needed to be balanced. A case in point is how to manage team work with diverse, cross functional groups, with competing interests, right from operator to the managerial level. Further, the challenge was to build in employee voice through appropriate suggestion schemes, line and HR support. This was in the context of absence of trade unions and results in proactive strategic HR role, which ensures industrial harmony. It was to make sure that competition and collaboration coexisted at Notel.

Notel believed in developing its people through their work. By promoting an open work culture, Notel ensured flexibility within its ranks to accommodate innovative thinking, which facilitated growth and fosters a culture of achievement. There was a clear mandate for top management and HR, as captured by one of the top management quotes:

> It is the responsibility of leadership and HR to create a culture of openness and trust, wherein the individual feels encouraged to realize his/her own potential and express it by being transparent with others, by feeling empowered and taking charge of one's actions, by seeking knowledge from where ever it was available, by taking calculative decisions, by learning from mistakes and still not losing one's enthusiasm or sight of the goal.

In 1990, an organization-wide program was put in place to create such an environment. Starting with every level, from operator to managerial levels, the organization instilled a sense of pride in each individual, inspiring them to perform to the best of their ability. Coupled with the work *samitees* (Hindi word for committee) and quality circles (QCs), this participative work culture led to smooth industrial relations. Notel also stressed progressive HRM, with an emphasis on experimentation, learning and development. At the time of this study, the company was in the growth stage of the organizational life cycle (Hendry and Pettigrew, 1992) with its attention on increasing technical specialization and dynamic growth. Notel added formality and structure, and expanded product lines and markets. All this had wide implications for its human resource department, which had to help employees adapt to the changing organization needs.

Integration of HRM into Notel's business strategy

Human resources department of Notel played an important role in shaping the organization's overall business strategy and realigning its business systems with overall business strategy. Its main focus is improving strategic as well as operational efficiency. The organization worked for a strategic perspective wherein the HR managers were no longer paper-pushers who handled administrative tasks, but played a central role in helping the organization reach its strategic objectives. For example, the HR department's vice-president was invited into each strategy meeting so he could offer ideas and suggestions to further the organization's strategic mission. In effect, HR served as a change agent in that it helped the organization develop new structural and cultural patterns to meet competitive demands. This was brought in via an increased focus on decentralization and by delegating authority and creating an entrepreneurial climate that encouraged risk taking and more interaction between employees and managers. The HR department from time to time planned OD intervention programs, for example, in the Notel color factory it arranged the "Art of Living" course for its employees (an intervention of Yoga, meditation and work–life balance philosophy based on controlling self and moving towards satisfaction and happiness).

Career development, job planning and promotion

Since Notel Group has been in existence for only twenty-five years, there had been no retirements at the time of the study and the staff were still young and enthusiastic. The company stated that it planned to fill vacant positions from within once retirements began. Thus, when a superior identified an individual as a potential candidate, the candidate would be groomed for that position. *Talent was developed from the grass-root level.* There were *role directories* available at each level in the organization. Unlike some other mature HR systems, there were *no assessment centers* and development centers for the selection, promotion and development of the employees. Yet it is based on standard psychometric tools, which facilitated identification of potential talent for grooming and nurturing. For example, employees were evaluated on inputs, processes and output and the company administered a psychometric test of MBTI (Myers–Briggs Type Indicator) for personal assessment to ensure that the right person has been promoted or selected. The MBTI tool identified how individuals gathered and processed information, as well as how they made decisions. This helped Notel identify talent for critical roles. In addition, an additional assessment is done to evaluate employees for promotions.

There were no labor unions at Notel but there were work samittees or working groups. These groups worked like task forces and addressed challenges. The approach is clearly solution-centric and helped control political muddiness, which trade unions are known for.

HR outcomes: workplace employee commitment

Employee turnover at Notel is low. Before the redesign exercise, the organization's emphasis was on *product* improvement, but after the redesign its focus is on *process* improvement, which has led to increase in productivity. Commitment and loyalty came as a subset of the HR processes. The level of loyalty at the operator level is very high. A strong vendor support to the organization helped in institutionalizing the commitment-based culture at the organization. The organization received the Transformational Leadership Award from the All India Management Association.

Implications on protecting talent

With global meltdown possible, Notel employees may join competitors like Bharat Electronics, BPL, Videocon, Mirc & JCT Electronics, and LG Electronics. One of the major challenges the organization faces is to protect its talent. This may be at operator or managerial level. It needs to be protected from being poached by competitors or the talent leaving on its own for better opportunities which the market may offer.

Key issues

The implications from the two case studies, though, cannot be generalized to the fullest extent, have important lessons for MNCs operating in India as well as for Indian organizations that are on their way to be tomorrow's MNCs. In effect the case studies examined a few lessons about how realignment of the entire HR value chain could lead to situation of competitive advantage. Important lessons on how restructuring and redesigning emphasized the trust and commitment of top management and HR leadership in people management practices. Further, the lessons highlighted that perhaps the key to success was the mapping of changing competencies in Indian managers in a complex, hypercompetitive, and changing market place. The chapter highlighted the importance of embedded role of HR in line management and its importance during a change process. Also it highlighted that communication and HR strategy needed to be synchronized while looking at both external and internal needs of the organization.

The cases identify that the ability to manage HR effectively time and again is a key competence that organizations have to face while doing business in India. This is partially because the business environment in India has been for the last fifteen years of a dynamic and turbulent nature that has witnessed liberalization, deregulation and globalization at the same time. Organizations such as BPCL and Notel have undergone phases of restructuring to ensure the focused HR processes and talent management that has ultimately differentiated these organizations from their competitors. Both organizations have undergone restructuring processes where the HR department has taken a strategic role and has delivered key success stories in the evolution of their respective organizations. Such has been the involvement of the HR department in both organizations that a systemic change in HR and organization development has led to an overhaul of the recruitment, career management, performance appraisal, retraining and redeployment and compensation policies of both organizations. This was a necessary step that was undertaken by both organizations to brace themselves from the rising competitive environment from within and outside India.

Clearly, the implications of the BPCL and Notel case studies (and the experience of other emerging MNCs) revolve around the ability to use HRM as a strategic tool that is aligned to the changing business dynamics of the environment. The present study holds a number of lessons that are potentially important for researchers and practitioners who are, or will be, trying to understand the emerging HRM practices in large business groups within the Indian context.

- BPCL and Notel's forceful redesign and restructuring focused on the trust and commitment of the top management toward people and HRM practices in the organization. Thus the first implication of this study is that *the role and commitment of top management are a key to the success of a redesign process.* Without the dedicated involvement of the top management change process of this nature might not get the required support from the middle or lower management. These change processes churn within the organization as the organization tends to focus, refocus, build and rebuild its competences to face the changing environment. Thus for MNCs entering India a key driver for success is to map the changing competences of their Indian counterparts while for Indian organizations would be to understand the complexities to operate in a hypercompetitive environment with both local and global competitors.

- The second implication of this study is to *develop and sustain the strategic and transformational role of the HR department* in Indian organizations. The transformational strategic role of HR that intervenes through quality and organizational development movement usually leads to a committed work force. Synchronization of HR and business strategy might provide the foundation for a culture where experimentation, learning, and development help the organization adapt to new structural and cultural patterns to meet competitive demands. While many MNCs already boast a strategic HR department, most Indian organizations are still in the process of acquiring key capabilities to make their HR departments proactive to the changes within the external and the internal environment. Thus for MNCs entering India it will be necessary to understand the HR role of an administrative expert and the employee proactiveness that generated a committed work force of their Indian counterparts. While for Indian organizations it would not only be necessary but to implement the strategic and change agent role of the HR department within the organization.

- The third implication focuses on *the vision/mission/goal/strategy statement of the organization and how the organization sees itself implementing these statements.* For Indian organizations such as Navratna, like BPCL, often times the stated statements get lost in the myriad tensions between the different stakeholders that drive the company strategy. For MNCs entering India it might be less true, as their stated objective is to enter the lucrative and growing economy of India. Thus Indian organizations need to restate and focus on their short, medium and long-term goals as BPCL and Notel have done in the past decade.

- The fourth implication reinforces *the embedded role of HR in change management* and explains how and to what extent *HR practices can help to create a self-sustaining progressive culture* that supports the change process and spearheads the change momentum. The way both BPCL and Notel spearheaded the HR change process through embedded support services is an example which both Indian organizations and MNCs entering or doing business in India might want to replicate.

- The fifth implication is *the necessity for building the capability of both internal and external communication by the HR Department* specifically due to conflicting demands of diverse strategies during change processes. For the redesign and change process by and large it has been observed that communicating the strategy by the communication department or by the HR department is one of the key factors for success. Usually communication is cited as an inherent weakness in the organization and which leads to a weak employee value proposition (Ulrich and Brockbank, 2005). In both the cases of BPCL and Notel they followed a well planned, detailed, clear, consistent and elaborate communication strategy with all the stakeholders. Indian organizations need to be sensitive to a well rehearsed communication strategy while MNCs in India need to balance the conflicting demands of a local and global, home and host country communication strategy that is in line with the overall stated objective of the company.

- The sixth implication follows *the need of the organization to recruit, build, motivate and retain diverse work teams* that are knowledgeable not only in the home market but have interest in foreign markets. This is a challenge that most Indian organizations are grappling with. Though the talent pool is large, development of these specific talents require time and resources that could lead to an effective strategy of global expansion in the medium or long term. The redesign is only the beginning of such an endeavor. On the other hand MNCs have already invested in this type of talent management when they have focused on emerging markets especially like India. The corollary of this implication is twofold. As local Indian companies will go global and compete with players in different markets, the capabilities of those who understand both or multiple markets will be in demand. A proactive role in developing talent and leadership roles will become a necessity. Both local organizations and MNCs will vie for such talents, which will remain scarce in the competitive marketplace. Secondly, in most industries there will be talent churn, which has to be managed judiciously, with proactive HR interventions which will be the key challenge in the future for HR departments.

The above six implications open a host of challenges for both Indian organizations and MNCs. To heed to the implication the future challenge will be to:

- Train managers for foreign assignments, to develop HRM policies appropriate for affiliates in emerging economies and to develop multicultural teams.
- Ensure adding value to business by executing strategy, ensuring employee contribution, building infrastructure and managing transformation and change. Further challenge would be the extent that HR managers can withstand to the pressure from the environment and rise up to the occasion for strategic choices.
- Institutionalize the strategic role of HR in the working processes of the organization.

With typical contextual cultural differences to manage, HR managers need to build a passionate, focused and out-of-the-box mind set that would address the simultaneous and conflicting local and global demands. Specifically, in the Indian context, senior managers are accustomed to this mind set while dealing with central and local issues. For MNCs they are also accustomed to deal with host and home country demands. The need will intensify in emerging markets such as India where the recession has been least felt, and most foreign firms wish to capitalize on the prosperity and innovative business model that have been created in India. As Barack Obama, the US President, pointed out in the G-8 summit on July 8, 2009, "the greatest resource of any nation in the twenty-first century is its people, and the countries tapping that resource are the ones that will succeed".

Note

1   Navratnas was the title given originally to nine public-sector enterprises, or PSEs, identified by the government of India in 1997 as its crown jewels or the most prestigious PSEs, which allowed them greater autonomy to compete in the global market. The number of PSEs having navratna status as of 2009 has been raised to eighteen. To be qualified as a navratna the company must obtain a score of 60 (of the total 100). The score is based on six parameters, which include net profit to net worth, total manpower cost to total cost of production or cost of services, profit before depreciation, interest and taxes (PBDIT) to capital employed, PBDIT to turnover, earnings per share (EPS) and inter-sectoral performance. Additionally, a company must first be a mini-ratna and must have four independent directors on its board before it can be made a navaratna.

References

Amba-Rao, S. C., Petrick, J. A., Gupta, J. N. D. and Von der Embse, T. J. (1994) US HRM Principles: Cross-country Comparisons and Two Case Applications in India. *International Journal of Human Resource Management*, 5 (3): 755–78.

Amba-Rao, S. C., Petrick, J. A., Gupta, J. N. D. and Von der Embse, T. J. (2000) Comparative Performance Appraisal Practices and Management Values Among Foreign and Domestic Firms in India. *International Journal of Human Resource Management*, 11 (1): 60–89.

Baruch, Y. and Budhwar, P. S. (2006) A Comparative Study of Career Practices for Management Staff in Britain and India. *International Business Review*, 15 (1): 84–101.

Bhatnagar, J. (2007) Predictors of Organizational Commitment in India: Strategic HR Roles, Psychological Empowerment and Organizational Learning Capability. *International Journal of Human Resource Management*, 18 (10): 1782–811.

Bhatnagar, J. (2006) Measuring Organizational Learning in Indian Managers and establishing firm Performance Linkages. *The Learning Organization*, 13 (5): 416–33.

Bhatnagar, J. (2009) Talent Management Strategies. In P. Budhwar and J. Bhatnagar (eds) *The Changing Face of People Management in India*: London: Routledge, 180–206.

Bhatnagar, J. and Sharma, A. (2005) The Indian Perspective of Strategic HR Roles and Organizational Learning Capability. *International Journal of Human Resource Management*, 16 (9): 1711–39.

Budhwar, P. and Bhatnagar, J. (eds) (2009) *The Changing Face of People Management in India*. London: Routledge.

Budhwar, P. and Boyne, G. (2004) Human Resource Management in the Indian Public and Private Sectors: An Empirical Comparison. *International Journal of Human Resource Management*, 15 (2): 346–70.

Budhwar, P., Bjorkman, I. and Singh, V. (2009) Emerging HRM Systems of Foreign Firms Operating in India. In P. Budhwar and J. Bhatnagar (2009) *The Changing Face of People Management in India*. London: Routledge, 135–58.

Budhwar, P., Luthar, H. K. and Bhatnagar, J. (2006) The Dynamics of HRM Systems in Indian BPO Firms. *Journal of Labor Research*, 27 (3): 339–60.

Economic Times (2009) Impact of Global Meltdown on Companies' Performance, 9 February. Ramkrishna Kashelkar and Priya Kansara Pandya, ET Bureau.

Hendry, C. and Pettigrew, A. M. (1992) Patterns of Strategic Change in the Development of Human Resource Management. *British Journal of Management*, 3: 137–56

Mathias, T. A. (ed.) (1994) *Corporate Ethics*. New Delhi: Allied Publishers.

Sodhi, J. S. (1994) Emerging Trends in Industrial Relations and Human Resource Management in Indian Industry. *Indian Journal of Industrial Relations*, 30 (1): 19–37.

Som, A. (2007a) What Drives the Adoption of Innovative SHRM Practices in Indian Organizations? *International Journal of Human Resource Management*, 18 (5): 808–28.

Som, A. (2007b) Organization Redesign at Bharat Petroleum Corporation Ltd: The Challenge of Privatization. In T. Agarwala (ed.) *Strategic Human Resource Management*, Delhi: Oxford University Press.

Som, A. (2008) Innovative Human Resource Management and Corporate Performance in the Context of Economic Liberalization in India. *International Journal of Human Resource Management*, 19(7): 1280–99.

Tayeb, M. H. (1988) *Organisations and National Culture*. London: Sage.

Ulrich, D. and Brockbank, W. (2005) *The HR Value Proposition*. Boston MA: Harvard Business School Press.

14 Living in India

Arup Varma, Bhaskar Dasgupta and
Pawan S. Budhwar

> So far as am I able to judge, nothing has been left undone, either by man or
> nature, to make India the most extraordinary country that the sun visits on his
> rounds. Nothing seems to have been forgotten, nothing overlooked.
>
> (Mark Twain, 1897: 544)

As earlier chapters have noted, India is a very diverse country, in every sense
of the term. Indeed, it is often said that however you describe India, the opposite
is likely to hold true also! While there is no doubt that each expatriate is likely
to have a different experience in any country, having some useful information
prior to travelling to that country can help the expatriate prepare better.

In this chapter, we present information that will prove useful for expatriates
who are on assignment to India, and have to live there for an extended period
(i.e., beyond a short trip, that one could spend in a hotel). We present
information on key issues that any expatriate would have to deal with in living
in a foreign land. Towards the end of the chapter, we present an interview
with an expatriate manager in India about his experiences of living in India
and also his suggestions for others.

Religion

India is a land of many religions coexisting together for centuries. While the
majority of the population is Hindu, other major world religions, such as Islam
and Christianity, have been present in India for a very long time. In addition,
other major religions, such as Buddhism, Sikhism, and Jainism were born in
India (see Budhwar, 2001). Not surprisingly, religion plays a major role in
the day-to-day lives of Indians. While there are numerous historical places of
worship of each religion, there are literally thousands of small shrines all over
the country. As one travels across India, either by train or road, one cannot
miss the ubiquitous presence of these shrines all across the nation (Sahay and
Walsham, 1997).

As one might imagine, India has perhaps the largest number of religious
celebrations of any nation during a calendar year. While one may sometimes

hear of communal tensions in India, the truth is that Indians of every religion have peacefully lived together for centuries. Indeed, many intellectuals and 'thought leaders' have argued that political parties often foment communal tensions for their own narrow gains and agendas. Indeed, this is a topic discussed in much detail by political scientists, sociologists and other experts.

Among the major Hindu festivals are Holi, which marks the beginning of spring, and Diwali, also known as the festival of light, which is celebrated as the Hindu new year. During Holi, people can be seen dousing each other with dry colours (called abeer) and also with water balloons and jet sprays (pichkarees). These water games usually end by mid- to early afternoon, after which people visit friends and relatives with boxes of sweets to exchange gifts. During Diwali, which is also celebrated as the victory of good over evil, people decorate their houses with lights to welcome Laxmi, the goddess of wealth. Families buy new clothes for each member and exchange sweets with neighbours and relatives. In addition to these pan-Indian festivals, there are several regional festivals that are celebrated with equal fervour. For example, West Bengal is known for celebrating Durga Puja and Kali Puja during the autumn months, while Mumbai, in the state of Maharashtra, is known for celebrating Ganesh Chaturthi with gay abandon. In addition to the Hindu festivals mentioned above, the Muslim festival of Eid is celebrated throughout the nation, as well as Christmas. What is remarkable about these festivals is that, for the most part, people of all religions join in the festivities without reservation. Indeed, one would be hard pressed not to marvel at the way Christmas is celebrated in Calcutta by almost every family. We hope it is clear from the above that the essential message of religious practice in India is tolerance and respect, and even atheists would have no trouble fitting into Indian society. A great way for expatriates to learn about India is to respectfully inquire about the religious practices or celebrations of colleagues, neighbours and friends. One might even participate in them: Indians generally welcome newcomers into their family and religious festivities. It is a good way to break the ice and one gets to learn about the culture and history of the nation, as well as experience different cuisines associated with religious festivals.

Eating habits

'Indian food' is in fact a misnomer. Indeed, there are as many varieties of cuisine in India as there are languages. It is true that Indian cuisine has gained in popularity all over the world, with Indian restaurants now being present in almost every part of the world. The truth is that the food served in most of the restaurants is derived from the north-western state of Punjab. Having said that, there are some commonalities across most Indian cuisine. For example, in general, Indian food is spicy, and a majority of Indians do not eat meat.

Let us next look at the key features of eating habits in the typical Indian home. Perhaps the most well known feature of Indian dining habits is that Indians eat with their hands. Without a doubt, this is true for a majority of the population. However it is essential to understand the source of this practice. Most Indian homes have sufficient utensils and silverware available and thus the habit is not a result of lack of silverware. On the contrary, Indians believe that using one's hands to feed one's body is a spiritual experience. As many Indians say, if you cannot trust your own hand to feed you, how can you trust foreign objects such as spoons/forks? We should, however, add that almost all restaurants will provide the customer with silverware and all Indian families will use silverware when guests are around.

Next the typical Indian family follows a regimen of four meals a day. They start the day with a hearty breakfast, followed by lunch, high tea and dinner. The breakfast composition varies from state to state and can include items such as toast, eggs, cornflakes, fruit, chapatti, poha, dosa, idli and so on. In addition chai (tea with milk, ginger, cardamom and sugar) is an important part of breakfast in the north, east and west, while coffee finds pride of place in the south. Lunch typically includes rice, chapattis, dal, vegetables and yogurt in the north, with numerous variations consumed in different parts of the country. An interesting addition to the meal regimen is the high tea consumed around five or 6 p.m. whereby tea (or coffee) is consumed along with a hearty plate of snacks, which often includes fried items such as samosas, pakoras, and the like. Not surprisingly many Indians have a very late dinner – given that they eat a hearty meal at around 6.00 p.m. In several parts of the country meat is an essential part of dinner, with fish replacing meat or accompanying it in the coastal regions. It should be pointed out that Hindus typically do not eat beef as such, lamb/goat or chicken are the most common meat items on the dinner table. While Indians eat a lot of vegetable and meat products, the food is rather oily and fatty, and questions have been raised about the health effects of Indian cuisine. Indeed, numerous reports have suggested that India is fast becoming the diabetes capital of the world. This should not surprise anyone, as Indians love sweets, and there are probably hundreds of varieties of milk and sugar-based confections available throughout the country.

When it comes to fruits perhaps the most popular across the nation is the revered mango, with numerous varieties available. In addition, Indians eat locally grown bananas, guavas, litchis, watermelon, papaya and coconuts, etc. Locally produced meat, fruit and vegetables are usually extremely cheap, while imported or exotic food can be significantly expensive to procure, if available at all.

Eating out

While the traditional Indian family prided itself on eating at home, the practice is slowly evolving and adapting to newer realities such as the rise in mobile nuclear families. With many families now seeing both husband and wife work outside the home, eating out or ordering in is not seen as such a foreign concept any more. Indeed, more and more families are known to eat out on a regular basis and the variety of options available is indeed staggering. From

McDonald's to KFC and Pizza Hut, almost all major chain restaurants are now present in India, though they have adapted their menus in deference to religious sensibilities. The fact that these and other chains keep adding to the number of their outlets is a testament to the growing practice of eating out. In addition, many of these and also the Indian restaurant chains will deliver food to individuals' homes.

It might surprise some readers that Indian restaurants have existed alongside restaurants serving Chinese (primarily Cantonese and to a lesser extent Sichuan) food for decades in almost all Indian cities. Indeed, Chinese food is so popular in India that it is often adapted by infusing local ingredients and spices, to the extent that it may not be recognisable as Chinese food any more. In addition, British cuisine (e.g. baked beans, toast, omelettes, etc.) has been a part of the Indian food scene for so long that it has made its way as a staple into many Indian homes, and is not seen as a foreign cuisine any more. However, the increasing number of expatriates now coming to India has led to a rise in the types of cuisine available in restaurants in all major cities. Thus, one is likely to find restaurants serving Japanese, Thai, Mexican, Lebanese, Greek and other international cuisine in all major cities.

Transport

Perhaps the first thing that strikes a foreigner arriving in India is the chaotic traffic almost everywhere. The roads are full of all manner of vehicles – cars, auto rickshaws, cycle rickshaws, buses, trucks, etc., with almost everyone's horn blaring constantly, not to forget some animals also found on the streets. Indeed, it is often difficult to believe that traffic moves at all! The traffic, at least officially, moves on the left of the road with the steering wheel located on the right side of the car. However, the lack of road space, the large number of vehicles on the roads, combined with a general lack of traffic sense, lead to almost utter chaos. For decades, only rich families could afford to buy a private four-wheeler while the majority of the population relied on public transport. This has changed over the last decade or so and with the easy availability of car loans, more and more families are buying cars instead of the typical two-wheeler that was ubiquitous on Indian roads. In the midst of all this, the cyclist and the pedestrian try and make the best of the situation. To give an indication of the situation, there is an old joke that says that traffic lights are only a suggestion. Most cities have state-run or -controlled public transit systems, which are usually packed, and a large percentage of the population continue to rely on them to get to and from work. Kolkata was the first city in India to build and operate an underground metro, though it continues to have just one line serving the north–south direction. More recently, New Delhi has built and operates an extremely efficient and extensive network of the metro. Several other cities are in the process of building underground metro lines – all with the aim of easing surface traffic.

The Indian railways have one of the largest networks in the world, reaching almost every corner of the country. The majority of the population continue to rely on the railways for travelling between cities and towns. The trains are usually packed to capacity (sometimes beyond), and reservations are made weeks or months in advance. The long-haul trains typically offer two classes of travel – a first/air-conditioned class with comfortable sleeper berths and a second class which is typically not air-conditioned and may offer wooden sleeper berths or seats. The majority of the population travel by second class and, given the high demand for the railways, there are usually unreserved compartments attached to trains whereby people can board at the last minute. While there is no doubt that the railway network is remarkably efficient, given its size and reach, trains can often run late. Food is available on most trains and all railway platforms. Once again, the Indian tea (the sweet chai) is available throughout the journey.

Air travel is still mostly reserved for the rich and the businessman. For decades, the air routes were controlled by the central government with only a state-run airline (Indian Airlines) which connected only the major metros and towns. In the last two decades the government has allowed private players entry into the airline business, with the result that there are now numerous private operators, helping passengers fly to more and more cities. However, the airline industry in India is still in its nascent stages and the coverage across the nation is fairly limited. Having said that, the typical business traveller will find that air travel is very convenient, comfortable and serves his/her purpose extremely well.

The road system in India was built during the reign of the Mughals, updated and expanded by the British, and suffered from extreme neglect. The roads are narrow, often full of potholes, and overcrowded beyond capacity. Given that almost one thousand new cars are being added daily in New Delhi alone, the road system is in urgent need of expansion and upkeep. The central government has embarked upon an ambitious project to create world-class highways connecting the four corners of the nation, though this is still a work in progress. One of the most travelled highways is between New Delhi and Agra, which is extremely popular with international tourists who want to see the Taj Mahal. This stretch has been upgraded substantially and is almost world-class. Having said that, it is still highly advisable to hire cars with a driver, given the often chaotic traffic.

Weather

India is a vast country with mountains, deserts, rivers and a long coastline. As such, the country experiences all kinds of weather, depending on where you are. Contrary to popular belief, India is not a 'hot' country. Up north, India experiences significant amounts of snowfall, while the coastal regions receive rainfall totals that are amongst the highest in the world. As such, as one travels across the nation, one is likely to witness different types of vegetation which are a result of the type of climate experienced by that region. The temperatures in the five major cities vary substantially. In New Delhi the weather is rather dry and temperatures can rise to almost 40°C in summer and fall as low as 2°C in the winters. Indeed, the winters in New Delhi are accompanied by dense fog, leading to cancellations of numerous flights at the airports. Given that most Indian homes are not centrally heated, one needs to be prepared. On the other hand, while summers are extremely hot, most homes nowadays have air conditioning, as do almost all offices. In addition, the newer cars plying on Indian roads are typically fitted with air conditioning, thus reducing the exposure of citizens to the extreme heat. It should also be noted that while the public transit system (i.e. buses) does not offer air conditioning, the Delhi metro is fully air-conditioned. On the east coast, Kolkata experiences temperatures going up to about 34°C in the summer, which can fall to about 10°C in the winter. However, as opposed to New Delhi, which is dry, Kolkata experiences extremely humid summers and a longer rainy season. An interesting aspect of the rainy season in Kolkata is that several streets tend to get waterlogged and pedestrians can be seen wading through knee-deep water. Farther south, Chennai experiences extreme temperatures and also a humid summer. It should be noted that both Kolkata and Chennai are close to the ocean. While Kolkata is some sixty miles from the Bay of Bengal, Chennai actually boasts beaches on the bay. The temperature in Chennai varies between lows of 18°C in the winters and highs around 40°C in the summer. Farther inland, Bangalore, which is often called the 'Garden City', experiences much more pleasant temperatures, with winter lows at around 10°C and summer highs up to 34°C. On the west coast, Mumbai, along the Arabian Sea, has temperatures ranging between 16°C to 20°C in the winters and 30°C to 33°C in the summers. Mumbai is also known to experience torrential monsoons during the months of July/August, when rain sometimes continues for days on end.

Shopping

Over the last two decades India has seen substantial changes in the availability and range of consumer products. Since independence in 1947 India has followed a socialist model of polity, with the emphasis being given to domestically produced products. Thus, for example, the only cars on Indian roads were the well known Ambassador and the Fiat (later known as Premier). Other brands were rarely seen and were typically imported by expatriates or those who had returned after living abroad. This phenomenon extended to almost all household items and the common refrain among the population was that the products often suffered from low quality due to a lack of competition. As of 1991, when the government changed its policy and allowed foreign competition, there has been a sea-change in the variety and quality of products available (see Singhania, 2006). As an example, not only is almost every brand of car now available India, many of them (e.g., Mercedes Benz, Honda, Ford, Hyundai, etc.) are manufactured or assembled in India. The reader will find that he/she is able to buy almost every brand of car, clothes, electronics, cosmetics, and so on. Another result of the government's policy change is the mushrooming of major malls across the nation, especially in the larger cities. While the previous mode had been to find the neighbourhood markets and grocery stores, these are now complemented by the larger chain stores such as Spencer's, Metro, and Reliance Fresh, etc. Interestingly, most middle-class families still rely on their local market to meet their daily needs in terms of fish, meat, vegetables and fruit, etc. Perhaps a carry-over from the days when the majority of the population could not afford a refrigerator, most families still take a trip to the vegetable market every morning. This, however, is changing – slowly but surely.

One final note about shopping in India: almost all shops expect and welcome bargaining over the prices, though many are known to raise their prices when the customer is an expatriate. Negotiation is all the more required, though the larger stores and supermarkets have introduced the fixed price concept.

Safety

The laws in India prohibit ordinary citizens from procuring or carrying weapons of any kind. In general, this has resulted in fairly safe cities and towns. Of course, like any other country with a large population and a substantial number of disenfranchised people, there are cases of purse snatching and pickpocketing, etc. For the most part, Indian cities have prided themselves on being safe for everyone. Indeed, the strong neighbourhood concept has led to the practice whereby people look out for each other. While this is sometimes seen as infringing on others' privacy, the flip side was that everyone in a neighbourhood knew each other and outsiders stood out.

Ironically, one outcome of economic growth has been that many neighbourhoods have changed drastically, with old two-storey homes being replaced by high-rise apartments, where most people may not know their neighbours. Increasingly, petty crime is on the rise and weapons sometimes seem to play a role in these crimes. While foreigners are rarely targeted in crime, taking precautions is best advised for everyone. Thus, for example, it is better to avoid being out at night in poorly lit areas specially if one is alone. In addition, the standard practices of locking one's front door each time and protecting one's valuables can help reduce the possibility of falling victim. In many neighbourhoods residents of a street or in a building complex come together to hire a security agency as a shared service. Of course, many of the new apartment complexes attract potential tenants by offering round-the-clock security guards, who are often supported by numerous CC-TV cameras and other electronic gadgets.

Medicine and medical insurance

The Indian health system is characterized by a vast public health system topped by an equally large private health system. Most expatriates, the middle and the upper classes rely on private medical health provided by a huge array of doctors, clinics and hospitals. Medical care, compared to Western countries, is much cheaper, faster and comes with better customer service, although the process of medical insurance, claims and reimbursement can be challenging. Indian-produced medicines are extraordinarily cheap compared with Western prices, and imported medicines can be very expensive. Finding and establishing good links with your local pharmacy is considered good practice. Your firm will be able to advise on local general practitioners (GPs) and, if not, asking colleagues is a good way to identify your local GP.

Housing

Housing is expensive in most Indian cities. Foreigners are not allowed to purchase property and, given the lack of space and increase in mobility by Indians, pressure on rental stock is very high. Consequently, rentals will be very expensive, and in some cases, could exceed what one would expect to pay in Western cities. A good real estate broker will be required, although expatriates are generally looked upon as good tenants, due to their better behaviour, long-term leases and payment in foreign currencies.

The softer side

A sense of humour is an absolute essential while living in India. The ability to laugh off the challenges due to bureaucracy, people responding with a 'yes' when they have no intention of helping you, transportation gridlock, linguistic issues, etc. will be a godsend for people moving to India.

Services such as household maids, servants and drivers, hairdressing salons, plumbers, electricians and telecommunications are considerably cheap and plentiful. Again asking your neighbours over a cup of tea or leaning over the fence will give you the real deal. There is an art to dealing with household servants, which can be learnt quite easily, although the language may be a challenge.

Generally one will find neighbours very helpful, if a bit nosy. Be prepared for the lack of personal space and some rather strange and perhaps surprising personal questions. If you feel a bit disconcerted, a gentle but firm negative goes a long way in clearing the air. One would also find that Indians tend to stare at the unusual or extraordinary. As a foreigner (perhaps wearing skimpy clothing or just the colour of the skin) be prepared to be stared at. It is just staring, nothing more, nothing less, and one is advised to simply ignore and carry on. Same advice applies to foreigners who are sometimes surprised at the level of garbage and trash which collects in the cities or the dichotomy between inner/personal hygiene and cleanliness versus public/city garbage and dirt.

Another potential jarring experience is the concept of time. Working in the West would generally mean that times and dates are rather sacrosanct. An arranged meeting usually happens on the committed date and time. In India, an agreed date and time is usually indicative, one would not be surprised if even the date got moved. Dinner invitation times are loose and one might find that guests appear anything between an hour or two later than specified.

We next present an interview with an expatriate who first came to India as a student, and has since stayed on and made India his home.

Dr Alexander Prokhorov (CEO, Nerthus Technology, Kolkata) interviewed by Arup Varma

A.V. Can we start by you telling us something about your background?

Alex. I am originally from Russia, and have been in India for eighteen years, three of which were spent studying at Shantiniketan. In terms of education, I hold a doctorate from the Institute of Afro-Asian Studies in Moscow State University. At the age of fourteen I started studying Buddhist philosophy, and my original intent was purely spiritual in nature. However, as I read more I became interested not just in the philosophy but also in the people and the land of Buddha, i.e., India. I decided to move to India to try my luck, if you will, and make a life here. The rest, as they say, is history.

A.V. What advice can you offer to those considering working and/or living in India?

Alex. OK, let's start at the very beginning. This might sound very basic, and perhaps applies everywhere, but I have found that one must love what one does for a living – this makes the transition to a new place that much easier. Next, it is important to learn about a country's culture, its language(s), and the people's psyche. Without a doubt, these are not easy concepts to master or even begin to understand, but the effort at understanding these is the starting point – the stepping stone – to success in anywhere, but more so in a country as diverse as India.

Next, I would advise potential expatriates coming to India to ask themselves a simple yet very meaningful question: 'How much do you want the experience?' In my opinion, India does not lend itself well to experimentation or half-hearted attempts at working/surviving here. It demands one's full dedication. Trust me, for those who are willing to give their all, the country will give back ten times the rewards. However, one has to be prepared for lots of disappointments along the way.

A.V. You mentioned a while ago that in order to understand and succeed in India, one must understand the psyche of the people. Could you please elaborate?

Alex. Sure. Let me give you a couple of examples. First, when working with Indian companies, one has to understand where the real decision-making power lies. So, for example, in Indian companies, both in the public sector and the private sector, the real decision-making authority often lies with the technical guys – most often, the engineers. The only exception to this rule is family-run businesses, where the power is typically centralized at the top. So, if I am trying to sell large machines to an Indian company I could spend all my time trying to convince the top boss(es) of the quality and price-competitiveness of my product, or I could approach the technical folks and get the decision done much faster. Also, if the product is really of a high quality, the chances of success are much higher, since it is the technical guys who will really understand the inner workings of the machines. This is just one example, from my experience – the point that I am making is that one has to learn how things operate around here.

Next, let me get to the question of penetrating the Indian psyche more specifically. As you know, there are numerous classes in Indian society, which is a rather touchy subject, and it is no wonder that many Indians shy away from discussing it. However, I have found in my experience that all you have to do is scratch the surface, and the recognition of one's place in society and relative standing is present in most cases. Let me sum this up by saying that, to succeed in business here, and especially for those who want to live here, it is critical that they make every effort to 'penetrate the core'. It is not going to be easy, but therein lies the irony – penetrating the core is the key to understanding India, and getting to know its people. Once you do that, you will be accepted into the inner circle, and both business and life become much easier, but it does require dedication.

A.V. Could you now talk a little bit about living in India?

Alex. First, as I said before, India demands 'dedication', and is unlikely to be like anything the expatriates have experienced before anywhere else. So my first recommendation would be to tell them to find as much as they can about India before heading out here. Next, it is critical not to come here starry-eyed, expecting mystics all over the streets to transform their lives as soon as they land here. Here's the deal – for most people, the first few experiences are bound to leave them disappointed . . . indeed, they might run into all the wrong people, because foreigners initially attract those that might try take advantage of them. The trick is to stay on course – with an open mind, and ultimately they will run into the right people.

Next, one of the biggest things that can make or break an expatriate's experience is his/her attitude. When I first came to India I travelled on crowded Indian trains, sleeping on newspapers on the coach floors, ate hostel and dhaba[1] food, and lived a very spartan existence. If one comes here expecting to find one's home replicated, one is likely to be very disappointed. But the one who comes here with an open mind is not only going to survive, he or she is going to thrive.

A.V. Any final words of wisdom?

Alex. Let's see . . . To sum up:

- It is absolutely critical that anyone attempting to do business here has an in-depth knowledge of the country. Superficial knowledge will not work. Absence of knowledge is absence of immunity!
- The individual(s) must have the ability and the desire to learn – India has a lot to teach! Trust me, I know.
- One must not give up easily – if you want to succeed here, be persistent. In my opinion, India is one of the best places for an ambitious person who is willing to tough it out. I believe it can be the ultimate business experience for a shrewd individual with a sharp mind, who is driven, yet open-minded enough to learn along the way.

Finally, the reward for those persistent enough is that India fulfils the human needs of dharma (righteousness), artha (wealth) and kama (desire).

Key issues

- Create a clear, transparent set of guiding business principles which will drive the relationship. Too many commercial relationships begin by trying to create legal contracts and very detailed master service agreements. Cultural factors and the speed of business change means that the relationship should be governed under a light-touch governance framework. Flexibility and the ability to review and renew are critical.
- Be very clear about the reasons for operating in India or operating in/with an Indian MNC. Are you operating to take advantage of lower costs? Or higher capacity? Or are you operating to access new markets? Or expand market share? Or a combination of the above? Given the nature of Indian business and the long-term culture, clarity and consistency are key.
- Recognise the cultural challenges and work with them. There are different angles and dimensions of culture. There are many subcultures emanating from differences in religion, language, region, gender, and so on – indeed, there are no hard-and-fast rules except for one: recognise the cultural factor and incorporate it in your plans.
- Apply the 'trust but verify' principle. Micro-management rarely works in the Indian environment or in Indian MNCs. High-level strategy, direction and guidance supported by good governance, tracking and reporting are a good starting point to establish a relationship or a business.
- It is important to be knowledgeable about, and devote resources (time, funding, employees) to, regulatory and government requirements. Non-compliance with stated and unstated regulatory, government (central, state, local and institutional) requirements can be problematic.
- Political involvement can and does play a part in business, and it is critical that managers be cognisant of that fact. While this may not be a huge issue

on the operating level, at the strategic level there is frequently a close and important link with local, state and central political institutions.

- Size does matter. India being India – the sheer numbers in almost any form of economic activity (ranging from number of customers, distribution channels, financials and economics, packaging, transport, etc.) can require some mental adjustments to be made for managers not accustomed to working with Indian firms or conditions.
- Be prepared for surprises, and be prepared to be patient. India does offer all manner of surprises, and sometimes disappointments, but if you are willing to wait, things will work out. Western models of time and efficiency do not apply in India.
- Learn as much as you can about India before you set out – while the country is too diverse and complex for anyone, including Indians, to claim they know all, it is essential to have a basic understanding of the country and its systems and people.

Note

1 Local roadside food stalls.

References

Budhwar, P. (2001) Doing Business in India. *Thunderbird International Business Review*, 43 (4): 549–68.

Sahay, S. and Walsham, G. (1997) Social Structure and Managerial Agency in India. *Organization Studies*, 18: 415–44.

Singhania, D. C. (2006) *Foreign Collaborations and Investments in India: Law and Procedures*. Delhi: Universal Law Publishing.

Twain, M. (1897) *Following the Equator*. Hartford CT: American Publishing.

15 Indian multinationals overseas

Tracking their global footprints

Mohan Thite and Bhaskar Dasgupta

The year 1991 was pivotal in the economic history as well as the psyche of India. It not only marked the transformation in the political and economic ideology of the Indian government but also changed the way the world looked at India and how India looked at itself and the world. It showed India not only what was wrong with the Indian economy but more importantly, what potential it possessed to transform itself and the world if it became truly world class. In that sense, it was a moment of self-discovery for Indians and Indian enterprises.

Since then India has made considerable progress to integrate with the world economy in tandem with the rapid globalisation of the world itself. The twenty-first-century knowledge economy is widely predicted to be dominated by Asia with China and India fast catching up with the developed world in the coming decades. While China is already fourth in the world economic rankings, India is not far behind, with both countries experiencing record economic growth rates. Both countries have distinct competitive advantages, with China being the manufacturing hub of the world under its government leadership whereas India is powering ahead in the service economy on the back of its knowledge workers and private enterprise. Together, the BRIC countries (Brazil, Russia, India and China) are spearheading the rising dominance of the developing and transition economies in the global economy.

The world investment report from UNCTAD (2008) indicates that although developed-country transnational corporations (TNCs) account for the bulk of global foreign direct investment (FDI), developing and transition economies have emerged as significant outward investors, with an investment of US$ 253 billion in 2007, 'mainly as a result of outward expansion by Asian TNCs', representing about 13 per cent of world outward flows as well as 13 per cent in global cross-border mergers and acquisitions in value terms, mainly in the services sector. Similarly, the growth rate of the number of TNCs from developing countries and transition economies over the past fifteen years has exceeded that of TNCs from developed countries. Asia dominates the list of 100 largest developing-country TNCs with an estimated foreign assets of US$ 570 billion. Further, the emerging economies are investing heavily in low-income host countries, generating considerable South–South investment flows.

UNCTAD (2008: 12) believes that 'in developed countries, FDI inflows and outflows appear to have peaked' whereas, on the other hand, 'relatively resilient economic growth in developing economies may counteract' the risk of recent global financial crisis (p. 8). It is therefore anticipated that in the new world economy the balance of power will shift to the East as China and India continue to evolve as two of the most attractive inward as well as outward FDI destination countries.

Some recent high-profile acquisitions by Indian multinationals, such as Tata Steel–Corus, Tata Motor–Jaguar and Land-Rover, and Tata Tea–Tetley have made headlines. In 2008, seven Indian multinationals featured in Global Fortune 500 and twenty in Boston Consulting Group's BCG 100 new Global Challengers. Indian multinationals are largely privately owned and cover a wide range of sectors in energy-related areas (mainly oil and gas), IT services, pharmaceuticals, engineering goods and natural-resource-based manufacturing firms (Ramamurti and Singh, 2008).

This chapter focuses on the nature and characteristics of multinational companies from India from an emerging market perspective. It tracks the global footprints of the Indian MNCs without reference to their operations and performance in the domestic market which are covered by other chapters in the book. It identifies the defining features that explain their internationalisation strategies, the rationale behind these strategies and how they compare and contrast with different time periods. It also pinpoints some of the crucial factors that underpin their success as well those that threaten their future growth and viability. It concludes with an optimistic view of the way ahead for these companies without losing sight of the current realities and challenges.

For managers doing business in India this chapter raises their awareness about the global competences and capabilities of Indian enterprises as potential competitors and strategic business partners. This would help them position their standing in the Indian market by identifying the management areas where they can add value that is distinct from local firms. For managers working in Indian MNCs, the chapter devotes a separate section on recommendations for improvement.

Key features of Indian MNCs' global odyssey

The heterogeneity of emerging-country multinationals and the global economic and political backdrop in which they have risen make it difficult to compare and contrast them with each other and with their predecessors. As pointed out by Ramamurti (2008), 'the countries from which they hail, the industries in which they operate, the competitive advantages they exploit, the markets they target, and the internationalisation paths they follow, vary quite widely'.

Reflecting the importance of the liberalisation process initiated by the government of India since 1991, analysts typically present the trends, patterns and determinants of outward FDI by Indian enterprises in two phases or waves, that is, pre- and post-1991 (Kumar, 2007; Pradhan, 2007; Jonsson, 2008;

Ramamurti and Singh, 2008). According to Pradhan (2007), the first wave, covering the period from the 1970s to the 1980s, restrictive government policies on firms' growth saw mainly a small group of large-sized family-owned business houses, such as the Tatas and Birlas, investing mostly in neighbouring developing countries, such as Malaysia, Indonesia, Kenya, Thailand, Singapore and Nigeria, in line with the South–South co-operation pursued by India. These Indian firms mainly went into greenfield investments by pursuing joint ventures with firms in host countries and held minority stake in line with government policy. The operations mainly consisted of exports of Indian-made machinery, raw materials, know-how and consultancy. During this period, the government policies created a large sheltered domestic market with hardly any incentive for internationalisation, and as a result India's share in global trade was below 1 per cent.

The main competitive strength of Indian firms at this time was the capability in reverse engineering by replicating foreign technologies in cost-efficient modes, particularly in the manufacturing sector that constituted over 90 per cent of its FDI stock. Despite low volumes, the industrialisation process in the first wave 'substantially improved India's locational advantages like skills (general, technical and managerial), physical and scientific infrastructures and institutions' (Pradhan, 2007: 6).

However, the second wave of internationalisation by Indian firms that started in 1990s is significantly different. Just as the government policy inhibited overseas expansion during the first wave, the trade and investment liberalisation and incentive policies since 1990s have spurred foreign investment. The South–South co-operation has been replaced by global competitiveness. A large number of Indian firms, including small and medium enterprises (SMEs), are flexing their muscles to expand globally in a variety of industries and services. 'Between 1991 and 2003 the number of outward investing Indian companies has grown at a rate of 809 per cent from 187 to 1700' (Pradhan, 2007: 1). In terms of ownership pattern, over 70 per cent of Indian multinationals have shown an overwhelming preference for complete control over their overseas ventures, mainly to protect their firm-specific advantages and also due to the relaxation of government policy restriction on Indian equity participation (Pradhan, 2007: 14). The Indian firms are also showing a clear preference for overseas acquisition as an entry strategy, largely in developed countries, 'as they are the centre of frontier technological activities globally and have large-sized domestic markets' (ibid.). Since 2000, the share of developed countries in Indian OFDI stocks has stayed above 30 per cent, mainly in North America and the European Union (Pradhan, 2007: 10). This is mainly due to the growing sophistication of ownership advantages of Indian manufacturing firms (for example in the pharmaceutical sector) and emergence of service firms like software companies catering to the demand of the developed countries (ibid.). In 2006, the share of service sector in Indian FDI stock stood at 38 per cent, mainly in IT, communication and software followed by media, broadcasting and publishing.

Box 15.1 Indian IT firms worshipping at the feet of the COBOL goddess

In the IT industry, the issue around Y2K and its required remediation went back quite a long time, to the early 1980s, but it was only around late 1997–98 that firms actually started to devote resources to try to resolve these issues that mainly related to large-scale transaction processing systems such as in banking, transport, etc. These industries were some of the earliest adopters of computers and it did not come as a surprise that these industries were the most impacted.

A significant proportion of these transaction-processing systems were written in an arcane computer language called COBOL, which had quite fallen out of programming use by the time 1997–98 rolled around. Organisations have invested an estimated US$ 1.5 trillion in COBOL systems and more than 30 billion transactions take place a day in COBOL systems (De, 2004). Given the sheer size of investment, history and use of these applications, there was simply no way that organisations could rewrite the code in a newer language such as Java or C or find the thousands of programmers who were very detail-oriented and able to handle COBOL programming to review and fix the existing code.

Enter India and its legions of high-quality programmers who were late entrants to the world of computing. Most of the educational institutions were still teaching COBOL, and the Indian technology MNCs were perfectly placed to service the needs of Western firms with low-cost but high-quality COBOL developers.

Estimates of Y2K remediation costs have run into trillions of dollars, with estimates for the United States itself ranging from US$ 50 billion to US$ 300 billion. A significant proportion of these amounts fed directly into the coffers of Indian technology firms, which gave them an opportunity to start moving into higher-value-added service offerings. And they can thank COBOL for it.

An empirical study of over 4,000 Indian enterprises in manufacturing for the period 1989 to 2000 indicates 'a shift in the geographical and sectoral focus of Indian investments' and suggest that 'Indian enterprises draw ownership advantages from accumulated production experience, cost effectiveness of their production processes and adaptations to imported technologies made with technological effort, and sometimes with the ability to differentiate the product' (Kumar, 2007: 1). 'Many Indian firms also have adopted overseas acquisitions as a strategy of acquiring new technologies, skills and expertise from developed countries' (Pradhan, 2007: 38). In addition, 'outward investment assists them to strengthen their trade-supporting infrastructure overseas leading to higher exports' (Pradhan, 2007: 2). Moreover, Indian firms are also using over-seas investment to secure sources of raw materials in industries, such as gas, oil, copper, aluminium and steel. As a result, the competitive advantages of Indian multinationals today are more broadly based and include technology, skills, management expertise, quality and scale of production.

According to the latest available statistics, India's outward flow of foreign direct investment in 2007 was about US\$ 14 billion as compared to just over US\$ 2 billion in 2004 (UNCTAD, 2008). While many of the dominant Asian TNCs are state-owned enterprises and operate in the primary sector (oil, gas, mining), Indian TNCs are mostly privately owned and many of them operate in highly competitive markets, such as IT services. The key driver of internationalisation for Indian TNCs is market-related factors, i.e. 'the need to pursue customers for niche products – for example, in IT services – and the lack of international linkages' (UNCTAD, 2006: 25). Competition from low-cost producers is seen to be of less concern to Indian TNCs, 'perhaps because of their higher specialisation in services and the availability of abundant low-cost labour. For them, competition from foreign and domestic companies based in the home economy is a more important impetus to internationalise' (p. 25).

Similarly, Ramamurti and Singh (2009) identify four generic inter-nationalisation strategies followed by Indian multinationals:

- 'The local optimiser', whereby firms optimised their products and pro-cesses to suit low-income consumers and underdeveloped infrastructure, using intermediate technologies that they then exported to other emerging markets (e.g., Mahindra and Mahindra's Scorpio SUV).
- 'Low-cost partner', whereby Indian MNCs leverage on their cost advantages, particularly in labour to serve the advanced markets (e.g., information technology enabled services (ITES)/business process outsourcing (BPO) sectors).
- 'The global (or regional) consolidator', whereby firms engage in strengthening their position in the growing Indian market followed by acquisitions in emerging as well as developed markets (e.g., Hindalco, an aluminium manufacturing firm of Aditya Birla Group acquiring Canada's Novelis and Tata Steel acquiring Anglo-Dutch steel maker Corus Group).
- 'The global first mover' in a new industry/segment with a firm adopting an innovative business model in 'what it does, or how it does it, relative to competitors both at home and abroad'. For example, Suzlon Energy, an Indian wind-power company's successful business model combined 'a low-cost Indian base with European technology and global marketing'.

Key success factors of Indian MNCs

The strategy literature on multinational firms mainly points to the competi-tive advantages in cost and/or quality that these firms develop in their domestic markets, which they then take to the rest of the world. The Indian multinationals on the other hand seem to 'represent a new breed of multi-nationals that build their competitive advantage in novel ways; multinational corporations that derive their advantage from service rather than technological innovations and manufacturing MNCs that straddle a low-cost and medium technology position' (Jonsson, 2008: 6). The growing internationalisation of capital markets and investor confidence in the capability and potential of emerging country enterprises have made it relatively easier for them to raise foreign equity capital and enlist on foreign stock exchanges to fuel their international growth (Farrell *et al.*, 2008). Indian multinationals are no exception to this trend.

Unlike Western country MNCs, Indian MNCs often acquire companies burdened with high costs and a declining domestic market but who have a good brand name, customers and know-how (*Economist*, 2007). Cost-effective engineering, also known as 'frugal engineering' is seen to be the hallmark of some of the Indian global success stories, such as Tata's Nano car, Mahindra and Mahindra's Scorpio SUV and Indian Space Research Organisation's (ISRO) space programme that launched Chandrayan satellite to the moon (Jonsson, 2008: 21). Similarly, firms in the Indian pharmaceutical industry such as Ranbaxy and Dr Reddy's have excelled in the manufacture of generic drugs by making use of recently expired worldwide patents and building on 'a strong skill in reverse engineering existing drugs, through synthetic chemistry, and good manufacturing process skills' (ibid.).

In the service sector, the Indian IT firms are seen to be at the forefront in acquiring the highest number of quality certifications and accreditations, including some world firsts, such as Wipro Technologies being the first company to get People Capability Maturity Model (PCMM) certification. The top five Indian IT firms have also pioneered end-to-end business service model with development and delivery centres situated in a combination of onshore, near-shore and offshore models.

Human resources are one of the key strengths of the Indian economy in the world. While most of the developed countries are experiencing falling birth rates and ageing population, Indian population is one of the youngest, with nearly 80 per cent under the age of forty, and the country boasts of the second largest pool of scientific and engineering talent in the world – one of the key resources in the services-based knowledge economy. For example, in the Indian IT and IT-enabled services (ITES) sector, nearly 90 per cent employees are under thirty years and tertiary qualified (Thite and Russell, 2007). Indian diaspora, estimated at more than 20 million worldwide, is the richest ethnic community in the United States and contributes to India's healthy foreign exchange balance through remittances. Considering that the intellectual capital is one of the key sustainable competitive advantages in the knowledge economy, human resources are one of the biggest strengths of Indian firms, both locally and internationally.

Some of the features discussed above (private ownership, emphasis on value-added services and availability of knowledge workers) augur well for Indian

Box 15.2 Something is brewing in the bio-technology petri dish in Bangalore

Bangalore is quite famous for the fact that companies such as Timken, Nortel, Texas Instruments, Nokia, AMD, General Electric, IBM, Intel have set up their technology R&D centres in that city. But few people know about the city's biotechnology research and development expertise and experience. With research and development what matters crucially is the availability of knowledge workers. To have knowledge workers, you need academic institutions as well as corporate firms closely tied together in a synergistic embrace.

The Indian Institute of Science is perhaps one of the most prestigious research-cum-teaching institutions in the city. Besides this, the National Centre for Biological Science works in the area of R&D in biochemistry, biophysics, bio-informatics, etc. Bangalore also hosts the Jawaharlal Nehru Centre for Advanced Scientific Research, which does sterling work in human genetics. The Institute of Bioinformatics and Applied Biotechnology was specifically set up and developed to concentrate on the advanced nexus of biology and information technology research and teaching. While the output of all these institutions is tiny compared to the massive output of the information technology colleges and institutes, this biotechnology output is very appropriate for the high-quality concentrated research that pharmaceutical and biotechnology firms look for.

For the past many years, a whole host of global firms have descended on Bangalore to set up their research and development laboratories to take advantage of the number of quality knowledge workers and research institute clusters. More than 100 firms ranging from AstraZeneca to Labland Biotechs to Agilent Technologies are based here. R&D and infrastructure investments have crossed Rs 2,750 crore, with yearly revenue of US$ 2.5 billion and exports worth Rs 5,733.68 crore in 2007. The total biotech revenues in 2015 are forecast to be Rs 64,466 crore.

Source: ABLE and Bio Spectrum, *The Sixth Survey on Indian Biotech Industry*, 2008, http://www.ableindia.org/html/resources/ind_overview_08.pdf.

multinationals' future in the knowledge economy. Supporting this view, Pradhan (2005: 13) states that 'the emergence of knowledge-based segment of Indian economy such as drugs and pharmaceuticals, software and broadcasting as the leading outward investors indicate the rapid pace at which India is enhancing global position in knowledge-based economy'. Similarly, Kapur and Ramamurti (2001: 20) suggest that:

India's emerging international competitive advantage – and the corresponding opportunities for multinational corporations – lies not in natural resource industries or low-skill, labour-intensive manufacturing (as in much of Asia), but in skill-intensive tradeable services, as exemplified by software . . . this success will generalise to other knowledge-based services. As a result, India is likely to emerge . . . in the medium to long term as a leading provider of knowledge-based tradeable services.

According to Ramamurti (2008), emerging market multinationals, including those from India, possess certain unique firm-specific advantages, such as the ability to extract maximum cost advantage using indigenously developed R&D expertise (e.g., Tata's Nano car), superior production efficiency and process excellence (e.g., Hindalco's aluminium plants), historic ability to turn adversity into an advantage (e.g., ability to work around poor infrastructure and corrupt bureaucracies) and sometimes world-class technological innovations (e.g., India's Suzlon Energy being a technology leader in wind energy). These unique competitive advantages set the emerging-country multinationals apart from any that have come before them.

Key challenges of Indian MNCs

The country of origin is seen to have a major impact on an MNC's effort to achieve the crucial balance between global integration and local adaptation (Harzing and Sorge, 2003). Most of the MNCs from emerging markets, including those from India, are in their early stage of internationalisation and are relatively small, with limited international experience. Accordingly, as compared to established MNCs, they face additional hurdles, such as liability of country of origin, with perceived poor global image of their home country (Engardio *et al.*, 2006), newness and smallness in their international-isation efforts (Contractor *et al.*, 2007).

While the challenges faced by an MNC are mostly firm and industry-specific, below is a list of common challenges that are faced by Indian MNCs moving forward.

The global economic crisis

The global economic slowdown is deepening by the day and is already considered the worst since the Great Depression of 1930s. Naturally this has slowed down the pace of globalisation that had picked up great speed in the past two decades and as a result growth has come to a screeching halt in most of the developed world, including the United States, Japan and Europe, the main markets for most Indian MNCs. As a result, even the most well established and renowned MNCs in virtually all major sectors of the economy, such as General Motors, General Electric, Citi Group and Sony have started announcing record losses for the first time in their long and illustrious history. This has raised the spectre of protectionism in the world's major markets to protect local jobs.

Box 15.3 The case of a global bank and Indian firms

A global bank decided to outsource its infrastructure and application development to Accenture, IBM, Infosys, Patni and Tata Consultancy Services (TCS), contractually worth a total of €1.8 billion. This was on top of the already existing €1.5 billion outsourcing deal with EDS. TCS and Infosys claimed that those were their biggest contracts to date. Despite the fact that the non-Indian firms such as IBM, Accenture and EDS were involved, these firms sourced a majority of their employees deployed on the contract from India. So, broadly speaking, India was supporting this record outsourcing contract either via Indian outsourcing firms or firms using their Indian operations and personnel.

Based upon personal experience of the second author in working with these firms, there were some clear challenges that the Indian firms faced. The first was the lack of strong domain knowledge relating to financial services and banking. Just being very good with information technology does not suffice to move up the value chain and be a trusted business partner for a bank. The lack of a sufficient number of qualified banking and financial services experts with technical expertise to partner with various parts of the bank was clear. One just does not hand over applications, one hands over intellectual property as well, which is built into the application. Given market, technical, economic and environmental changes, if domain knowledge is missing, then the technical application will start falling behind in its appropriateness and partnering will become increasingly difficult.

The second challenge is the comparatively low productivity of Indian resources. Roughly, an offshore team will end up being anything between 20–50 per cent bigger in number compared to the onshore team. Obviously it was not just due to low productivity but also due to the fact that the attrition rates offshore were higher, so one needed a higher bench strength. The organisational structure of Indian firms is deeper and less flat, less initiative is allowed or taken, sometimes too high-quality standards are applied, which causes a higher amount of work to be done when less documentation, testing, QC, etc., could have sufficed, etc.

Lack of employable personnel and high wage inflation meant that employees were reaching managerial grades without commensurate experience of managing onshore activities. Furthermore, there were also instances that employees were promoted based upon seniority rather than managerial experience. The final challenge was a cultural one. In general, Indian managers would not like to say No to the onshore business partners for fear of offending them. Another way of looking at this was an inability of Indian firms to manage risks and point to potential problems so that mitigating action could be taken.

Infrastructure bottlenecks in Bangalore and other Indian cities were another sore point. Ranging from the lack of hotel rooms, bad airline connections, the challenging state of electricity and power, the high inflation and lack of good housing stock, etc., meant that, several times, contracts were actually shifted to other countries.

The Indian firms are taking action on each of these points. The firms are hiring a significant number of Western and domain professionals to improve their domain knowledge. Productivity is improving, and with the downturn the attrition rates are falling as well. Plus contracts are frequently built with cost reductions and productivity improvements in mind. Further development on the trust equation between the bank and the Indian firms is improving the cultural factors relating to saying 'No' and proper risk management of the relationship and contract.

The emerging and transition economies are caught up in the global economic meltdown even though countries like China and India are still expected to continue to register positive growth. It is only natural that the more globalised the local economy the more pronounced are the effects it feels from global developments, both positive and negative. Indian MNCs have to quickly learn to surf the violent global economic waves and still come on top, which would be a steep learning curve. One of the immediate consequences of global economic crisis is the drying up of investment funds (Jonsson, 2008). Cash is considered king in the current environment and the huge foreign exchange reserves built by countries such as China can now be put to use to acquire assets abroad, as illustrated in the efforts of Chinalco to increase its stake in Australia's Rio Tinto. Similarly, the crisis has thrown open new opportunities for cash-rich Indian firms to buy undervalued overseas assets that fit their strategic game plan (Chawla, 2008).

Fundamentals of the Indian economy

As the country of origin affects the global image of an MNC, the fundamental weaknesses of the Indian economy such as poverty, overpopulation, reliance on agriculture, illiteracy, poor and fragmented political leadership, corruption, red tape and poor infrastructure will continue to blunt the edge that Indian MNCs seek to achieve in their effort to globalise. The country 'must address problems of poverty, infrastructure, and governance to achieve its potential' (Wilson and Keim, 2006). The Indian government is acutely aware of the need to evenly spread prosperity for long-term sustenance and accordingly the Indian prime minister, Manmohan Singh, 'laid out a ten-point social charter for widening the benefits of India's economic boom by creating "socially, politically, environmentally, and financially sustainable growth processes"' (Walia, 2008). Sustainability on all fronts will be the key to India Inc. going forward.

Human resource issues

The rapid growth of the Indian economy is causing 'concern about running short of key resources and inputs for [its] economic expansion', including natural and human resources (UNCTAD, 2006: 26). The human resources are at once the greatest strength and weakness of Indian firms. For example, in the Indian IT and ITES/BPO sectors, lack of trainability and employability of Indian graduates, escalating wage costs, high employee turnover and super-visory skill vacuum are some of the key HR challenges that threaten the long-term viability of Indian firms (Thite and Russell, 2007). Similarly, talent management is key to Indian pharmaceutical firms in their quest for inter-nationalisation (Bassett *et al.*, 2005).

Global mind set

One of the key indicators of a truly global company is the extent of internationalisation of its key management team, including the board of directors. It is still the case with Indian MNCs that their top management mostly consists of Indian nationals. As long as it is the case, it would inhibit the global mind set that is required to go global (Jonsson, 2008).

Corporate governance

The case of Satyam Computer Services, where the founder and chairman of the company resigned after admitting to a series of misdemeanours, such as falsifying company accounts and inflating profits, is a timely reminder about the importance of corporate social responsibility (CSR) and its impact on the national image (India Knowledge@Wharton, 2009). Similarly, a plant owned by Indian pharma major Ranbaxy has been found to have falsified data and test results by the US Food and Drug Administration (FDA, 2009). Companies such as Infosys Technologies are leading the way with world-class initiatives in this regard. Government and industry associations also need to play an active role in improving CSR standards of Indian enterprises, both in India and abroad, as the image of Brand India is everybody's concern.

The way ahead

As described in 'India Inc. Going Global', a forum set up by the Confederation of Indian Industry (CII) to develop 'an ecosystem which can accelerate the creation of multinational corporations from India' (http://www.indiainc goingglobal.com):

> The world's fastest-growing free market democracy is rapidly establishing its footprint across the globe. Leveraging the competitive advantages accruing from – easy access to a vast pool of skilled knowledge workers; scale-neutral, high-quality manufacturing processes and global services

delivery models; strength in home markets and global investors' willingness to finance their plans, Indian companies are scouting across borders
seeking opportunities and challenges.

It is true that India is still one of the poorest countries in the world, with a
miniscule share of world trade and a majority of its population is illiterate,
lives in villages and relies on agriculture. It is largely because of the socialist,
inward-looking and growth-inhibiting government policies that have dominated much of the country's post-independence era. It is no coincidence that
ever since the government adopted pro-liberalisation, pro-growth and pro-
globalisation policies the spirit of the country has started soaring to new heights.
This process is now seen to be irreversible despite continuing bureaucratic
hurdles, poor infrastructure and government apathy. The future of India lies
with its young, educated and outward-looking population eager to break the
shackles of the past and look to the future with renewed enthusiasm and
determination.

The Indian economy can only benefit by its outward-looking overseas
expansion. In the process, Indian MNCs 'gain knowledge, which potentially
benefits them in two ways. First, they learn from experience and improve their
ability to operate internationally. Second, they gain expertise and technology
to enhance their firm-specific advantages, thereby improving their competitiveness and performance' (UNCTAD, 2006: 27). The success story of Indian
multinationals indicate that they have reached a critical mass to realise their
global ambition to become one of the key economic super powers of the world
by the middle of this century. They may not yet have the size, speed and state
support of some of their counterparts but they certainly have the entrepreneurial
spirit and talent.

Key issues

The below-mentioned recommendations are not rules for doing business, nor
are they checklist methodologies for operating an MNC. They are key issues
based upon the second author's experience of personally operating in
international business mainly in the Organisation for Economic Co-operation
and Development (OECD) countries as well as working with a large number
of organisations pitching for business to international firms. Many of these
takeaways might not be applicable in a variety of countries, regions, markets,
industries and products hence caveat emptor.

External business environment

- Understand the challenges and rigour of *regulation*. Unlike what one might
  find operating in India, regulations (on a federal, state, municipal, market
  or industry) are of a considerably different nature. They are quite
  challenging and rigorous. These regulations are usually brought in after

consultations with business associations, market participants, civil society and the like. Hence the regulations have a much greater weight in driving business environments than usually imposed non-consultative regulation found in India. Also, as they are consultative, they are more reasonable and pragmatic, which means that the underlying assumption is that one should comply with the regulations and not try to see how to skip them or cut corners.

- *Business and industry associations* occupy an important role in the external business environment. They actually listen to individual members and do act on their behalf. Besides the IT industry associations in India, one will find it difficult to see any other industry association which has the kind of social networking and political engagement that one would find in the OECD countries. As usual, the more one puts into these associations, the better it is.

- The *unique selling proposition* (USP) which works in India could very well fail in the foreign markets. USPs such as low cost might not be appropriate in many OECD countries that have much more sophisticated customer and business segmentation perspectives and experience. So a market, service, solution or product strategy has to be much more sophisticated than what one may implement for Indian conditions.

- Understand the *role of law* and the courts in foreign climes. In many cases, business is done more in the courts than in the market. OECD countries generally have a timely, strong, complex and rigorous legal system. Unlike India, where legal systems can be extremely slow, having a legal system which works means that disputes frequently end up in arbitration or court and resolution happens within business operating parameters. The flip side of this point is that one needs to have good legal representation that can handle international commercial aspects and getting good legal advice might be a challenge from India. The legal angle of almost all external business decisions has to be explicitly considered.

- Appreciate the fact that *failures are part of doing business*. For example, being bankrupt is not an indication of personal failure. The whole positive orientation towards business failure and bankruptcy is what makes for a thriving business environment. This assists in the creative destruction mechanism, which keeps capital, ideas and innovation forever churning. Compared to India, where bankruptcy or business failures seem to be seen as the end of the world, this is a refreshing change which many people find difficult to incorporate into their business lives.

- Understand that *suppliers* are there to do business just as you are. Don't abuse them, which is a far too commonly seen syndrome in India. Abuse in terms of delaying payment for way too long, pushing too hard on costs and prices, quality control or simply ignoring them does not make for a good productive relationship. The golden rule applies here, do unto your suppliers how you want your customers to do unto you.

- *Dealing with the media* is also a new skill for most Indian managers. Public Relations are a crucial part of getting your message about your firm, service and product out. And as with everything, this requires specialist advice and being smart about the timing, channel and message.

Internal business environment

- One needs to make a distinction between hard work and quality. While hard work is measurable and absolute, quality is more relative. So when asked to perform some work or deliver a product, what matters is the ultimate quality and end results. Quite often, hard work seems to be equated with deliverables. At end of the day, what the customer or client is looking for is a quality deliverable. Far too frequently, one gets a lesser quality deliverable and then the explanation is 'But I worked so hard.' That might well be true, but that is not enough.
- Sweat the cost and financial statements and give good commentary. Provide actionable explanations for costs, revenues and financial statements rather than just reporting the bare costs and financials leaving the reader to summarise, identify significant points and then take action. This ranges from basic cash flow analysis to complex deal structures.
- Invest more in your *communications*, both internal and external. By and large, OECD firms spend more on their internal and external communications. A significant proportion of this spend relates to formal communication in a variety of channels, whether intranet, blogs, written, spoken, team meetings or the like. This is not something that is fairly common in Indian firms. This includes taking employee feedback on regular intervals, which is also fairly uncommon in India. Opening oneself up to open communication and feedback means that one has to be prepared to hear bad news or feedback, but that allows one to address the issues. This, in turn, assists in better employee engagement. Using e-mail productively is also a good communication skill to pick up. Some common mistakes are to copy all and sundry, to confuse an e-mail with Microsoft PowerPoint or Word, to hide behind e-mails when a phone call could have worked, etc.
- Learn to *cut losses* if a deal has gone down or is not working: one should walk away rather than keep on plugging away at it. A way of looking at this would be to consider the cost of sales. A frequent assumption is that there is no cost of sales and one can persist at trying to sell goods and services long after there is no practical chance of that sale going through. This can be thought of as a risk-adverse mechanism, which believes in trying to plug away at a known issue rather than release the opportunity and pick up a new one.
- *Leadership* is much more visible and in-your-face in 'foreign' countries than in India. This involves facing or leading many more (formal and informal) team events, team communications, face-to-face employee

meetings, frequent feedback (upward and downward) sessions, team briefings, etc. This, in particular, extends to all ranks of managers rather than just the top management as might be seen in Indian firms.

- Understand the difference between the behaviour of the managed Indian rupee (INR) and the freely floating USD, EUR or GBP. Curiously, this phenomenon was observed many times, where the inner concept of having fixed and managed costs denominated in Indian rupees finds itself significantly out of sync in a world where currencies are freely floating. In other words, one has to not only to undertake analysis based upon direct costs but also indirect costs such as non INR invoice currency exposures. In so many cases, one can see the lack of planning for the potential foreign exchange (FX) exposure.

- *Transparency* is a good thing to adopt as default. Generally, corporate information is to be hidden and safeguarded on the basis of 'need to know'. That said, outside commercially sensitive information such as pricing sheets and intellectual property, the amount of transparency on internal corporate matters comes generally as a surprise to many Indian firms and managers stepping into foreign firms. While this is not to say that silo-based thinking does not occur in foreign firms, only that the amount of transparency and openness on each silo, department and function is considerably higher than what a manager might be experienced in India

- Learn to *take risks and be aggressive* while improving risk management. By and large, the risk-taking ability of managers is comparatively low, whether it relates to a new product/feature development, bidding for work or taking jumps or providing commentary or thinking imaginatively. This area of Indian management can be improved significantly, but at the same time, risks need to be managed actively and systematically. This will immeasurably improve business performance.

References

Bassett, P., Buxton, C., Pathania, R. and Sharan, M. (2005) Talent Management is Key to India's Pharma Future. Korn/Ferry International. http://www.kornferry.com/Publication/3259 (accessed 3 March 2009).

Chawla, P. (2008) Crisis offers Chances for Indian Companies to acquire Firms abroad. *Press Trust of India*, dated 5 October, 2008.

Contractor, F. J., Kumar, V. and Kundu, S. K. (2007) Nature of the Relationship between International Expansion and Performance: The Case of Emerging Market Firms. *Journal of World Business*, 42: 401–17.

De, R. (2004) The ghost lives on. *Dataquest* India, 5 June.

Economist (2007) They're Behind You. Print edn, 6 December.

Engardio, P., Arndt, M. and Geri, S. (2006) Emerging Giants. *Business Week*, New York, 40. 31 July.

Farrell, D., Folster, C. S. and Lund, S. (2008) Long-term Trends in the Global Capital Market. *McKinsey Quarterly*, February.

FDA. (2009) FDA takes New Regulatory Action against Ranbaxy's Paonta Sahib Plant in India, http://www.fda.gov/NewsEvents/Newsroom/PressAnnouncements/ucm 149532.htm (accessed 22 June 2009).

Harzing, A. W. and Sorge, A. (2003) The Relative Impact of Country of Origin and Universal Contingencies in Internationalization Strategies and Corporate Control in Multinational Enterprises: Worldwide and European Perspectives. *Organization Studies*, 24 (2): 187.

India Knowledge@Wharton (2009) Scandal at Satyam: Truth, Lies and Corporate Governance, http://knowledge.wharton.upenn.edu/india/article.cfm?articleid = 4344 (accessed 2 March 2009).

Jonsson, S. (2008) *Indian Multinational Corporations: Low-cost, High-tech or Both?* Ostersund: Swedish Institute for Growth Policy Studies.

Kapur, D. and Ramamurti, R. (2001) India's Emerging Competitive Advantage in Services. *Academy of Management Executive*, 15 (2): 20–33.

Kumar, N. 2007. Emerging TNCs: Trends, Patterns and Determinants of outward FDI by Indian Enterprises. *Transnational Corporations*, 16 (1): 1–26.

Pradhan, J. P. (2005) *Outward Foreign Direct Investment from India: Recent Trends and Patterns*. GIDR Working Paper No. 153. Ahmedabad: Gujarat Institute of Development Research.

—— (2007) *Growth of Indian Multinationals in the World Economy: Implications for Development*. MPRA Paper No. 12360. New Delhi: Institute for Studies in Industrial Development.

Ramamurti, R. (2008) What have we Learned about Emerging-market MNEs? In R. Ramamurti and J. V. Singh (eds) *Emerging Multinationals from Emerging Markets*. Cambridge: Cambridge University Press.

Ramamurti, R. and Singh, J. V. (2009) Indian Multinationals: Generic International-ization Strategies. In R. Ramamurti and J. V. Singh (eds) *Emerging Multinationals from Emerging Markets*. Cambridge: Cambridge University Press.

Thite, M. and Russell, B. (2007) India and Business Process Outsourcing. In J. Burgess and J. Connell (eds) *Globalisation and Work in Asia*. Oxford: Chandos, 67–92.

UNCTAD (2006) *FDI from Developing and Transition Economies: Implications for Development*, World Investment Report 2006, New York: United Nations Conference on Trade and Development.

UNCTAD (2007) *Transnational Corporations, Extractive Industries and Development*. World Investment Report 2007. New York: United Nations: United Nations Conference on Trade and Development.

UNCTAD (2008) *Transnational Corporations and the Infrastructure Challenge*. World Investment Report 2008, New York: United Nations: United Nations Conference on Trade and Development.

Walia, V. (2008) India Inc.: Triumph or Time Bomb? *Green Futures*, http://www.forumforthefuture.org/greenfutures/articles/indiainc (accessed 3 March, 2009).

Wilson, B. A. and Keim, G. N. (2006) India and the Global Economy: Vast Potential but also Difficult Challenges. *Business Economics*, January.

Appendices

Appendix 1
Useful resources

- A. T. Kearney:
  http://www.atkearney.com/index.php/India/at-kearney-india.html
- Census of India:
  www.censusindia.net
- Central Statistical Organization (Ministry of Statistics and Programme Implementation):
  www.mospi.nic.in/cso_test1.htm
- Department of Industrial Policy and Promotion:
  www.dipp.nic.in
- Directory of Official Websites of India:
  http://goidirectory.nic.in/exe.htm
- Export–Import Bank of India: www.eximbankindia.com
- Government of India:
  http://business.gov.in/
- IAOP:
  http://www.outsourcingprofessional.org/
- India Brand Equity Foundation (IBEF):
  http://www.ibef.org/
- India Direct Marketing Association:
  http://www.direct-marketing-association-india.org/
- All India Trade Union Congress:
  http://aituc.org/
- Infrastructure Services:
  http://infrastructure.gov.in/
- The Internationalist:
  http://www.internationalist.com/business/India.php
- Key Reports:
  http://www.indiainbusiness.nic.in/
- Law Commission of India:
  http://lawcommissionofindia.nic.in/

- Ministry of Commerce and Industry:
  http://commerce.nic.in/
- Ministry of External Affairs:
  http://meaindia.nic.in/
- Ministry of Human Resource Development (MHRD):
  www.education.nic.in
- Ministry of Finance:
  www.finmin.nic.in
- Ministry of Law and Justice:
  http://lawmin.nic.in/
- National HRD network:
  http://www.nationalhrd.org/
- National Disaster Management:
  http://ndmindia.nic.in/
- NASSCOM:
  http://www.nasscom.in/
- neoIT global outsourcing and captive advisers:
  http://www.neoit.com/
- Opportunities for investments:
  http://www.investmentcommission.in/index.html
- Planning Commission:
  www.planningcommission.nic.in
- Press Information Bureau:
  www.pib.nic.in
- Reserve Bank of India:
  www.rbi.org.in/home.aspx
- SBPOA:
  http://www.sharedxpertise.org/index.php
- Union Budget and Economic Survey:
  http://indiabudget.nic.in/
- US Commercial Service India:
  http://www.buyusa.gov/india/en/motm.html

Appendix 2

Useful links for expatriates living/working in India

- Birth certificate:
  http://www.india.gov.in/howdo/howdoi.php?service = 1

- Adoption:
  http://www.india.gov.in/outerwin.php?id = http://www.adoption india.nic.in/

- Death certificate:
  http://www.india.gov.in/howdo/howdoi.php?service = 2

- Marriage certificate:
  http://www.india.gov.in/howdo/howdoi.php?service = 3

- Domicile certificate:
  http://www.india.gov.in/howdo/howdoi.php?service = 5

- Driving licence:
  http://www.india.gov.in/howdo/howdoi.php?service = 6

- Registering land/property:
  http://www.india.gov.in/howdo/howdoi.php?service = 9

- Registering a vehicle:
  http://www.india.gov.in/howdo/howdoi.php?service = 13

- Registering with state employment exchange:
  http://www.india.gov.in/howdo/howdoi.php?service = 12

- Applying for a PAN card (Permanent Account Number):
  http://www.india.gov.in/howdo/otherservice_details.php?service = 15

- Applying for a TAN card (Tax Deduction Account Number):
  http://www.india.gov.in/howdo/otherservice_details.php?service = 3

- Registering as an employer:
  http://www.india.gov.in/howdo/otherservice_details.php?service = 17

- Registering a company:
  http://www.india.gov.in/howdo/otherservice_details.php?service = 19

- Registering the IN domain for online use:
  http://www.india.gov.in/howdo/otherservice_details.php?service = 18

- Checking the status of stolen vehicles:
  http://www.india.gov.in/howdo/otherservice_details.php?service = 1

- Land records:
  http://www.india.gov.in/landrecords/index.php

- Cause list of Indian courts:
  http://www.india.gov.in/howdo/otherservice_details.php?service = 7

- Court judgements (JUDIS):
  http://www.india.gov.in/howdo/otherservice_details.php?service = 24

- Daily court orders/case status:
  http://www.india.gov.in/howdo/otherservice_details.php?service = 21

- Acts of the Indian Parliament:
  http://www.india.gov.in/howdo/otherservice_details.php?service = 13

- Speed Post status:
  http://www.india.gov.in/howdo/otherservice_details.php?service = 10

- Agricultural market prices on line:
  http://www.india.gov.in/howdo/otherservice_details.php?service = 6

- Train tickets on line:
  http://www.india.gov.in/howdo/otherservice_details.php?service = 5

- Air tickets on line:
  http://www.india.gov.in/howdo/otherservice_details.php?service = 4

- Income tax returns:
  http://www.india.gov.in/howdo/otherservice_details.php?service = 12

- Complaint with Central Vigilance Commission (CVC):
  http://www.india.gov.in/howdo/otherservice_details.php?service = 14

- Search for government services:
  http://www.india.gov.in/howdo/advancedsearch.php

Note While we have provided some important links, clearly there would be other links that the reader would need. In such cases, please search the relevant domains for the links.

Index